*Hubert Crackanthorpe
and English Realism
in the 1890s*

Hubert Carr-Gomm

Hubert Crackanthorpe
and English Realism
in the 1890s

David Crackanthorpe

Foreword by William Peden

University of Missouri Press
Columbia & London, 1977

Copyright © 1977 by the Curators of the University of Missouri
University of Missouri, Columbia, Missouri 65201
Library of Congress Catalog Card Number 77–269
Printed and bound in the United States of America

Library of Congress Cataloging in Publication Data

Crackanthorpe, David.
  Hubert Crackanthorpe and English Realism in the 1890s.

  Bibliography: p. 183
  Includes index.
  1. Crackanthorpe, Hubert Montague, 1870-1896.
2. Authors, English—19th century—Biography.
I. Title.
PR4515.C45Z6   823'.8   77–269
ISBN 0-8262-0224-1

Frontispiece, Hubert Crackanthorpe, aged twenty-three, as
he appeared in the frontispiece to *Last Studies*.

To Doreen

Foreword

Every piece of imaginative work must be a kind of autobiography of its creator, significant, if not of the actual facts of his existence, at least of the inner workings of his soul.

Hubert Crackanthorpe, "Reticence in Literature"

It is one of the paradoxes of English literary history that the short story was a minor and undistinguished literary form during the century that produced England's highest achievements in the novel. But in the 1890s, primarily under the influence of Continental realists like Maupassant, the form suddenly came of age. Conrad and Kipling and James were producing some of their best work, just around the corner were George Moore's *The Untilled Field* and James Joyce's *Dubliners,* and after that the deluge: Walter de la Mare, D. H. Lawrence, Saki, Katherine Mansfield, A. E. Coppard, V. S. Pritchett, H. E. Bates, and a host of others.

Of the lesser-known fiction writers of the nineties, many of whom were associated with the *Yellow Book* and the *Savoy,* the most talented, the most important, and the most undervalued is Hubert Crackanthorpe. Dead at the age of twenty-six, the man labeled by some of his contemporaries as the English Maupassant was soon, to all intents and purposes, forgotten or ignored. Only now, more than eighty years after his death, is this gifted author the subject of a biographical and critical study that does justice to the man and his work.

Hubert Montague Cookson (the family name was changed in 1888 for reasons of inheritance) was born in London, May 12, 1870. His parents, as this biography by his grand-nephew amply attests, were liberal and well-born intellectuals. His father, Montague Hughes Cookson, was kin to the poet William Wordsworth, a graduate of Oxford, a barrister and Queen's Counsel, and a writer of articles on social subjects and a book on *Population and Progress*. Blanche Alethea Holt, Hubert's mother, similarly espoused liberal causes and was well known among literary circles of the period as a novelist and critic who defended such controversial novels as *Tess of the D'Urbervilles* and *Esther Waters* or the writings of Zola and Ibsen. At their Rutland Gate receptions or at Newbiggin Hall in Westmorland they entertained such established authors as Meredith, Hardy, and James, along with new and younger novelists, including Galsworthy and Somerset Maugham.

Crackanthorpe began writing early but apparently did not contribute to any of the many school magazines during his years at Eton, nor, unlike his two younger brothers and many of his forbears, did he attend Oxford or Cambridge. Shortly after leaving Eton in the spring of 1888 he lived in Orthez, in southern France, which later became the setting of his most interesting collection of short fiction, *A Set of Village Tales;* at Orthez he met the poet Francis Jammes who was to become one of his closest friends. Back in England, his professional career really began in 1892 when, aided by his parents who apparently encouraged him throughout his life, he became coeditor of a significant but short-lived periodical, *The Albemarle*.

His first book, *Wreckage,* a collection of short stories that shocked and outraged staid Victorian sensibilities, was published in March 1893, a month after his marriage—on St. Valentine's Day—to Leila MacDonald, allegedly a descendant of Flora MacDonald of Bonnie Prince Charlie fame and a granddaughter of the chemist Sir William Grove, and a not untalented young author in her own right. Though on friendly terms with many of the *Yellow Book* coterie where both he and Leila published some of their best work, the Crackanthorpes left England and returned to Orthez shortly after their marriage. They traveled on the Continent often, with frequent returns to England, where they moved from a flat to an "expensive house" in Chelsea the year of Crackanthorpe's death. Though Hubert was said to have "adored" his young wife, their marriage ranged from an almost light-opera *ménage à quatre* (involving Leila; a "French adventurer of the name d'Artaux"; Hubert; and Sissie Welch, the sister of Richard Le Gallienne and wife of the actor James Welch) to a series of disasters that eventually included a miscarriage, charges of adultery, threatened lawsuits and even more sinister accusations that David Crackanthorpe discusses at length and with tact and understanding. Whatever the rights and wrongs of these dark and tangled human relationships, in the late summer of 1896 Hubert left London with Sissie Welch for what was to be his last sojourn in Paris. On the night of 5 November, after a series of family conferences, he disappeared and was never again seen alive. His body, identified by his brothers Dayrell and Oliver by his signet ring, cufflinks, and "certain medals that he habitually carried" with him, was found in the Seine the day before Christmas. Rumors of foul play and other speculations were rife, but there seems little or no reason to doubt that Hubert Crackanthorpe had taken his own life.

In addition to *Wreckage,* Crackanthorpe published two other books during his lifetime: *Sentimental Studies* and *A Set of Village Tales* (1895) and *Vignettes: A Miniature Journal of Whim and Sentiment* (1896). *Last Studies,* a posthumous collection assembled by his mother, contains two long stories, including his most frequently anthologized single piece, "Anthony Garstin's Courtship," and "The Turn of the Wheel," the best of his longer fictions; it also contains a warm-hearted elegiac poem by Stopford Brooke and a curiously ambivalent essay on Hubert and his work by Henry James.[1]

Many critics have attempted to dismiss Crackanthorpe as little more than a moderately gifted amateur who attempted, rather unsuccessfully, to "transplant Maupassant on English soil." Nothing could be further from the facts. Crackanthorpe *was* influenced by the French realists in general and by Maupassant in particular; the similarity between some of the *Wreckage* stories and the French *conte* is immediately apparent. Crackanthorpe learned a great deal from the French master

---

1. I have discussed these fictions in "Hubert Crackanthorpe: Forgotten Pioneer," in *Studies in Short Fiction,* 7, no. 4 (1970), and in my introduction to *Collected Stories of Hubert Crackanthorpe* (Gainesville, Florida: Scholars Facsimiles & Reprints, 1969).

and praised his work in his most important critical essay, "Reticence in Literature"; but however derivative some of his stories are, he was seldom if ever merely a facile imitator. Though he began as a realist, he avoided the excesses of what was to become the school of sociological realism. "Realism," he wrote, could be as "ridiculous as any other literary creed"; the business of art, he maintained, is "not to explain or to describe, but to suggest," and his increasing concern with the inner lives of his characters suggests that he learned as much from James and the "new psychology" as he did from the French realists.

The matter of "influences" aside, the important thing is that Crackanthorpe took his art seriously, perhaps because he took life seriously. His fiction, from *Wreckage* to *Last Studies,* shows remarkable growth, increasing depth, and impressive variety, ranging as it does from a single-episode piece like "The Struggle for Life," in *Wreckage,* to the impressionistic stories of *A Set of Village Tales,* or the delineation of the most complicated human relationships in "The Turn of the Wheel," from *Last Studies,* which anticipates in no small way the best of D. H. Lawrence.

The tragedy is that Crackanthorpe's art was only beginning to mature at the time his marriage was disintegrating. His career, like his life, was finished before it had really begun, and when for the first time he was really finding his own subject matter (or, in Faulkner's phrase, *being found by it*) and his own narrative voice and his own dualistic and ambivalent process of vision: a vision at once simple and complex, a lust for life and a morbid drift toward death that manifested itself almost simultaneously in such antithetical concepts as "I awoke all a-glad and hungering for life" and "life is but a little thing, and love a passionate illusion."

In his biographical and critical study of this gifted and bedeviled artist, David Crackanthorpe has made effective and judicious use of family papers, records, and other materials (including, for example, Hubert's books with their revelatory underlinings and particularly Hubert's copies of Amiel's *Fragments d'un journal intime,* themselves often characterized by morbid introspection and an obsessive concern with sexuality) that illuminate clouded areas in his subject's life, clarify misconceptions, and correct errors of both fact and interpretation. *Hubert Crackanthorpe and English Realism in the 1890s* is an important addition to the body of indispensable books about the 1890s, a moving portrait of fin de siècle aspirations, achievements, and failures.

William Peden
University of Missouri
May 23, 1977

Preface

Any study of Hubert Crackanthorpe's work could only be very incomplete without a biographical study fuller and more truthful than the brief, often misleading references to be found in memoirs and literary histories of the 1890s. And no biography could ever have been feasible without the help of Hubert's younger brother Dayrell, who survived for fifty-four years after Hubert's death. Dayrell, however, maintained an extreme reticence about his brother's life, and several biographical attempts were frustrated by his silence. This determined reticence was due to a deep but disturbed affection for Hubert's memory, and to a fear of intrusion into family privacy. Although the predilection for privacy owed more to mistrust of family life than to liking for its intimacies, Dayrell still undoubtedly thought it his duty to shield Hubert from biographers and, for the sake of secrecy, to leave uncorrected the various biographical misconceptions that appeared and were repeated. On this subject Dayrell preferred inaccuracy to investigation, and so he contributed greatly to the neglect, both critical and biographical, into which Hubert's career soon fell.

It was in his old age that Dayrell, whose grandson I am, spoke more freely of his brother, of their childhood and youth, and of Hubert's death. By putting into my hands his letter to Hubert's widow, which describes the character of the marriage and the circumstances of Hubert's death, Dayrell showed that for all his secretiveness he wanted the truth to survive him; perhaps he thought that a fuller study might some day appear. These conversations, the letter, and other family papers that came into my possession after Dayrell's death in 1950, provide an essential basis for this biography.

At the same time I inherited Hubert's library in which he had made many revealing markings. In both the biographical and the critical parts of my study I have quoted widely from these marked passages, the majority of which are from French nineteenth-century authors. Some of these works are not in translation; some are admirably translated in rightly celebrated renderings; and some are available only in translations that now seem dated. Therefore, for the sake of stylistic consistency both in the translated passages and in the book as a whole, I have provided my own translations of all the passages quoted. For the benefit of readers of French who may like to form a judgment of these versions, I have included the original texts in the notes.

Acknowledgments

I am deeply indebted to William Peden, who has generously provided a Foreword for the book, and with equal generosity has helped me with advice at all stages of its preparation. And in the final stage of work on the manuscript I received invaluable help from my wife. I am very grateful to Caroline Dilke who showed me letters from Hubert and Blanche Crackanthorpe to her grandmother Ethel Clifford (Lady Dilke), and Ethel Clifford's account of Crackanthorpe's funeral service. The Dowager Countess of Iddesleigh, who knew Hubert Crackanthorpe's parents and their world, was able to give me a first-hand account.

My thanks are due to Mercure de France, for permission to quote from Francis Jammes's poem "Albion en Béarn"; to Pierre Seghers for permission to reproduce the photograph of Jammes, which appears in Robert Mallet's *Francis Jammes, une étude;* and to the Librarian of Liverpool City Libraries for supplying the photograph of Richard Le Gallienne and his sisters. Some of the details of Crackanthorpe's life at Eton, and the research at the University of Geneva, I owe to the late Dr. N. A. Khalil of Manchester University.

D.C.
August 4, 1977

Contents

Hubert Crackanthorpe as a young boy, "the happiest of fortunate youth," according to Richard Le Gallienne.

Blanche Crackanthorpe in 1886, aged forty, in the house in
Rutland Gate where she entertained her literary friends.

Montague Crackanthorpe in about 1898, aged sixty-six. As a father, he believed that only those children "who are desired before, and are warmly welcomed after, birth" should be conceived.

Hubert (*left*) and Dayrell Crackanthorpe on the tandem quadricycle they rode from London to Sedbergh, Westmorland, in
1887.

Hubert (*right*) and Dayrell Crackanthorpe aged about seventeen and sixteen. Dayrell, as his pose suggests, was much the more accomplished sportsman.

Newbiggin Hall in Westmorland as it appears from the Cumberland bank of the Crowdundle River. The oldest remaining part of the house is the small projecting tower in the center, known as "Jerusalem" and built in about 1450.

Newbiggin from the south. Hubert Crackanthorpe was buried in the church to the left of the house. The central "pele" tower with its four corner turrets was built on the foundations of an earlier tower after the Wars of the Roses.

The hall at Newbiggin which occupies the ground floor of the "pele" tower. The date on the fireplace, with the monogram "H. C.," is 1564. The small window set in a curved section of wall to the left of the fireplace is believed to be a surviving part of the earliest house, which was probably built in the thirteenth century.

Hubert Crackanthorpe aged about twenty at Newbiggin.

Professor Selwyn Image, Hubert's tutor and later Slade Professor of Fine Arts at Oxford. He was described by Ernest Dowson as "the most dignified man in London."

Villa Baron,
Sault-de-Navailles,
(Basses-Pyrénéss)
France.

April 21.

My dear Image,

It was very good to have news of you after all this while, & to read your appreciation of "Wreckage". Thank you. But especially, thank you for those two very sound criticisms. Yes, they are entirely true, both of them. & you may be sure that I will remember them.

Under the circumstances the book is, I hear, selling well: but W. H. Smith & Son, when they refused to have it on their bookstalls, blocked the best opening that exists for a book published at three and sixpence. One Arthur Waugh (do you know him) has said some most delightful things about it & one in the 'Literary World'; so has William Archer in the 'Westminster Gazette'; the 'Daily Chronicle' gave me a column of "unwilling praise", as Johnson puts it; &, besides a mass of paragraphs have appeared elsewhere good, bad & indifferent.

A letter from Hubert to Selwyn Image, written soon after the publication of *Wreckage* in 1893 and referring to reviews by William Archer and Arthur Waugh.

The poet Francis Jammes in 1898. He was one of Hubert Crackanthorpe's most intimate friends and in 1893 dedicated *Vers* to him.

Henry Harland, editor of the *Yellow Book*. Hubert dedicated his *Sentimental Studies* to Harland and collaborated with him in writing a comedy, *The Light Sovereign*.

Richard Le Gallienne and his sisters. Mary Elizabeth (Sissie) is seated on Le Gallienne's right. She became Hubert Crackanthorpe's mistress in 1896 and was not separated from him until the day of his death.

Lindsey House (center) on Chelsea Embankment. The house was built in 1674 and is shown as it appeared about 1890. Hubert Crackanthorpe's last home, which had formerly been the home of James McNeill Whistler, was the projecting wing at the further end of the building. Hubert commissioned Roger Fry to decorate the interior.

Dayrell Crackanthorpe in about 1896. On Christmas Day of that year he identified his brother's remains at the Morgue, and on January 30, 1897, he was appointed third secretary at the British embassy in Madrid.

1

A Marvelous Instrument of Education

I

Hubert Crackanthorpe was born in London on May 12, 1870, the brightest and most favored of his parents' three sons. From the first, the auguries for his life seemed fair, and the promise generous. His friend Richard Le Gallienne, whose own background was less propitious and certainly more severe, described Hubert as "the happiest of fortunate youth."[1] He was the eldest child of a passionate and comprehensive love, and his early literary development was to some extent the work of a parental alliance, the issue of a union that was as fruitful intellectually as it was emotionally close and enduring. But the precocious growth of the much loved child and of the fostered talent were perhaps too green and tender to withstand much misfortune. William Wordsworth, a near kinsman of Hubert's family,[2] noted a bitter contrast between the aims of nurture and the casualties of temperament:

> Amid the groves, under the shadowy hills,
> The generations are prepared; the pangs,
> The internal pangs, are ready.[3]

The marriage of Montague and Blanche Crackanthorpe was so much a *succès pyramidal,* in the words of their second son Dayrell, that their children must have seen in it a paradigm of the ideal; a full guarantee of security no doubt, but one that imposed on them a special identity, not always comfortable, of being the offspring of an idyllic match. None of them succeeded in repeating the triumphant marital unison of which the parents, happy in their achievement, were apt to boast. Probably this ideal was implicitly presented as an example, and an example that others were not likely to emulate with success. Dayrell, who had doubts about the pleasures of family life, described the relationship ironically but with a certain awe: "They formed a mutual admiration society in ceaseless operation. Day and night." And he considered that the admiration reached as far as his elder brother Hubert, included by virtue either of primogeniture or of talent. Nevertheless, all three sons of this apparently flawless marriage betrayed flaws of temperament in different ways; if Hubert's early death was by suicide, as has usually been supposed, then evidently the fault ran more deeply in his personality than in those of his brothers.

The base of the *succès pyramidal* was established in two letters of proposal written shortly before Christmas 1868. Montague was then aged thirty-six, a scholastically inclined Chancery barrister who, though the youngest of six sons, was already supporting his mother and sister, as well as the family of an elder brother who had died young. Some nervousness, possibly a fear of rejection, could explain this offer of marriage made in writing:

> In spite of a natural reserve of manner, which I often regret, you must have discovered that my affections are centred in yourself, and whatever the result it is a pleasure to me to tell you so. . . . If you think I cannot make you happy, I am content that you should burn this letter. . . . But, my dear Blanche, I hope you will not do anything of the kind, but write me a little letter with your own hand and tell me I have not been so very foolish after all.[4]

The hand is strong and flowing, precise but not pedantic. Excitement appears, not in the dry and formal tone, but in a number of erasures and blots in this scholar's proposal and in the precipitancy with which lines trail downward at the margin of the paper. The script of the second letter is firmer and shows the exultancy of a man who knows his mind and is to have his desire:

> I owe you a thousand apologies, my dearest Blanche, for putting you to the pain of answering on paper a question which ought to have been put to you by word of mouth. But I think you understand. . . . When I read as far as the words which told me that I had no superior rival in your heart of hearts I felt very happy. . . . You will aid, stimu-

late, console, and spiritualise my efforts with God's help. In
return, I will love cherish respect (is not respect an element
in love?) your dearself, and thus we shall each be the gainer
by the other both in this life and in another.[5]

Something of Montague's character emerges despite the apparent restraint of language: deliberate, vigorous, and re-
served, but with strong feelings, which once engaged were
constant. The marriage took place on April 6, 1869, and after
the birth of the first son the family made its London home in
Rutland Gate, on the south side of Hyde Park.

On both sides of the "mutual admiration society" there was
some reason for admiration, certainly for respect; both husband and wife displayed in their published work an intellectual energy which they transmitted to their eldest son, and an
independence of thought that enabled them, when he wished
to take up the improbable career of a writer, to encourage and
approve. If the marital unanimity was sometimes oppressive
to the sons, it was at least a continuous source of strength to
the parents. Montague expressed his ideal of marriage in an
essay entitled "The Morality of Married Life" in the
Fortnightly Review of October 1872, which reappeared in his
Population and Progress in 1907. The wider purpose of the essay
was to advocate birth control by means of what he called the
"voluntary principle," but in writing of the married relationship itself his tone was almost panegyric:

> The end and aim of marriage . . . is a great deal higher and
> grander than the one crudely put forward by the Church.
> Marriage is a marvelous instrument of education. . . . The
> sweet companionship of well-matched minds, whose most
> potent bond of union lies in the very fact of their difference,
> is in itself almost a religion, for it quickens the spiritual
> instincts and enlarges the social sympathies.[6]

Montague, who had many scientists as friends and who was
one of the founders of the Eugenics Society, was probably
agnostic in his inner mind, and certainly his sons were
brought up in a semiagnostic intellectual atmosphere. The
exalted, almost mystical view of the possibilities of marriage
was evidently to some extent a substitute for religious experience which his rationalism denied him; unfortunately for his
sons, this powerfully formative influence could eventually

only reinforce, by painful contrast in the memory, any sense of failure arising in their own marriages.

Montague Crackanthorpe was the youngest of the seven children of Christopher Cookson of Nowers, in Somerset. It was not until the death in 1888 of his cousin William Crackanthorpe of Newbiggin, that he took the name Crackanthorpe. The Cooksons were a prolific and vigorous family, stemming from the southern part of Westmorland and passing, during the seventeenth and early eighteenth centuries, through the rapids of the mercantile class; by the end of the eighteenth century no less than five contingents of Cooksons had reached the still waters of the landowning oligarchies of Northumberland and Cumberland where four of them remained becalmed.[7] For the fifth, represented in the issue of Montague's great-grandparents, William Cookson of Penrith and his wife Dorothy Crackanthorpe whom he married on December 9, 1741, the only daughter of Richard Crackanthorpe of Newbiggin, there was to be a recurring academic and sometimes creative aspiration, shared by the Wordsworth family who also descended from that marriage.

Dorothy Crackanthorpe was her father's eventual heiress; her granddaughter Dorothy Wordsworth mentioned in a letter of 1790 that her grandmother had inherited "a very handsome estate"[8] from which she hoped to benefit the Wordsworths. The Newbiggin inheritance was heavily mortgaged, and greatly neglected, but it had a medieval origin and character irresistible to any historic or romantic imagination. The name "Newbiggin" is not uncommon in the northern counties and means "new building." The term is relative; the house had been the family home since the middle of the twelfth century, with reconstructions and additions, especially after the dynastic and civil wars. In 1671 Daniel Fleming alluded to it in his *Description of Westmorland:* "A fair old house, which hath a long time been the chief seat of the Crackenthorps [*sic*], and being a family very antient and of good esteem."[9] A century later the house was semiruinous and the family almost equally advanced in decay. As for the house, the prescription composed by John Ruskin for the care of an old building had been long applied and the last stage almost reached:

> Count its stones . . . bind it together with iron where it
> loosens; stay it with timbers where it declines . . . and
> many a generation will still be born and pass away beneath
> its shadow. Its evil day must come at last.[10]

Dorothy Crackanthorpe began the work of repair but died
within two years, leaving two sons and a daughter; her elder
son Christopher—Montague Crackanthorpe's great uncle and
"Uncle Kitt" to William Wordsworth and his sister Dorothy,
with whom he was unpopular—completed the restoration,
leaving the house much as it stands today. Christopher was
followed in ownership by an only son, at whose death in 1888
Newbiggin fell to Montague Crackanthorpe, who was the
grandson of Dorothy Crackanthorpe's second son, William
Cookson.[11] Dorothy's daughter, Ann, was the mother of
Wordsworth who described her in *The Prelude:*

> she who was the heart
> and hinge of all our learning and our loves.

Although the Wordsworths had harsh things to say of "Uncle
Kitt," they were well-disposed to their other uncle, Montague's grandfather William Cookson, for whom the poet had
a high regard. Cookson was a fellow of St. John's College,
Cambridge, and it was he who accompanied the young
Wordsworth on his first journey from Cumberland to Cambridge where they arrived on October 30, 1787. On the way,
either at Stamford or Grantham, Wordsworth's eye fell for the
first time on a prostitute, and he heard "the voice of woman
utter blasphemy."[12] Shortly afterward, Cookson obtained a
Foundress Scholarship for his nephew; and he remained always rather endearingly interested in his career, though with
an increasing disapproval of the poet's way of life.

From 1781 to 1787 William Cookson had been one of the
tutors to the younger sons of George III: the princes Frederick; William, later King William IV; and Edward Augustus, who was to be the father of Queen Victoria. The preceptors were appointed from Cambridge, and the post required
them to live a celibate life at Kew and Windsor; for a man
waiting to marry, the life must have been frustrating, and for
an academic singularly unrewarding. Ambition was no doubt
the inducement, as several of the preceptors later became

bishops; in Cookson's case there was a long servitude and a very modest reward, a canonry of Windsor.[13] Throughout these years he exchanged with an increasingly impatient fiancée a series of ironically regretful letters. Occasionally, gossip may have been some compensation:

> You have no Doubt heard of the Marriage which has taken place in *this* Family—This *Mrs. Wales* alias Fitzherbert, this Wife and no Wife is about one and thirty, has been already twice married, is handsome, perhaps rather too much embonpoint and as her third Husband says, the only Woman in the World worth talking Sense to.[14]

When the royal youths were released from the schoolroom William wrote: "I am now a free Man. . . . Our final Parting was affectionate enough."[15] The six years of exposure to the Hanoverian mind had evidently so blunted the edge of academic ambition that Cookson gave up his fellowship at St. John's in 1789. It was his hope that he would be succeeded in it by Wordsworth who, however, departed for Paris in the summer of 1790, having written to his sister:

> You will remember me affectionately to my uncle . . . as he was acquainted with my having given up all thoughts of a fellowship, he may, perhaps, not be so much displeased at this journey. I should be sorry if I have offended him by it.[16]

In 1791 Dorothy wrote to a friend:

> William, you may have heard, lost the chance, (indeed the certainty) of a fellowship, by not combating his inclinations.[17]

But kindly, avuncular interest and irrelevant advice were still bestowed upon the poet, who wrote in November 1791:

> My uncle, the clergyman, proposed to me a short time ago to begin a course of Oriental literature, thinking that that was the best field for a person to distinguish himself in, as a man of letters. . . . But what must I do amongst that immense wilderness, I who have no resolution?[18]

However, once Wordsworth's relationship with Annette Vallon and the existence of an illegitimate daughter became known, the kindliness seems to have been withdrawn.

Dorothy wrote: "I have been much disappointed that my Uncle has not invited Wm. to Forncett, but he is no favorite with him alas! alas!"[19]

Dorothy Wordsworth lived for six years in her uncle's household and described herself happily, in 1793, as "head nurse, housekeeper, tutoress of the little ones or rather superintendent of the nursery."[20] Christopher Cookson, Montague Crackanthorpe's father, was William Cookson's eldest boy, born in 1791. He and his brothers, like their numerous Northumberland cousins, were educated at Eton; he won a scholarship to Cambridge in 1809 but did not take to the scholastic life. In 1809 Dorothy revisited her uncle's family and wrote:

> Christopher the eldest son . . . is a fair, tall, manly affectionate & good young man, a very good scholar too, but Alas! he is not so studious as my uncle wishes, & after having had him a year at Cambridge, my Uncle feels it right to consent that he shall go into the Army. . . . It is a pity for he is a noble youth.[21]

The "noble youth" for whom the army was thought an unworthy career served in India from 1810 to 1818; he returned to England and married in 1821, fathered seven children, and died in 1834, two years after the birth of his last child and sixth son, Montague.

Four of Montague's five elder brothers were sent to school at Eton, but for this fatherless boy a less expensive education was required. Luckily, he was a natural scholar able with fluent ease to turn his genius for examinations to a wide variety of disciplines. After his death Blanche wrote that "in his youth he had many troubles, which to a sensitive nature like his were very acute."[22] Whatever these troubles may have been, they did not impede academic progress; indeed he earned his own education from a very early age. As a schoolboy at Merchant Taylor's—the school attended by Coleridge—he won prizes in such disparate subjects as mathematics, Hebrew, and Greek; clearly he entered for prizes that were remunerative and by winning them showed a precocious self-reliance. At eighteen he was appointed to a fellowship at St. John's College, Oxford, where his brother Christopher was also a fellow. After gaining a double first in classics and mathematics, he went on to win the University Mathematical Scholarship and the Eldon Law Scholarship. He became doctor of civil law in 1860 and Queen's Counsel in 1875; from 1893 to 1899 he was standing counsel to Oxford University and, from 1895, an honorary fellow of St. John's. The ease and apparent inevitableness with which the academic successes were achieved probably intimidated his three sons, rather like the shining marital example; for although two of them went to a university, none took a degree. Montague himself continued throughout his life to write learned essays on legal, political, sociological, and eugenic problems, which appeared in the leading journals. From 1909 to 1911 he was president of the Eugenics Society, which he and his friend Francis Galton had helped to found. To his sons he was the object of a deep respect tempered by cautious mockery; Dayrell, though not himself noted for generosity with money, criticized what he considered a certain parsimoniousness in his father's character. But even in Dayrell's old age these criticisms were produced with a somewhat defensive irony. To his wife, Montague remained always and altogether admirable:

> It was not so much his extraordinary intellectual power that differentiated Montague from other men. . . . It was his character—the power of self-denial and single-mindedness, the power of feeling *with,* instead of *for,* other people.

And she added her *passe-partout* maxim:

> The twin motives of his life were:
> 1. Never put up with anything but the best.
> 2. Learn to do without.[23]

In the law courts, where much of his life was spent, he was known as a refined speaker and ingenious reasoner, indeed by some accounts overingenious and too subtle. It was said that he never quite overcame the appearance of great nervousness in public speaking, an impediment that may have contributed to his failure in two attempts, in 1885 and 1886, to enter Parliament as a Liberal. In an obituary, which to Dayrell's amusement and his father's fury was by accident prematurely published, and which reappeared after his death in 1913, the *Times* remarked:

Montague Crackanthorpe was one of the few leaders at the Bar who did not reach judicial promotion, of whom most lawyers would have said 30 years ago that his early elevation to the Bench was inevitable. A brilliant career at Oxford was followed by a career scarcely less brilliant at the Bar, and yet the result is not so inexplicable perhaps as it seems, for he did not appear to follow his profession with the whole-hearted seriousness of some of his competitors, and had many interests outside of his professional work. . . . Always something of a critic, and even a journalist, he wrote many articles on social subjects. . . . He dealt with the Malthusian question so called, as many thought not with absolute discretion.[24]

The *Times* also described him as "something of a wobbler" in politics, and this political unreliability may have been a factor. Yet, "if his judgment was not always to be entirely trusted, his knowledge of public affairs gave a value of its own to his intervention in political discussion."[25]

Some of the family believed that Blanche's outspokenness in print on social subjects, a certain arrogance in conversation, and her championing of the new literature that was thought corrupting, had impeded Montague's career. But there seems no doubt that it was his own "indiscretion" on the Malthusian question that was disliked by those responsible for judicial appointments, stalwart upholders of polite opinion. Even in 1913, in the *Times* obituary, the term *birth control* was prudently avoided, although Montague's views on the subject had first been expressed in 1872 when he was still a junior member of the bar; and by 1907, when he again advocated the "voluntary principle" at greater length in *Population and Progress,* it had already been too widely adopted to be either unfamiliar or taboo: "Another illustration . . . of the truth that the discoveries of one generation become the commonplaces of the next."[26]

"The Morality of Married Life" first appeared when the taboo was still in operation, and ignorance or fear of contraception were prime causes of social misery; it was addressed to those "who are still under the popular delusion that, in this particular department of conduct, no man is his own master, therefore no man can lend a helping hand to his brother."[27] With the voluntary principle, "those children only are born who are desired before, and are warmly welcomed after, birth."[28] He seems never to have regretted this advocacy of liberal views; the essays of 1907, written when he was seventy-five, are quite unrepentant, and it is unlikely that he had ever looked for advancement that could have restricted the scope of his interests or freedom of expression. His attitude in this was thoroughly patrician, in the Victorian manner; after his death the *Eugenics Review* said of him: "If Crackanthorpe's independence of thought was an impediment to his progress in the legal world, he paid heavily for his mental temerity."[29] A certain temerity was characteristic too of his son Hubert's literary career.

II

Hubert's mother, Blanche Alethea Holt, was born in 1846, the younger daughter of a clergyman, Eardley Holt of East Sheen in Surrey. She was fourteen years younger than her husband and was born in an age when even the most intelligent of daughters suffered educational deprivation and, at least until marriage, fettering social and moral restrictions about which Blanche was later to write with some irony. In her own case, the disadvantage was mitigated by the energy of her character and, later, by her husband's sympathetic views:

> Excessive child-bearing tends to arrest the education of the woman at its most critical stage. . . . the complexities of modern life require that a wife should be something more than the chief domestic of her establishment. Should she come to realize that her head is empty, she will hardly be consoled by the reflection that her nursery is full.[30]

In appearance, Blanche was small, elegant, and of a markedly sardonic expression of face. She had a dominating presence derived from inner vehemence that expressed itself in opinion and in speech, and that made her, in later life, seem overbearing and alarming to the young despite her known sympathy with their problems.[31] However, it is clear from her writings that in her prime she was gifted with a capacity for argument, and with wit to contribute to the "sweet companionship of well-matched minds" that her husband wrote of. And in it she must have found intellectual scope far larger than could be expected by most young women of intelligence in an age when, in Montague's words, "Woman was the apanage of Man, and whether her position was that of lawful wife or hidden mistress, this was the settled point of view."[32] The completeness of the companionship is testified in a letter to her son Dayrell, written after Montague's death:

> You will have I think, known intimately, how it has been—how it is—with me. Life's main-spring broken—& a blank hopelessness against which it is vain to struggle, filling the emptied life. Of course I have known it was coming. . . . There is no blinding the eyes of love.[33]

The letter goes on to propose movements of her various grandchildren during the coming holidays and to suggest arrangements rather transparently for her own solace:

> If the children come to Newbiggin at Christmas they shall have as happy a time as they can have without you. . . .Life only holds the helping of others, and love, if one can find that chief blessing in a broken life, for me now.[34]

Blanche's mother was of French descent and, according to Dayrell, this contributed to her partiality for French literature, an element in her personality that repeated itself in Hubert. Her Huguenot antecedent Jean de Motteux came to England from Normandy in 1685. His son Peter became a successful dramatist and opera librettist in London, and completed the work of Sir Thomas Urquhart as translator of Rabelais;[35] Pellegrini did a handsome portrait of Peter and his family in 1708, which is in the collection of the British Museum.[36] On her father's side, Blanche was a descendent of Sir John Holt, Lord Chief Justice of England from 1689 to 1710, and of Sir John Eardley-Wilmot, Lord Chief Justice from 1766 to 1791; Eardley-Wilmot had been at school in Lichfield with Samuel Johnson and David Garrick. Through the Eardley-Wilmot and Talbot families, she descended from the Pastons, and so from the issue of John of Gaunt and his third wife, Katherine Swynford, whose sister was the wife of Chaucer.[37] This Plantaganet genealogy, not devoid of literary associations, was a source of half-ironic pride. "My mother liked to apply her favourite rule of life (never put up with anything but the best, or learn to do without) in the matter of ancestors," Dayrell would say.

Literature was the chief interest in Blanche Crackanthorpe's life, apart from the inexhaustible concerns of marriage. It took precedence even over her interest in her sons, except in Hubert's case where literary and maternal interests coincided. She was herself a writer, and so were many of her friends; for many years she presided vigorously over a well-known literary and social salon at her house in Rutland Gate. After her death the *Times* said of her: "She was a lady of remarkable social and intellectual gifts. . . . There must still be many who will recall with pleasure her amusing parties in Rutland Gate and at Newbiggin Hall."[38] Marie Belloc Lowndes, the sister of Hilaire Belloc and wife of F. S. Lowndes of the *Times,* was a frequent guest at these parties and for a time a close friend of Blanche, of whom she wrote in the third volume of her autobiography:

> I have never seen, in any published diary or book of memoirs, any allusion to Mrs. Crackanthorpe, a considerable figure in the literary world of the late 'nineties and of the early part of the present century. The Crackanthorpes had a house in Rutland Gate where they entertained all the established authors—I met there not only George Meredith, Hardy, and Henry James—as also the new writers whose work attracted the brilliantly intelligent hostess. I well recollect a dinner-party where, among the guests, was John Galsworthy, just after he published *The Man of Property,* and his beautiful wife, who was believed to be the "Irene" of the book. It was there I first met Somerset Maugham.[39]

Two other young writers whom Blanche encouraged and who became her friends were Robert Hichens, whose *Green Carnation* appeared in 1894, and the prolific Horace Annesley Vachell.

The parties at Rutland Gate seem to have been devised with some flair. In the spring of 1896, Thomas Hardy recorded attending "a most amusing masked ball" at which he and Henry James being "the only two not in domino, were recklessly flirted with by the women in consequence."[40] Perhaps Hardy found this more stimulating than James, who recorded dryly in his diary, "last night at Mrs. Crackanthorpe's, Stopford Brooke suggested to me 2 little ideas";[41] one of these was to provide the basis of *The Sacred Fount.* On another occasion, Marie Belloc Lowndes recorded a political lunch at Rutland Gate:

> I went yesterday afternoon with the Crackanthorpes, and certain of the gentlemen concerned, to see the new Cabinet at Madame Tussaud's. Most of them were half afraid, half wishful, that the public would recognise them. To my secret amusement *no one did*—in fact they were looked at with a certain suspicion, as we were a rather large party, and laughed and talked so much. I thought Asquith's wax counterpart quite good, Grey and Haldane quite bad.[42]

One of Blanche's closest friends, described by Marie Belloc Lowndes as "one of the twin feminine stars" of her circle,[43] was the American actress Elizabeth Robins, the successful Hedda Gabler of the London production of 1893; she too was a friend of Henry James, appeared in his plays and published a considerable correspondence with him. Another of what Dayrell called "my mother's old cronies" was Arthur Mackmurdo, the architect and pioneer of *Art Nouveau,* who was in turn an associate of Hubert's future tutor, Selwyn Image. And with the poet Stopford Brooke, Blanche carried on a correspondence from 1888 until his death in 1916. Brooke had an unusual career; he was a clergyman of the Church of England and honorary chaplain to the queen, a flamboyantly handsome and fashionable preacher who seceded from the Church in 1880 and took to literary work. His letters to Blanche were published in *The Life and Letters of Stopford Brooke* in 1917. Brooke once expressed surprise at the breadth of Blanche's reading of fiction, in French and German as well as in English, and professed his own contempt for novels. Nevertheless, he recommended to her topics for the "studies in selfishness" on which she was engaged in 1896, the year of her son Hubert's death; and he contributed a valedictory poem to *Last Studies,* Hubert's posthumously published work.

When Brooke produced a book on Browning in 1902, he was delighted that Blanche saw in it something of himself unnoticed by other readers:

You only, of all the people who have spoken to me (of my "Browning"), have recognised how much of myself is in the book, and that its interest to me is there, and less in that which I have said about Browning, and it was balm to my soul that some one had seen that.[44]

But her proposal that he should write a play was less cordially received:

Write a play indeed! . . . Do you want me to prove my inability in order to amuse you . . . or to say to your friends, as no doubt you said of Henry James . . . "Mr. Brooke tried too, he also failed. If men can do one thing, they think they can do all things. We women know our limits."[45]

Knowledge of limits did not prevent Blanche from making literary efforts in several forms. She published a novel, *Milly's Story,* several one-act plays, and many articles. Among the best known of these were "The Revolt of the Daughters" and "A Last Word on the Revolt," which appeared in January and March 1894 in the *Nineteenth Century*. Both the topic and the title of the first of the two articles caught on; by November, Richard Le Gallienne, something of a womanizer if not a feminist, was creating a stir with a lecture concocted under the same formula. In some sections of London society, as part of the general unrest of the fin de siècle, there existed a state of "war, open or concealed, between mothers and daughters." Blanche herself, being the mother only of sons, was in a position of observer which made it easier for her to find herself "ranged on the side of the younger generation" in its claim for an enlarged liberty and the right to make its own mistakes. "And why not," she asked, "since mistakes have to be made?" Education of girls was, of course, the heart of the matter:

Caste, so far as men are concerned, is dead and buried. . . . One stronghold, however, still remains in our midst, and it is to be found in the accepted handling and treatment of upper and upper-middle class girls. . . . For our own part we have no hesitation in saying that the girl who sees her brothers equipped for any professions they may choose, whilst she herself is confined to the single one of marriage, is a really ill-used person.[46]

She commended the example of the upper working class, whose daughters "do not sit at home eating the bread of idleness until called higher by a husband." While pointing in a friendly way to the egoism of the daughters and their "inner barrenness of spirit," she directed most of her advice to the mothers:

> These same daughters are not barrels of gunpowder only to be safely stored between layers of the sand of convention. It is when mothers have not lived in full confidence with their girls that they become so terribly afraid of them.

She ended with a sanguine prophecy of

> the woman of tomorrow . . . fearless of speech, who demands of herself and of every one else, not a flimsy and superficial "correctness" but that inward sincerity which enables her both to say and to hear "I have erred," with equanimity.[47]

These pieces provoked much discussion in print and drew strong attacks for suggesting that girls be allowed a *Wanderjahr* of self-discovery. In retrospect, the articles give an impression of great common sense and openness.

Between April and September 1898 Blanche contributed, to the *Westminster Gazette,* a series of fictional letters that to some extent satirize the kind of mother she had criticized in the articles. These letters were published in book form by William Heinemann in 1909 under the title *Letters of Diana, Lady Chesterfield, to her Daughter and Sister.* Stopford Brooke wrote a succinct appreciation of this work:

> Read Mrs. Crackanthorpe's *Letters of Diana Lady Chesterfield* with much pleasure. She has really created the Victorian lady of good society in the fifties and sixties, well-born, well-bred, of a fine, honest, tender character, but with the prejudices of an aristocrat, and a cultivated woman who has known the world for many years.[48]

From her sickbed the fictional Lady Chesterfield endeavors to control her daughter's actions, tastes, and even her thoughts, by methods combining emotional blackmail with sheer maternal autocracy: "Do I not know that my child would never neglect one opportunity of keeping her mother informed of her slightest movement?"[49] While instructing her daughter in the "Art of Pleasing," the mother comments briskly and acidly on contemporary manners and their decline, making many references that no doubt would have been recognized by contemporary readers. The rather acerbic irony of style was, according to Dayrell, very characteristic. Half concealed below this presentation of a deeply possessive and dominating matriarch there are signs that, as with Stopford Brooke's work on Browning, a good deal of the author's self went into the book. Lady Chesterfield advises her daughter to conceal her talent: "It must lie close hidden, folded in a napkin till . . . marriage shall have put you into possession of *yourself*."[50] The hymeneal image seems notably apt. There are also allusions to Plantaganet blood—"not on the wrong side of the blanket either"—and to the daughter as a "Latin of Latins . . . . sensitive, highly-strung, capable of the utmost devotion when your imagination is alight,"[51] that could equally be a self-projection of the writer, conscious of Gallic antecedents, or a posthumous vision of her eldest son, who had been dead little more than a year when the letters first began to appear. One letter contains a striking sentence that could be applied to the real-life relationship between mother and son: "To your service I then dedicated myself, and whatever of energy or of talent I might possess."[52]

Another of Blanche's essays, "Sex in Modern Literature" which appeared in the *Nineteenth Century* of April 1895, attracted wide attention and publicly expressed literary sympathies of a kind that were thought to have adversely affected Montague's career. This article was written in the context of the furious attack provoked by the presentation of the work of Ibsen and the publication of Zola in England. The efforts of those who hoped to have Ibsen's work banned were frustrated by the formation, following the success of *Hedda Gabler* in 1893, of a society for "Subscription Performances." As for Zola, the reaction was, at first, even more hostile: Ernest Vizetelly had been imprisoned in 1889 for publishing his work and that of Flaubert. Much of Blanche's article dealt with Zola, whom she supported unreservedly, despite the repudiation of him by some of his followers in France in 1887 on account of the brutality of *La Terre:* "Brutal as his facts often are, they are always grouped round a great central principle, a great governing idea, and so far may M. Zola be counted as an idealist."[53] The central principle she defended was that of the "sex-motif," and she described as "at once healthful and health-giving" the public hunger for reality in this sphere, and its insistence on "the right to know."[54] Praising Hardy's *Tess of the D'Urbervilles* and George Moore's *Esther Waters,* both of which had been indignantly attacked, she asserted that the mystery of sex, no matter how interpreted, "remains and will remain, the most beautiful *motif* for all creative work in every department of Art. It is the most powerful and the most convincing factor in life."[55] Such views were therefore among the molding influences in Hubert Crackanthorpe's youth.

At the end of the *Letters,* there is an obituary notice of the fictional Lady Chesterfield that, allowing for a touch of parody, foreshadows with curious prescience some of the newspaper accounts of Blanche herself after her death in 1928. More than anything else in the book, this obituary gives an impression of shrewd and ironic self-portraiture:

> Although of late years but little seen in London, she was at one time a very well-known figure in Society there. . . . She was noted for her keen observation of men and manners. Her mode of speech being a little impetuous, with a marked predilection for satire and epigram, she was apt to be misunderstood by strangers who did not know the sterling worth of her character.[56]

III

In January 1888 the way of life of Montague and his family was affected by the death of William Crackanthorpe of Newbiggin, a bachelor and almost a centenarian. During the last years of William's life, Montague had taken his two elder sons to visit their ancient cousin at Newbiggin; William addressed the boys with Regency formality and told them stories of the Grand Tour and of his visit to Napoleon in exile on Elba, which took place a few weeks before the escape to France in 1814.

[Napoleon] asked many questions about our militia, in all the details of which he seemed much better informed than any of us. He asked whether we were not formed when he was at Boulogne with his army, fearing an invasion. . . . He spoke with . . . an ease and good nature which I can assure you pleased us extremely. At intervals, though, he seemed to relapse into a kind of reverie, when his countenance wore an almost fiendish expression; the light of the moon shining on it perhaps increased and exaggerated it, and I doubt not that he breathed vengeance within himself against us for having dared to come and see him in his humility.[57]

Hubert was seventeen when his father inherited Newbiggin.. The estate then comprised six manors and some seven thousand acres of farmland, woods, and moor. The house and village lay in a deeply wooded valley on the bank of the river dividing Westmorland from Cumberland, the Crowdundle; in the rude epoch when border raids from Scotland made a defended tower a necessity to every northern town and village, the river had been used to supply a system of defensive moats. The earliest surviving parts of the house dated from the period of peace following the Wars of the Roses, but they stood on earlier foundations and incorporated portions of the original building that had been damaged, possibly sacked, during those wars. This fifteenth-century structure retained the defensive character of the original, typical of the Border country and consisting of a rectangular central or "pele" tower abutted by two lesser towers, one of them separated from the pele by a raftered hall built in 1533.[58] Despite the repairs and alterations made by Christopher Crackanthorpe in 1790, the interior remained rather dark, window openings within five-foot deep embrasures being in low ratio to somber, paneled wall space. A potential oppressiveness seemed to attach to the house and the adjoining church, shadowed by trees, as if too much diurnal family history, of births, senescence, and mortality, had been soaked up like blood and dried into the fabric, the deep red sandstone of these buildings. From the outside, the somewhat squat and frowning aspect of a Border stronghold was softened by that warm color, and by refraction of light from the surface of the river whose wide, shallow, trout-thick water runs fast below the windows and over a bed of the same stone, enouncing a constant song, eroding banks, gently shifting course, transcending the passage of generations, and bearing away with each flood a reddish detritus of earth, like a periodic infusion of ashes, or spent memories, toward the river Eden and the sea.

2

La Maladie de l'Idéal

Hubert and Dayrell Crackanthorpe were so near in age and intimacy that they grew up, despite fundamental differences of temperament, to think of themselves almost as twins. Hubert as a boy was physically slight and small, while Dayrell, though not tall, was from an early age as big as his elder brother and more robust, with an innate sense of being at home within his own body that photographs of Hubert, however sporting, do not quite convey. The personality of Dayrell, who became a diplomatist, is relevant to the history of Hubert's career, to his life, and especially to the events surrounding his death. Dayrell held discretion to be almost the first of virtues, and he developed, to a high degree, manipulative skills in dealing with those around him, particularly within his own family where, living to some extent in the shadow of a gifted and preferred older brother, he regarded self-protection as diplomacy's main aim.

The closeness of the brothers may have been the reason for their parents' decision to separate them at school; competitiveness perhaps produced strife, though love between the brothers was constant and, certainly on Dayrell's side, very deeply rooted. Endowment led to development of contrasting accomplishments: Dayrell had a facility for all sports but especially for individualistic forms such as fencing, dependent upon anticipation of an opponent's move; while Hubert showed a precocious interest in literature and politics that enabled him to keep pace with his parents' conversation. These exchanges were described by Dayrell, with studied ambiguity and emphasis, as "like guns of big intellectual *bore*, booming away from opposite ends of the table. It was all over our heads but Bertie managed to hold his own." And as

Hubert grew up, his commitment to literature become exclusive, drawing him away from his brothers, while Dayrell had many interests none of which was so obsessive. In the atmosphere of the family, Dayrell and the youngest son Oliver alleged a certain intellectual oppression, and as young men they would take the earliest chance of escape from the literary salon and its inhabitants, to lighter company: "There goes Oliver, out into the night," their mother would remark, a little histrionically. Dayrell felt that there existed between Hubert and his parents an intellectual sympathy and approval which diminished their interest in their younger sons; and though there is no reason to suppose from Dayrell's letters that either he or Oliver suffered from any lack of affection, there is little doubt that some idolization of Hubert was a part of the family pattern. Dayrell grew up with a severe, at moments crippling, stammer, traces of which remained all his life, in the deliberateness of his speech and in a kind of punctuating hiccup which had originated in breathing techniques, and which gave careful emphasis and idiosyncratic phrasing to his conversation. But in childhood any unhappiness could quickly reduce him to a wretched muteness; no very abstruse speculation is needed to connect this with the presence, just ahead of him, of a brother with a gift for words. Hubert's position as the firstborn boy was in any case a special one; after her husband's death Blanche wrote: "It was the most beautiful life *I* have ever known, and the son who has gone before him was made of the same *stuff*."[1]

Even the sons of liberal and progressive parents had to suffer some of the barbarities of Victorian education, though Dayrell's surviving school letters show that any complaints made to his mother were vigorously taken up with the authorities. Some of his accounts of school life, which must have been the same more or less for his brother, are horrifying enough:

> Mr. Cazalet . . . has a beastly caddish dodge of twisting your arm and hitting you with all his might on the back. He says it's impossible to break your backbone. . . . I called him a brutal cad, he gave me two more on the same place.[2]

He and Hubert had already been separated when in one letter he remarked: "When I come to think of it I think Bertie has a little the better school. I do not say this because I am unhappy (because I am perfectly happy)." The stammer was treated by a London specialist and required performance of drills and exercises, which Dayrell as a small boy felt made him disagreeably conspicuous. "I think it would help me to attend to the rules if you were to tell Bertie not to laugh. . . . I found this one *great* drawback last holidays. I feel sure you understand what I mean." There is already an unmistakable attempt at manipulation. Later, he used the stammer and the need for regular sessions with the specialist to engineer his early withdrawal from school at Winchester, where he was unhappy. Meanwhile Hubert and Oliver went to Eton; Oliver later entered Trinity College, Cambridge, and Dayrell spent two years at Merton College, Oxford, before taking his education into his own hands. Hubert's training and apprenticeship were quite unusual and specialized, forming by no means the least unusual part of his history.

Dayrell was inclined to be sardonic about the ways of Victorian parents, but a surviving series of handwritten holiday magazines, which he and Hubert edited, shows that the early upbringing of the brothers was not in an atmosphere of unrelieved intellectual or moral aspiration. The magazines suggest a mode of life in which an almost ebullient enjoyment found its characteristic expression in a frequent irony. The personalities of the brothers cannot usually be distinguished in the writing of the features, which include unsigned short stories and poems and such items as: "Drama," "Police News," "Expeditions," and "Cricket." The "Athletic Column" and "Fishing" were the most regular features, and the tone of the entries is humorous but not facetious. The magazines were named after the places where holidays were spent; the earliest, written when Hubert was twelve, is the *Mayes Gazette* of August 22, 1882, Mayes being an early Victorian country house near East Grinstead, in Sussex. The following item is characteristic:

ADVERTISEMENT.
EXCHANGE WANTED. Two large schoolboys are offered in exchange for a nice little girl. Apply at the Study, Mayes. A premium given for an arithmetician.

The initials of Hubert and Dayrell appear at the end of the

magazine: "Published at our office at Mayes in the County of Sussex. H. & D. C. proprietors."

Nine papers in all have been preserved, and it is clear from the numbering that many more were written.[3] Between 1883 and 1887 the Crackanthorpes spent the summer holidays in Westmorland, though one item speaks of the parents as having been "obliged to seek a more thorough change on the shores of the Mediterranean." In Westmorland, they stayed at a small and very picturesquely sited hotel, the Howtown, at the head of one of the two arms of the most beautiful of the Cumbrian lakes. A verse in the *Howtownian* celebrated the choice:

> A party this year into Westmorland went,
> A lady three boys & a middle-aged gent,
> Her nerves were worn out with society's duties,
> And he was exhausted with opposing the Q. C.'s.
> They therefore determined on trying the air
> Of the Lakes, their lowered tone to repair.
> The spot that our friends fixed on for their stay
> Was on Ullswater's shore in a sweet little bay.

Six issues of the *Howtownian* have survived from this time, including one that covers the period in August 1884 when George Gissing was staying at Bonscale on the same lake with the family of Frederic Harrison in the capacity of tutor.[4] In April 1885 there appeared an item, over the initials H. C., which noted the possibilities of the multiple negative in Cumbrian dialect:

> Yesterday as I was taking a stroll over the Hawse, I came across a crowd of farmers, boys and girls, in the midst of whom a man, gesticulating violently, was saying, "Han't none o' you chaps nowhere never seen nothing of no hat?"

In the same issue, in "The Ullswater Alphabet," is found the line, "H stands for Howtown, the place we love best," and until his death in 1950 Dayrell would make summer visits from Newbiggin to Howtown, to sit on the hill above the hotel, from which there is a view commanding both arms of the lake, or to ride into Martindale and the higher fells, as he and Hubert had done as boys. It was from Howtown that expeditions by carriage were made to Newbiggin to visit William Crackanthorpe at the end of his life.

The last holiday to be recorded was that of 1887. On the first of August, Hubert and Dayrell set out from Rutland Gate on a heavy tandem quadricycle to travel the two hundred and sixty miles to Sedbergh in Westmorland. Part of the journey by this cumbersome machine, on roads that were often rough, is described in the two surviving issues of the *Sedbergh Gazette*. On the first day they rode for eight and a half hours, covering a distance of sixty-one miles and stopping for meals at Rollins Tavern in Dunstable and at the Cock Hotel in Stony Stratford. At the first of these they composed a verse, to be set to the tune of "Two Lovely Black Eyes," which they wrote into the landlady's book, recording it "for the benefit of Lord Tennyson, Mr. Browning, and others":

> Cycling so wearily down the street
> Two sad youths one day did meet,
> A haven of rest, so clean, so sweet,
> Oh! What a surprise—
> If you would be wise,
> Never when passing through this little place,
> Past Rollins Tavern put on the pace,
> But stop and refresh and your mind solace,
> If you would be wise.

At the Cock in Stony Stratford they wrote another humorous verse, which they did not record; the first example suggests that the loss is slight. An account of the second day describes the departure from Towcester in the morning and a journey through Coventry that brought them by evening to Lichfield, where John Eardley-Wilmot had begun his schooling at King Edward's School.

The holiday magazines show that Hubert was fond of sport, though perhaps less so than his brother, and that he had a love of travel, which soon led him to France where he would discover more of his individuality, his talent, and his literary passion. Strangely enough, there is no trace in these schoolboy papers of any somber or ominous note, no melancholy verse or descriptive pieces, nothing to contradict Henry James's remark about Hubert in his preface to *Last Studies:*

> The author of *Sentimental Studies* was so fond of movement and sport, of the open air, of life and of the idea of immediate, easy, "healthy" adventure, that his natural vo-

cation might have seemed rather a long ride away into a world of exhilarating exposure, of merely material romance.[5]

The series of journals ceased after the inheritance of 1888, and the new immersion in the rural freedom and delights of Newbiggin, and in its deep historical and feudal perspectives. Even in the late nineteenth century, the feudal element was still much alive; the last traces of the system of feudal landholding did not disappear until the passing of the Enfranchisement Acts, some thirty years after Hubert's death, and records of manor courts continued to be kept until that time. So far as sport was concerned, the Newbiggin rivers, woods, and moors, fell and farmland, became home ground to the brothers and literary interests were probably temporarily overshadowed. The inheritance also brought a new and unusual social experience. The country population of Cumbria, containing Norse and Celtic elements and separated from Scotland by nationality and feuding, and from England by rings of mountains, remained self-contained, enclosed, and somewhat static. Most of the inhabitants of Newbiggin and of the surrounding villages and farms were the descendents of manorial families that had been *in situ* for many centuries. The manorial records, which were preserved in great quantities in the house at Newbiggin, show the same family names recurring from the time of the earliest documents. It is probable that many of these families were related by blood to the Crackanthorpe family whose innumerable daughters and younger sons, unless they migrated on marriage into other parts of Westmorland or Cumberland, would receive legacies of land at Newbiggin, or simply remain in the manors as tenants themselves. The resulting connections, although their precise origins whether legitimate or not would be forgotten with time, nevertheless produced a sense of community that helps to explain why in much of his work Hubert was able so naturally to study the lives of those apparently less fortunate than himself.

Hubert was at Eton from 1883 to 1888; he left in March, two months before his eighteenth birthday and without having entered the sixth form. The obvious conclusion must be that he belonged to the class of individualists who do not flourish in schools, especially in English boarding schools, and that by the end of his time at Eton he had grown impatient to embark on his proper life. This supposition is supported by the almost complete absence of notable achievement at Eton, the exception being the aptitude for French and the interest in French literature, which were probably first fostered by Hubert's house tutor, Francis Cristall Tarver, who was also senior French master.[6]

Although there were a number of school magazines, ephemeral and otherwise, Hubert seems not to have contributed to any of them nor to have belonged to any literary society. Eric Parker noted this surprising fact in his *Eton in the Eighties:*

> Journalists and authors of later life have usually given some hint of the future while still at school: but I do not know what (if there is any) Eton journalism to connect with the name of Hubert Crackanthorpe, who had a personality which won him many readers in the *Yellow Book* and took other readers to his published work.[7]

Parker himself was assistant editor of the *St. James' Gazette* in 1906 and edited the *Country Gentleman* from 1902 to 1907. Other Eton contemporaries of Hubert were Arthur Clutton-Brock, one of the early supporters of James Joyce, and Geoffrey Robinson, who became editor of the *Times* in 1912. In 1902 L. V. Harcourt compiled an *Eton Bibliography,* but there is no mention of Hubert among the editors and authors of the magazines and pamphlets that Harcourt unearthed, nor does his name occur in the correspondence between Harcourt and the editors concerned, in which nearly all the writers of unsigned contributions printed between 1883 and 1888 were identified. Hubert's classical tutor was Edward Lyttelton, one of the most distinguished of Eton masters and headmaster from 1905; but there is no sign that Hubert ever won any prize, exhibition, or any distinction in trials. The conclusion is that he had no particular academic success and that during his years at Eton his abilities remained hidden or latent. A few mentions of his name in accounts of football matches are almost the only traces of his passage through the school, and it would be hard to think of a record less relevant to the development of an adolescent sensibility. It has always been said of Eton that the cultivation of individuality is possible because of the degree of liberty the boys enjoy; Parker claimed that "Eton teaches those who teach themselves," and another apologist, Wasey Sterry, said that "Etonians had leisure to be idle . . . maybe it is turned to good account in various ways."[8] The willingness of Hubert's parents to see him leave school before completing his time, and the later substantial help they gave in setting him, or allowing him to travel, on a literary path, might be some evidence that his tutors had given encouraging reports of talent and that the parents were convinced of a potentiality, needing another sort of cultivation. Edward Lyttelton seems to have maintained an interest in him since it was Lyttelton who conducted Hubert's funeral service.

Montague Crackanthorpe, who had himself worked so hard in his academic youth, expressed surprisingly tolerant views on the subject of academic pressure indiscriminately applied:

> It is strange that a child should be crammed before he has power to digest, but this is now the accepted plan. Under a system of excessive competition we turn out prigs and pedants by the gross, thick with honour in more senses than one, whilst at the same time we strew the educational path with a quantity of waste products.[9]

It seems that Hubert profited by this generosity of opinion and was released at his own request into the outer world with its painful but stimulating tensions. In this real world he made friendships that had nothing to do with caste: in spite of Blanche's belief that caste was "dead and buried," it is obvious that the Victorian public schools were impregnated with class preconceptions and feelings, from which a writer of the kind that Hubert had the ambition to become—an empathic realist and psychologist—must free himself. The author of *Last Studies* cannot be identified with an ex-Etonian persona; in other words, he seems to have enfranchised himself, and this may partly have been achieved by lying low while at school, and escaping comparatively unmarked and unmolded.

Another aspect of public school life that may have repelled Hubert was the notorious and inescapable obscenity and homosexuality rampant in Victorian boarding schools. He himself, in one of his stories, mentioned the "unwholesome atmosphere of an expensive public school,"[10] a matter that was not often brought into the open until at least a generation later; and Dayrell, from Winchester, made many complaints on this score:

> I am sorry to say the fellows are just as much brutes in every way, and the school is in a frightful condition. Du Boulay [his housemaster] had me into his study a few days ago and said I was always to remember I was a Wykamist, not a thing to be proud of if he knew the condition of the house, which I'm afraid he doesn't.[11]

These letters from Winchester show the young diplomatist influencing his father by playing on his mother's natural disgust of this side of school life. The maneuver succeeded, Dayrell left Winchester at sixteen and then studied with a tutor in London before going on to Oxford. Hubert, in his copy of Paul Bourget's *Un Crime d'amour,* one of the books for whose publication Vizetelly was imprisoned in 1889, marked this passage, referring to the same problem in French schools:

> What ignominy and shame, in this world where the oldest boys were nineteen, and the youngest eight! There could not but be infamous sorts of love between the older and the younger.[12]

And next to these lines he placed a double marking:

> Alfred and he had been among the small number of those whom the contagion had not touched. But the greatest advantage of this disgust had been, for him at least, to lead him on quite early to the pursuit of girls, and his initiation to natural pleasures took place with the humblest of prostitutes.[13]

Naturally, it would have been easy enough for a young man in the London of the eighties to have had a similar experience and for similar reasons; there is some evidence to suggest that Hubert's initiation was of this kind, though whether it occurred in London, in Paris, or in some lesser center— Windsor, Stamford, Grantham—it is impossible to know.

II

Four years elapsed between Hubert's departure from Eton as a schoolboy of intelligence and sensibility but no apparent note, and his emergence in 1892 as coeditor of a new and spirited London literary journal, the *Albemarle,* which, presumably on paternal funds, ran a course of nine monthly issues. These four years must have been of great formative value and it was probably during them that he wrote his first stories. But the period is a misty one; many of the often repeated stories of his activities are either false or unsupported by convincing evidence. Katherine Lyon Mix in *A Study in Yellow,* in general so valuable and sound a source, states that Hubert matriculated at Cambridge and that his academic career was cut short by "having come home within a year on the losing side of an argument with the authorities,"[14] whereupon he turned to the writing of short stories. It is an attractive idea, but unfounded. It is certain that he was never a member of either Cambridge or Oxford universities, and although he might have spent some time at either place without belonging to the university, there is no other evidence to suggest that he did. After his death the *Kendal Mercury,* a Westmorland newspaper which could easily have checked facts, stated categorically:

> His parents desired that he should grow up to be unconventional, and to that end they caused him to be educated unconventionally. In the ordinary course of things he would have gone to Oxford or Cambridge. Instead of that he was sent to pursue his studies at the University of Geneva, and while there he improved his time by writing articles in the French language for many of the newspapers of the neighbourhood.[15]

There is clearly some truth in the first sentence, but the second is without foundation. It is not impossible that Hubert briefly attended a Continental university between 1888 and 1892; but his movements that can be traced during those years rule out any full-time university study, and a search at the University of Geneva excludes any possibility of his having been a student there. As for the articles in French mentioned by the *Kendal Mercury,* it is interesting that after Hubert's death the Paris paper *Le Journal* remarked that he wrote French with as much elegance as English, but no examples of this proficiency have survived.

One of the most sensitive and appreciative of the critics who have written about Crackanthorpe was Professor William C. Frierson who, in an article in 1928 on "Realism in the Eighteen Nineties and the Maupassant School in England," helped to perpetuate some of the myths:

> Bertie Crackanthorpe, a slim and sensitive youth, was expelled from Cambridge during his first year for some boyish prank. Thereupon he went to France and joined a traveling circus as a bareback rider. Returning eventually to England and the patronage of his family he began to write stories distinctive for their impersonality and unconcern with conventional values. . . .He lived a life of uncompromising revolt which fittingly terminated in the chivalric gesture of his death.[16]

Frierson repeated this account, in which the criticism is as apt as the biographical detail is mythical, in *The English Novel in Transition* in 1942; he was disposed to see revolt as "the dominant factor,"[17] in Hubert's life, but in fact the account given by the *Kendal Mercury* is nearer the truth. The circus incident belongs to a later period and is well evidenced, and described by Hubert himself in an ingenuously graceful piece in the *Yellow Book* of October 1895; it was a chance adventure and had nothing to do with education or revolt. That he cut short his formal academic training and turned to literature as a profession probably helped to produce a supposition of revolt in the minds of commentators who had little hard fact to rely on in the conspiracy of family silence that followed Hubert's death. Still worse, he was known to associate with writers and artists called "decadent" and even incurred that description himself by producing work that, in subject and technique, was seen to be French inspired and thought to be pessimistic. An incongruity between social "station," to use Frierson's word, and a full-blooded commitment to letters—a conjunction that in France would hardly have seemed incongruous in itself—in England led to the mistaken inference that Hubert's parents must disapprove of his literary passion or be unable to understand it. The exact contrary seems to have been the truth.

The contrast between what Hubert was, and what on a conventional assumption he might have been expected to become, seems to have caused as much mystification to Henry James as to anyone else. Some of James's remarks in his preface to *Last Studies* show signs of resentment, as in one whose preconceptions have been annoyingly disturbed:

> Was not the grossly obvious, more or less, what he had inevitably been brought up to—the pleasant furniture of an easy, happy young English family, the public school and the University, the prosperous society, the convenient chances, the refined professions, the placid assumptions, the view of the world as through rose-coloured gauze. . . . I sought an issue in the easy supposition that nothing is more frequent in clever young men than a premature attitude and a precipitate irony, and that this member of his generation differed from many others . . . only in the degree of his emphasis and his finish.[18]

Frierson thought this preface patronizing and gave his opinion that the choice of James for the purpose was an unhappy one.[19] Perhaps from one point of view he was right; Henry James knew Hubert's parents and might have seen that in intellectual matters he had been brought up without the complacency of any "placid assumptions."

Parental tolerance was even more marked in the period after Hubert left Eton; the story of his apprenticeship is an unusual example of understanding of adolescent literary aspiration. All the evidence suggests that Blanche and Montague endeavored to obtain for him a good and practical training for a career of letters, using such inflence as they and their friends could bring to bear, in place of the more conventional approach through academic work or the professions. Perhaps to spare a young writer conflict and disappointment was not the best way to help him, an insufficiently tempering experience, but the intention and practice were, at least, unorthodox and audacious.

It has often been said that Hubert was tutored by George Gissing and although there is no conclusive evidence of this, it is a possibility full of interest. K. L. Mix refers to it, the source being Richard Niebling's *The Early Career of George Gissing:* "According to Austin Harrison, Gissing tutored 'a son of Mr. Montague Crackanthorpe K.C.' The latter was the father of Hubert Crackanthorpe, a prominent realistic writer of the 'Nineties."[20] Apart from the fact that there were three brothers to whom Harrison's description could apply, there is no mention of a date that might help to identify the pupil. In his article on Gissing, which was written two years after the novelist's death, Austin Harrison recorded affectionate memories of him as tutor and friend. In an attempt to show that the story of Gissing "starving in garret and cellar" was "fiction of fiction," he described how his father, Frederic Harrison, had helped Gissing in his early career;[21] Frederic Harrison himself, in a letter to H. G. Wells, had debunked the myth of Gissing's penury and ascribed his self-projected image of misery to inner psychological causes.[22] Austin Harrison mentioned a Crackanthorpe son as one of several pupils to whom Gissing had been introduced through the Harrison family. It is true that the Harrisons had a house at Bonscale on Ullswater, and that Frederic Harrison was a lifelong friend of Sir Charles Cookson, Hubert's uncle, and that both of them, together with Montague, were members of the Athenaeum Club; all of which renders it quite possible and even likely that the Crackanthorpes would have been among those who gave employment to Gissing.

In August 1884 Gissing was at Bonscale with Austin and Bernard Harrison, and in the *Howtownian* there is mention of joint activities—in particular, a cricket match—of the two families. On August 12 and 14 Gissing wrote to his family describing in detail an expedition made on foot on August 11[23] that may have been the same as one described in the *Howtownian* of August 18 as "A Remarkable Pedestrian Feat." But Gissing's letters make no mention of the Crackanthorpes, nor is there any mention of Gissing by name in the *Howtownian,* although under the headings of "Arrivals" and "Departures" there is often a list of their friends and guests. The only possible reference could be this, in an "editorial note": "Several eminent literary performers have again offered their valuable aid and it is estimated that the forthcoming series of papers will eclipse in brilliancy those of all preceding years." This opens the fascinating but untestable possibility that Gissing was among the anonymous contributors to the *How-*

townian, the editorial purpose of which was "to give publicity to none but original compositions, whether prose or verse, & the name appended to each contribution as sent in to the Editor is a guarantee of the writer's good faith. Nothing which has already appeared in any other publication is admissible into our columns."

In view of Austin Harrison's remark, a stronger but equally untestable possibility would be that Hubert was tutored in literary studies by Gissing in the period between leaving Eton in March 1888 and his next emergence from obscurity, in France in the spring of 1889. The special interest is that this was the beginning of the period in which Hubert's literary character was formed and his orientation determined. Gissing was an admirer of French realism, and much of his own work was intended as a development of it. Hoping to free the English novel from moral ties, he propounded a version of the theory of naturalism advanced by Emile Zola and Edmond and Jules de Goncourt:

> Let the novelist take himself as seriously as the man of science; be his work to depict with rigid faithfulness the course of life, to expose the secrets of the mind, to show humanity in its eternal combat with fate.[24]

Gissing was in London from January 1888 until his departure for Paris in September. It would be quite in keeping with the literary sympathies of Hubert's parents to have sent him to Gissing, and if they did, it may be supposed that Gissing's view of the novelist's vocation would be inflaming to a young imagination and that it was under the influence of Gissing that Hubert turned so earnestly to the study of French contemporaries.

Apart from these speculations, the first known stage in Hubert's preparation for a literary career was his stay in France in 1889, when he transformed his schoolboy French into the fluent speech of a lover of the language. He lodged with a Protestant clergyman in the ancient town of Orthez in the Béarn, under the Pyrenees. In the nearby town of Pau, the birthplace of Henri of Navarre, and in its vicinity, a discriminating English colony had established itself in the nineteenth century. Some of the settlers were the families of soldiers who had discovered the delights of this country when campaigning

with Wellington in 1814; it was before the walls of Orthez that
Wellington's army had engaged that of Marshal Soult, who
commanded a force one third smaller than Wellington's and
who retired only after fierce fighting. At Orthez, Hubert had
the good fortune to make one of his deepest and must fruitful
friendships. The poet Francis Jammes, in his autobiography,
described his first meeting with Hubert at the *Cercle d'Orthez,*
and his first impression of him:

> A very distinguished young Englishman came at this time
> to stay at Orthez and brought an unexpected distraction
> into my life. He was called Hubert Crackanthorpe . . . and
> in his heyday was to achieve a resounding success. His first
> book, *Wreckage,* full of bitterness and lofty scepticism, was
> thought scandalous but captivating. This misanthrope re-
> mained my friend until his tragic end. But in 1889, he was
> still no more than an elegant youth, highly-strung and
> highly-bred, who rather disappointed his family by show-
> ing no desire at all to follow their centuries' old tradi-
> tions. . . . He was introduced to me at the *Cercle* by M.
> Vidal, the man with the fluffy side-whiskers, who scarcely
> knew what to make of this gentleman with the Byronic
> glance, who would icily propound . . . the most perturbing
> theories.[25]

This is both the first and the most detailed description of
Hubert's personality to find its way into print. The mention
of the Byronic glance and of the uttering of disturbing
theories contributes to a picture of a clever adolescent still in
search of himself. So far as family disappointment at neglect
of age-old traditions is concerned, it is likely that Hubert felt
that until he could prove his literary ability his father would
remain disappointed that he had not gone to a university; but
the facts suggest that, if Hubert did have such a feeling, it was
less a reality than the result of filial sympathy or the memory
of scholastic pressure in childhood. Francis Jammes also stated
that Hubert was kept on a tight financial rein by his father.
This may well have been an aspect of Montague's policy
toward his sons, a result of his own early struggles, and it is
to some degree confirmed by a letter written many years later
by Dayrell to his wife, from the British Embassy in Tokyo
where he was serving as first secretary. She had returned
alone to England to canvass Montague's help in a financial

crisis, evidently by no means the first in Dayrell's life: "I know so well by now with what a bad grace my father consents to put his hand in his pocket, and how he makes one feel it whenever he is compelled to do so."[26]

There is no reason, however, to think that in this vital matter Hubert had any ground for complaint against his father; his literary earnings can hardly have supported him, yet he was soon able to marry and live comfortably in London, traveling whenever and for as long as he wished, free from the anxieties that beset Le Gallienne, for example, or Gissing, or Francis Jammes himself, and with no profession but that of writer. An understandable resentment of privilege is evident in the tone of some of the remarks of English contemporaries, particularly those of William Rothenstein in *Men and Memories,* written thirty-five years after Hubert's death but with a still noticeable animus. The criterion of need applied by Montague to his sons' affairs was that of work and the liberty to do it without harassment. In another letter, Dayrell explained to his wife:

> I know my father well enough to feel sure that the only way for me to count on a continuance of his help is my remaining at my post and at my work. . . . He would not have the same feeling of responsibility towards me if I were to absent myself from the public service.[27]

The most significant part of Jammes's account is his description of Hubert as highly-strung and misanthropical, both these rather vague terms being equally applicable to Jammes himself at this period of his life. The combination of qualities recalls the character of the literary man Charles Demailly in the Goncourt novel of that name, in a passage marked by Hubert in his copy: "This nervous sensibility, this continual jarring of impressions . . . had made of Charles a melancholic—he was melancholic like a man of spirit, with good manners."[28]

The exact length of Hubert's first stay at Orthez is not known. From a remark of Jammes it seems that it lasted several months at least: "Hubert Crackanthorpe hardly knew the French language when we first met. Two or three months later he spoke it fluently and even with charm."[29] No doubt he stayed away from England as long as he could. His mother later described in general terms her view of this period of self-discovery:

> The wiser and more catholic the woman, the quicker she will be in realising that her best-loved son must have his *Wanderjahre.* She cannot hold him back. She can only gaze after his retreating form from the watch-tower of her love; too often he departs with never a backward glance at her.[30]

The friendship with Francis Jammes was a happy accident, traveler's good luck; but as a planned part of his literary apprenticeship Hubert seems also to have been introduced, between 1889 and 1891, to a number of distinguished French authors of an older generation. The second issue of the *Albemarle* contained an interview by Hubert with Emile Zola, which had taken place in 1891, but which makes it clear they were already acquainted; "I am very glad to have seen you," said Zola jovially, "I wish you all success." And Hubert remarked on "new changes in Zola since we last met." By 1893 Hubert's relations with several French authors had become well enough established to allow him to introduce to them the poetry of their compatriot Francis Jammes; among those whom he certainly knew were Stéphane Mallarmé, André Gide, and Henri de Régnier. From the evidence of contributions and of promises to contribute to the *Albemarle,* the names of Maurice Barrès, Paul Bourget, and Guy de Maupassant can be added with less certainty to the catalogue.[31] Some of these he may have met in the small apartment in the rue de Rome where Mallarmé, according to R. H. Sherard, "Used to hold once a week a reception for his young literary friends. . . . One drank mild rum punch, and one listened to the master as he discoursed on art and literature."[32]

III

For an uncertain time after his first visit to France in 1889, Hubert studied in London under Selwyn Image, a disciple of John Ruskin, who from 1908 to 1914 was Slade Professor of Fine Arts at Oxford, a chair first occupied by Ruskin himself. Image preserved a number of letters received from Hubert over a period of years which are among the very few letters known to have survived.[33] The first of them, undated, was written from Newbiggin at the end of the period of tutelage:

> My dear Image,
>   My father tells me that he has arranged with you for our meetings to end with this month and I want to tell you how much I feel that I owe to you—in more ways than one. I am really sensible of all that you have done for me, and I am very grateful. And though, I am no longer to come to you at Fitzroy Street on Wednesdays and Saturdays, may I still, from time to time, ask for your advice & criticism with regard to my work? I value it so highly that I should be indeed sorry to lose it—at least all at once.
> Always yours, Hubert Crackanthorpe.

Evidently the tuition by Image included discussion of Hubert's own literary efforts as well as more general aesthetic guidance, and the letter shows how seriously Hubert took himself. The absence of a date makes it impossible to know when the arrangement ended; the *Albemarle* first appeared in January 1892, so it seems probable that the tuition covered at least the two preceding years, from the time of Hubert's return from France in 1889.

Selwyn Image was born in 1849 and was one of the central figures of influence in the eighties and nineties, though not himself a major creative personality. But as scholar, artist, and poet his opinion was much respected by many of the young men of the period, who came to his house in Fitzroy Street to seek it. He was a friend and admirer of Walter Pater, ten years his senior, and it is possible that the profound influence of the ungregarious Pater on the writers of the fin de siècle—Le Gallienne described him as "something like an English Flaubert"[34]—reached many of them through Image's mediation. Hubert, as Image's pupil, was naturally much exposed to the flavor that became, in Bernard Muddiman's words, "disseminated like a perfume from the writings of Pater in the men who came after him."[35] Occasionally, there are unmistakable Paterian traces discernible in Hubert's writing; for example in a studied, rather slow rhythm of prose, or in the idiosyncracy of opening a paragraph with a conjunction and closing it on a preposition, a device which effectively spreads the flow of rhythm. And even at moments in his life, it is easy enough to find parallels with *Marius the Epicurean:* "There was everything in the nature and training of Marius to make him a full participator in the hopes of . . . a new literary school." Hubert too had "early laid hold of the principle . . . that to know when one's self is interested, is the first condition of interesting other people";[36] while in his literary character there was, perhaps to a fault, the Paterian passion and seriousness — *la passion et le sérieux qui consacrent.*

If Hubert's tutelage to Image was arranged with a view not only to introducing him to congenial literary contemporaries and groups of artists, but also to preparing him for editorship of a literary magazine, the plan was well judged. Image was one of the foremost of those who began the fight against the watchdogs of Victorian moral and aesthetic austerity; in a letter to Herbert Horne, with whom he was joint editor of the *Hobby Horse,* one of the most notable periodicals of the time, he spoke of the "gospel of sensuousness, as the very foundation of all fine art. . . . We must exterminate the impudent creatures who oppose and seek to rule us; or be ourselves exterminated."[37] Edgar Jepson described Image as "a man of an unerring soundness of judgement, and capable too of immense indignation, as violent as those of his friend Ruskin himself, though far more coherent."[38] Like Stopford Brooke, he had been a clergyman whose vocation was eroded by doubt; the influence of such figures was noted by Blaikie Murdoch who surmised "that the upheaval of the nineties was largely due to the marked increase, during the eighties, of agnosticism . . . in whose wake there lurked . . . a desire for freedom in art."[39] Not all the young men who came under Image's influence, however, regarded him with excessive reverence. Ernest Dowson described him in a letter:

> Image, the most dignified man in London, a sort of cross in appearance between a secular *abbé* and Baudelaire, with a manner *du 18me siècle*—waiting in a back passage of the Alhambra to be escort to ballet-girls.[40]

Image shared the house in Fitzroy Street with Herbert Horne and Blanche Crackanthorpe's friend Arthur Mackmurdo, the three of them having formed the *Century Guild* in 1882, to bring together artists and craftsmen for the cooperative study of design.[41] Mackmurdo was the architect of the group and was another friend of Ruskin, with whom he had traveled in Italy in 1874. The so-called Fitzroy Group soon became an intellectual center for the arts in London and was the gathering place of contributors to the *Hobby Horse*. During his period of tutelage Hubert must have met there most of the young men who became his friends and whose reputations were being, or were about to be made, such as Lionel Johnson, Richard Le Gallienne, Ernest Dowson, and others. In one of his letters, Dowson referred ironically to "the sacred house in Fitzroy Street";[42] and Victor Plarr, who lived there for a time, as did Lionel Johnson and Augustus John, gave an account in his book on Dowson:

> The house was at one time referred to as "Fitzroy" and . . . "Fitzroy" was a movement, an influence, a glory. . . .Professor Image . . . kept a studio there, as did the late Mr. Maclachlan the landscapist. . . . the late Hubert Crackanthorpe was for a time a pupil of Professor Image. Numbers of other distinguished people visited this artistic colony. The list of them would include . . . Mr. Walter Crane, the late Oscar Wilde, Mr. Dolmetsch . . . Mr. W. B. Yeats, Mr. William Rothenstein, Father John Gray, the Rev. Stewart Headlam, and a host more.[43]

Ernest Dowson wrote of "Fitzroy" to Arthur Moore with the gusto that marks his letters:

> Plarr and Image . . . contemplate a colony *à la* Thoreau, of *Hobby Horse* people and a few elect outsiders each with a "belovèd"—(please mind the accent) where there will be leisure only for art and unrestrained sexual intercourse.[44]

There was some overlapping between the Fitzroy Group and the Rhymers' Club, which included among its official members several of those who habitually met at Fitzroy Street: Plarr, Johnson, Le Gallienne, Dowson, Arthur Symons, and W. B. Yeats.[45] All of them were in the habit of congregating at the Crown in Charing Cross Road, where drinks were served after midnight, and of whose Saloon Bar it was said that there the "spirit of the nineties found its freest and fullest expression." Stories of self-conscious excess seem to be mythical; Grant Richards remarked that "a visit to the Crown was not a dissipation; it was the end of the day's work, a chance of meeting and talking with congenial friends, of exchanging ideas."[46] Mark Longaker described the ambience and some of the clientèle:

> To the passer-by in the hours before 11 o'clock, the Crown seemed to be nothing save an ordinary public house. . . . When the music halls let out, however, the Crown took on an atmosphere. . . .then it became a sort of Mermaid Tavern for the younger generation of artists. From eleven o'clock until the lights were dimmed at twelve-thirty there was an ever-widening group of figures who were devoting themselves seriously or in appearance to the arts. Here one was sure to find a convivial group, some of whom appeared with the ladies whom they had recently applauded for their singing or dancing at the Alhambra, others with their models. . . .On weekday nights one was almost certain of finding Arthur Symons, Conal O'Riordan, Herbert Horne, . . . Lionel Johnson, Max Beerbohm and occasionally Aubrey Beardsley and Hubert Crackanthorpe. Even Paul Verlaine, on a visit to London in November 1893, was taken to the Crown.[47]

According to Rothenstein, hot port was the usual drink.

Hubert had connections also with the Independent Theatre Society founded by J. T. Grein in 1891. In that year Grein put on Ibsen's *Ghosts* and earned a scandalous reputation in consequence—"the best-abused man in London." Grein made himself the center of a group parallel to that in Fitzroy Street, both being concerned with the freeing of the arts and the war on hypocrisy; the society was formed in order to stage plays before a membership audience and so evade the Lord Chamberlain's censorship. Grein's declared object was to "nurture realism, but realism of a healthy kind." The realism of *Ghosts* was not in general found healthy by the critics; in a famous leading article it was compared to "an open drain, a loathsome sore unbandaged."[48] The Victorian dread of the revelation of any venereal infection that might prove intractable to treatment is easily forgotten; Ibsen's play, and the revulsion it provoked, have a gruesome kind of relevance to Crackanthorpe's career, the end of which was to be overshadowed by a like problem. But the emancipating results of the endeavor of literary men can be measured by the fact that in 1897, only six years after the first presentation of the play, a new production of *Ghosts* was attended by Queen Victoria as part of her jubilee celebrations.

Both Hubert and his parents joined the Independent Theatre Society, and he wrote one or more one-act plays for the September 1894 program. Grein also organized the Sunday Popular Debates, some of which Hubert attended and at one of which, in February 1894, he lectured on the art of fiction. Conal O'Riordan, who was on Grein's committee, wrote in his foreword to *J. T. Grein: The Story of a Pioneer:* "Two of that committee and two of our lecturers, committed suicide; no small feather in the cap of the *Sunday Observance Society.*"[49] The logic is obscure, but the reference is to Hubert, among others, and to his supposed manner of death. Grein also edited a monthly review, *To-Morrow,* to which Hubert contributed an article on Maurice Barrès and Paul Bourget that appeared in February 1897. Grein's determination to depict in the theater "human beings . . . speaking human language and torn by human passions" was not reduced by the reception of *Ghosts.* In the same year he produced Zola's *Thérèse Raquin,* and Zola expressed his pleasure at this during the interview with Hubert:

> Our work is attracting more attention in England, is it not? It is more freely discussed that it was. And your stage too is getting emancipated. This Independent Theatre is an excellent sign. My Little *Thérèse Raquin* excited quite a little battle, they tell me. All that is good.[50]

George Bernard Shaw's *Widowers' Houses* was produced at the Independent Theatre in December 1892 and was uproariously received. It has been said that "on the night of December 9th 1892, at the Royalty, two men became famous in the theatre; G. B. S., the author, and James Welch the comedian."[51] Welch was Richard Le Gallienne's brother-in-law, having married Sissie, Le Gallienne's closest and beloved sister, who was one of the embodiments of the feminine spirit of the fin de siècle and who, by taking her *Wanderjahr* after marriage rather than before it, was to play a dramatic part in the life of Hubert Crackanthorpe.

The movements of the nineties in England met resistance but were irresistible at the moment of flow, a tidal surge onto an island coast. It is obvious that much of the reputation for decadence of artists and writers originated in what then seemed extravagances of behavior by contrast with a severely restrictive convention; as Zola pointed out in the interview with Hubert, "You have got under the yoke of Puritans, and as long as you remain so, you will never have a really fine outburst,"[52] If the groupings of intellectuals in London often seem to be slightly lame versions of more spontaneous, less hampered associations in Paris, nevertheless it was the members of these groups who gave, against Victorianism, what Ezra Pound in another context called the "first great heave." And their shared ideals, especially the hatred of cant and the determination to approach and render reality freely, gave them a cohesion and integrity from which minor figures gain a deserved prestige and a right to be remembered. Blaikie Murdoch aptly described them as "seceders."[53] As a very young man, with the help of his parents and their friends, Hubert placed himself at a point of liaison and advantage with the central figures of these movements. In 1894 he wrote: "In the little bouts with the bourgeois . . . no one has to fight single-handed. Heroism is at a discount";[54] and, "young men of today have enormous chances, we are working under exceedingly favorable conditions."[55] In his first public literary activity, the editorship of the *Albemarle,* Hubert was able to attract contributions from many writers, critics, and artists who were already exploiting the cultural springtime, and he soon became one of them himself, though he was to take his own particular orientation; "the reception of theory, of hypothesis, of beliefs," declared Pater, "depend a great deal on temperament."[56]

All of this background makes little sense of Henry James's reference to Hubert's "comparatively unassisted and isolated state."[57] But in an interior application, the phrase is true. The bright youth and apt pupil—"charming creature," said Ella D'Arcy, "every one loved him"[58]—was exploring his own temperament and examining his responses to the world, gauging his emotions in the light of his reading; and transforming himself into a writer by pupation, through experiment, and with the help of others' writings, a process strikingly described by Bourget in a passage that Hubert marked:

To write, is to transform oneself into a field of experiment. . . . What Claude Bernard did with his dogs and Pasteur does with his rabbits, we must do with our own heart, injecting it with all the viruses of the human spirit. . . . And there we have another fine page to add to the literary patrimony.[59]

IV

Hubert Crackanthorpe's library, mainly of nineteenth-century French works, has been preserved. The many markings he made in these books provide evidence both of influences on his own work and of alignments, leanings, affinities of taste and temperament, and parallels of experience. All quotations from French works in the present study, except those from Francis Jammes and his biographer Robert Mallet, are taken from passages marked by Hubert himself in his own copies of the books quoted.[60] The marked passages, a small fraction of which are quoted, fall with notable consistency into three rough categories. Some concern literary theory and criticism; some are passages exemplifying techniques of narrative, description, or characterization obviously made in the process of self-instruction, in the attempt by a young writer to find his place in the literary sequence; the rest, a great many, seem to have nothing to do with technical matters but are expressions of temperament introspectively viewed, passages of self-analysis by writers who, whether speaking in their own voice or through their personages, appear to be carrying on, often in face of disillusionment and a final despair of happiness, a process like the one described above by Bourget. "Midnight strikes," wrote Henri-Frédéric Amiel in his journal of August 8, 1865, "one more step taken towards the grave."[61] Flaubert himself expressed something of the same feeling in a letter to George Sand: "Each one of us carries about in himself, his own Necropolis."[62] By no means all the marked passages falling within the last group are as pessimistic or as death orientated as these two; nor would it be safe to conclude from their emphasis on melancholy and despair that Hubert was himself irrevocably depressive or despairing, any more than Pater's obsession with death imposes that conclusion. But it is not surprising, especially in view of his youth, that details of Hubert's life frequently give the impression of being, so to speak, extrapolations from the works he studied, or even from his own. In his work there is repeated reference to an overlapping between life and literature, tending to produce confusion and psychological enervation. Bourget, writing on Flaubert in his *Essais de psychologie contemporaine,* pointed out that in a man who lives for letters, the facts of literary rhetoric become identical with facts of the psychology of the writer, because of the degree to which theories of art engage the personality, and so "the way one writes blends into the way one feels."[63]

Nevertheless, the consistency with which, throughout a wide reading, Hubert noted expressions of despair and of consciousness of mortality clearly indicates that behind the bright exterior was a mind preoccupied by the painful contrast of the real and the ideal, between the excitements of free imagination and the restriction, the triviality, of experience. Amiel spoke of this "maladie de l'idéal,"[64] a sickness that can produce great searching and striving followed by, or alternating with, the collapse of reasonable hope. Unhappiness was widely thought to be a literary prerequisite; Georges Pellissier ascribed all of Alphonse de Lamartine's faults to his being too happy.[65] And the unhappiness must be a sensual one, seen as a failure of experience to supply matching satisfactions for what Paul Verlaine called "la fureur d'aimer."[66] Frustration produces a tempest of demand in youth that supply cannot appease; Bourget spoke of the torment of physical desire as so painful that "some timid young men experience, merely in crossing the threshold of establishments where ready pleasure is sold, an almost intolerable racing of the heart."[67] Libido thus accumulated would have a tendency, at least in complex natures, to clash with the sense of moderation and of shame, and this could be a version of the clash between real and ideal. The Goncourts spoke enviously of those "lucky fellows—not such analysts as we are: grosser natures that fuddle themselves regularly with effortless pleasure . . . even the mind in rut."[68]

The two volumes of Amiel's *Journal intime* carry more numerous and more emphatic markings than any of Hubert's other books. Amiel was professor of philosophy at the University of Geneva, a poet, and a diarist who tirelessly studied his own feelings and traced his sense of debility to its source in fear of action. "All action is my cross," he wrote, and "I have cancelled myself out by analysis";[69] born in 1821, he died, self-observant and self-detracting to the last, in 1881. Hubert seems to have felt a profound recognition of fellowship with this misanthrope who felt that the vast majority of mankind represented no more than "la candidature à l'humanité."[70] Amiel's friend Edmond Scherer described him as the martyr of the ideal who could not accept himself: "Amiel was the victim of a very special psychological constitution. . . .a modest and tender spirit, he was torn between love, tending to possession, and the profane satisfaction."[71] These marked passages in Amiel that do not seem to have anything to do with a study of the art of fiction relate unmistakably to the emotional experience of Hubert himself: "The ideal poisons for me any imperfect possession,"[72] and "fear of the thing I love is my undoing."[73] The last word on this problem inside the personality may be allowed to the brothers Goncourt, who so often defined in lapidary phrases the dilemmas that beset the literary men of their day:

> Modern love is no longer the healthy love, the almost hygienic love of the old days. We have built upon woman something like an ideal model of all our aspirations. . . . in her and through her, we hope to satisfy the insatiable and the unbridled in us. We no longer know how to be simply and stupidly happy with a woman.[74]

Another perturbing mental duality, often the product of a too agile and comprehensive imagination, may produce ambivalences of feeling and the instability to which artists are specially prone: "I am divided, and perplexed,"[75] said Amiel, and Jules Michelet defined the duality: "The artist is a manwoman. I mean a complete man who, having the two genders of the mind, is fruitful."[76] Amiel in a beautiful image described this state:

> There are two forms of autumn: the vaporous and musing kind, and the highly colored and lively; almost the difference of the sexes. . . .Is each season bisexual in its own way? Does each have its minor and its major scale, its two sides, of light and dark, gentleness and strength? It is possible. Every complete thing is double.[77]

George Meredith, another significant influence for Hubert and his contemporaries, also wrote of "men who have the woman in them without being womanised; these are the pick of men."[78] So it is not until fear of self-knowledge is dispersed that the writer can have all his temperament at his disposal and know what Pater called "the special felicities of his own nature";[79] he is then free to measure his extent and discover his limits. Hubert seems to have sought this self-knowledge through literary contacts and affiliations of which these markings in his library give some evidence. It is possible, too, that a close relationship with a clever mother, an ardent identification perhaps, would contribute to the duality and lend certainty, later on, to a young man's literary empathy with feminine subjects.

V

During 1891 and 1892 Hubert was writing his first stories, to be published in 1893 in the collection entitled *Wreckage*. Meanwhile the first issue of the *Albemarle* appeared in January 1892, with the stout declaration that the periodical was to be characterized by "individual independence of thought."[80] Hubert's twenty-second birthday fell roughly halfway through his editorship, which lasted from January to September; the four years of his apprenticeship, culminating in this public trial of capacity, curiously resemble a course of academic study leading to an examination, as if his father's scholastic habit was imposing itself unconsciously.

The *Albemarle* was a rather haphazard synthesis of artistic, political, and social elements; the lively tone of the material and the elegant presentation were noted in a number of contemporary reviews. Financial backing was evidently supped by Montague who "put his hand in his pocket" to the tune of whatever sum was necessary for the nine months of this trial. He also contributed two articles on legal topics, and his and Blanche's social and political connections seem to have been used to obtain contributions from some prominent political and social figures. The political features were of a Liberal tendency; contributors included Sir Charles Dilke, Herbert Gladstone, David Lloyd George, R. B. Haldane, Auberon Herbert, and Ben Tillett. Articles on feminism were provided by Elizabeth Holland Hollister, and on women's education by the Countess of Malmesbury; the Earl of Desart supplied a story in three parts that was described in one review as "intensely amusing."[81] Stopford Brooke contributed two poems, and the name of Sir Charles Cookson appeared among those who had promised to contribute. The March issue had Selwyn Image's poem "La Rose du bal"; Herbert Horne's poem "Dissipabitur Capparis" and Richard Le Gallienne's "Orbits" appeared in May. Lionel Johnson contributed two short stories, "A Commentary on Love" and "Mors Janua Vitae." One of the early poems of Ernest Dowson, "To One in Bedlam," later reprinted in *The Second Book of the Rhymers' Club,* appeared in August. John Gray's lecture on "The Modern Actor" was included in July, and an article was promised on the same subject by Herbert Beerbohm Tree. The last issue, in September, contained an article by Shaw entitled "Shaming the Devil about Shelley," in which he accused Edmund Gosse of talking "bogus Shelleyism" by ignoring Shelley the hardened sinner, republican, and atheist: "If it were only to keep ourselves from premature putrefaction, we must tell the truth about somebody, and I submit that Shelley has pre-eminent claims to be that somebody."[82]

Each issue had as frontispiece a lithograph by a contemporary artist, and some of these were so much appreciated at the time of their appearance that copies of the *Albemarle,* which was published at sixpence, were a few weeks later changing hands at ten shillings. The first number had Whistler's famous lithograph "A Song on Stone," on which Zola congratulated Hubert on the occasion of their interview: "You have been lucky to get a drawing from Whistler for your first number . . . a great artist. . . . I wish you all success. Send me your review when you get another Whistler!"[83] Later issues had works by Walter Sickert, Wilson Steer, Frederick Leighton, and Fantin-Latour. The editors evinced an obvious interest in impressionism. In May, L. Baynard Klein discussed and defended the work of Monet, Renoir, Degas, Pissarro, and Sisley in a piece entitled "Modern French Art and its Critics." In August the English impressionist Charles Furse contributed an article on "Impressionism—What it Means," in which he discussed Whistler, Degas, Monet, Manet, and Puvis de Chavannes. He described pitilessly the strain put on the conventional critic by the development in contemporary arts:

> The academician is fond of picturing to himself the impressionist as a young man, eager for a place in the vanguard, . . . whose maxim is to find out what people most dislike and then to perpetrate it, who uses the public indignation and disgust as stepping-stones to notoriety. . . .The mass of intelligent people . . . are bound to remain a generation behind the painter, whose whole life and energy are devoted to the study of his art. . . .The same remark applies to both literature and music.[84]

The experimental approach of the impressionists and their choice of the ordinary as subject for technical exploration were discussed in a solicited contribution by D. S. MacColl, whom Rothenstein described as the "Ruskin of the Impressionists" and "a power in the land." MacColl's article, "The Logic of Painting," gave a clever analysis of the impressionist method by contrasting it with that of the great landscapists of the early part of the century:

> The order of thought [in Turner] is:—a Place—under an explanatory effect of light. The order of thought in a landscape by M. Monet is:—Effect of Light—on something somewhere. . . . By the Impressionist then the wave will be represented by some symbol and summary of its agitation, and the leading character of its life [that is a flux of forms] thus preserved.[85]

Avoidance of the explanatory in favor of an impassive presentation of natural phenomena of course suggests a parallel to the supposed impassivity of the realists; and in both cases the artist's passion is as fully conveyed as in work governed by any other theory of presentation. Flaubert's remark, "In the ideal I have of art, I believe that one should show nothing of one's own, and that the artist should no more appear in his work than does God, in nature,"[86] does less than nothing, by bringing the Divinity into the comparison, to reduce the artist's position in relation to his own work or to the world; indeed to a very young writer the scale of the conception must have seemed wonderful, as it already had to George Moore.

Hubert Crackanthorpe's first contribution to the *Albemarle*, in January 1892, was a short piece entitled "Mr. Henry James as a Playwright." The subject of the theater and of dramatic work of literary quality was, naturally, one much discussed in the wake of Ibsen's first successes in England. James was one of many novelists of standing who tried to adjust their talent, without much success, to writing plays or to dramatizing their novels. Hubert too was drawn to the theater, and with Henry Harland was to write a comedy for the stage as well as the one-act plays offered to Grein. However, he now used the occasion of a review to offer criticism going far beyond the realm of theater, perhaps recklessly far for a critical novice.

There is no doubt, despite some sharp words in this review, of Hubert's deep admiration for James, who in his preface to *Last Studies* mentioned that Hubert and two other young men of letters had recently offered to him a "substantial token of esteem."[87] And in 1896, in the last work written before his death, an article on Barrès and Bourget that appeared post-humously in *To-Morrow,* Hubert expressed his admiration hyperbolically: "For one tale by Mr. Henry James one would willingly barter all the countless volumes by the English novelists of the eighteenth century."[88] This spendthrift declaration contrasts sharply with the criticism in the *Albemarle:*

> Mr. James' play is eminently unsatisfactory, and it is to me, in spite of my admiration for much of his work, unsatisfactory because it is characteristic. Mr. James' talent is essentially the product of culture. He has studied, and studied very carefully, the best French models. His talent has no singular defects but it has also no singular virtues. It is a talent of negatives: not shallow rather than subtle, not slovenly rather than polished, not brutal rather than refined, Un-American rather than European. Too fragile, too delicately nurtured to battle with the strain of human passions, it is better suited to skim their surface than to sound their depths. Mr. James does not rise to the emotional passages: for *he has no real sense of situation;* and being unable to grapple with the passions of his characters, seeks refuge in rhetoric. . . . It is said that he has in hand another play. I, for one, sincerely hope that this is so; for it is only because I am confident that he will one day give us a light comedy of sterling value, that I have ventured to touch upon one or two weak spots in *The American.*[89]

It would be hard to say whether the criticism or the encouragement is the more impertinent. The critic's age—twenty-one—and the negative method, which leaves on the page a catalogue of literary faults that the older writer, by implication, is judged to have barely avoided, could only have increased James's annoyance if the review ever came to his notice. In the circumstances it is probable that it did. The special, youthful characteristic of the piece is that it is cutting and yet innocent. Memory of the impertinence may have outweighed appreciation of the "token of esteem," and, associated with other bad memories of James's adventure into the theater, it might account for some of the grudging tone of the preface to *Last Studies,* described by Wendell Harris as "one of the most cautiously ambiguous 'appreciations' ever produced."[90]

W. C. Frierson was of the opinion that Hubert's work showed a better grasp of "l'esprit des naturalistes français" than that of James and promise of a greater vigor; he went on to define what it was in James's temperament and in Crackanthorpe's work that in his view made James an inappropriate critic of it:

> The coldness and equanimity of his temperament made him ill-fitted to respond to the coarseness and warmth of the characters. . . . he could only imperfectly understand Crackanthorpe's insistence on considering sexuality as an important factor in understanding human nature.[91]

VI

Some prospective contributors to the *Albemarle* whose work never appeared because of the periodical's abrupt demise in September included Maupassant, Degas, and Bourget, on whom there was an essay in the issue of August, by R. Gurnell. In March there was a contribution by another of the French authors whom Hubert admired, Maurice Barrès, "Les Beautés de l'interview." But by far the most notable of the pieces reflecting Hubert's interest in French literary affairs was his own interview with Zola which appeared unsigned in February; because of the attention it attracted, the following notice was printed in the March issue: "The inter-

view with M. Émile Zola which appeared in the February
number of the *Albemarle* was written by Mr. Hubert Crackanthorpe. We mention this as its authorship has been wrongly
attributed in some of the many press-notices which this contribution evoked."

The characteristic tone of the piece is one of respect light-
ened by ironic observation of literary egoism in full flight.
Zola's first words are, "What are they saying about me in
England?"[92] Hubert's own part in the conversation is self-
effacing and designed to draw Zola more toward discussion
of movements than to consideration of particular examples.
Only in the opening sentences, before the entry of Zola, does
he allow himself subjective comment:

> "The self-made always fit out their drawing-rooms in the
> manner they had aspired to when they were young and
> poor." I had never completely realised the truth of this
> remark of Balzac's until I stood in M. Zola's gorgeously
> furnished study in the Rue de Bruxelles.[93] I called to mind
> the struggles of his early years: how having failed in the one
> examination which in France leads to everything, he had
> started in a wretched situation. . . . I thought of the years
> . . . adrift . . . doing nothing, with no future before
> him. . . ."The furnishings betray the man." M. Zola began
> his literary career under the influence of Victor Hugo and
> the poets of 1830, and it is singular how every object in the
> workroom of the great realist of today answers to the
> romanticist of thirty years ago . . . the heavy Oriental
> carpet, mediaeval tapestries on the walls, stained glass in
> the windows, old Italian and Dutch furniture scattered here
> and there, the splendidly carved black oak writing-table,
> with an enormous high-backed chair—almost a throne—
> behind.[94]

That Zola recognized the traces of romanticism in himself is
indicated by the words spoken by Sandoz in *L'Oeuvre:* "Yes,
our generation is soaked to the innards in romanticism, and
. . . all the washings in the world will never remove the odor
of it."[95]

In the early nineties, opposition to French realism in England was fast fading. The trial of Vizetelly had naturally made
the public eager to read Zola, so much so that is was said that
several thousand copies of French naturalist novels were sold

in London every week. And English fiction was beginning to show a taste for *le vrai et le réel* while critics were becoming more tolerant. In 1894 Hubert wrote:

> Books are published, stories are printed, in old-established reviews, which would never have been tolerated a few years ago. . . .The opposition to the renascence of fiction as a conscientious interpretation of life is not what it was. . . .It is not so long ago since a publisher was sent to prison for issuing English translations of celebrated specimens of French realism; yet, only the other day we vied with each other in doing honour to the chief figurehead of that tendency across the Channel.[96]

The last sentence refers to a complimentary dinner given by the Authors' Club on September 28 in honor of Zola, at which Oswald Crawford, as chairman, greeted the "very illustrious guest" declaring that "it was in this country, where he had formerly encountered the greatest resistance, that he had now been received as emperor in the field of letters."[97]

Hubert's opening question to Zola concerned the "supposed death of realism in France" and "the signs of a reaction"; Zola replied that "realism, naturalism, whatever name you give it, is but the result of man's continued search after truth. And that search for truth will exist as long as the human race continues to progress." He acknowledged that the conception of realistic fiction in France was developing, that Flaubert, Daudet, the Goncourts, and he himself might have been "a little sectarian, a little dogmatic," and that he expected an expansion of their literary formula. But in answer to Hubert's question whether "a reaction was near at hand," Zola affirmed that until his death "the present naturalistic formula will find it hard to die. . . .We have perhaps been too absolute. . . .We have studied the human being a little too much from the point of view of the senses," but the movement was essentially "the outcome of the temper of the age. . . .No more realism! You might as well say there will be no more sun, no more stars, no more trees."[98]

Zola referred scathingly to the work of the symbolists as "vague scribbling, in obscure, stuttering verses,"[99] and when Hubert attempted to turn the conversation to a discussion of Ibsen the response was discouraging:

"And Ibsen, too," I put in. "We have had several of Ibsen's plays produced in London this year, and one of them at least was a great success." M. Zola was turning over the uncut pages of M. Ferdinand Fabre's last novel: he did not seem to hear what I was saying.

"What do you think about Ibsen's work?" I continued.

"Ibsen!" he answered without raising his eyes. "C'est bien obscur."

"But wouldn't you say—?"

"C'est bien obscur. Tout cela est bien obscur," he repeated, shrugging his shoulders—"parlons d'autre chose." It was hopeless, I saw. The great man declined to be drawn.[100]

When asked by Zola about writers in English who shared the aims of the realists, Crackanthorpe rather tentatively replied, "Well, there is Mr. George Moore"; Zola was immensely pleased:

Ah! Yes, of course, my friend Moore. Il a beaucoup de talent. . . . But he is almost alone is he not? Ah! I thought so. You English are so essentially Protestant. We over here cannot understand your Protestantism, just as you can never understand our Catholicity. All this puritanism of yours is very curious, it would seem as if it were almost an element in your national genius, yet I know no literature more healthily brutal and vigorous than that of Shakespeare, Jonson. . . .Il vous faut de la patience en Angleterre . . . de la patience. Tout vient à qui sait attendre.[101]

Clearly, the theories of realism and naturalism were expected to do great things for the practice of English fiction in its effort to rediscover what Zola called its healthy brutality; by the time of this interview, emulation of the French school was more advanced than Zola realized, George Moore being certainly a foremost disciple:

The idea of a new art based upon science, in opposition to the art of the old world that was based on imagination, an art that should explain all things and embrace modern life in its entirety . . . filled me with wonder, and I stood dumb before the vastness of the conception.[102]

Although the naturalists resorted to scientific parallels for the sake of apparent theoretic precision, the rather fine distinction between naturalism and realism was in part a matter of literary expediency, as Zola himself admitted when pressed by Flaubert on the genuineness of his professions of faith: "Good God! I don't care any more than you about this word 'naturalism,' and yet I will go on repeating it, because one needs to baptize a thing for the public to think it new."[103] However, Zola differed from Flaubert on a fundamental point, Zola's position being by no means the equivalent of that of his scientific contemporaries: while Flaubert believed that one should not write with one's heart, and that one must "stifle the ego," Zola was no believer in the absolute impersonal: "You have not understood that art is the free expression of heart and intelligence, and that the more personal it is, the greater it is."[104] The doctrinal contradiction is relevant to Hubert's early work, which illustrates the difficulty of reconciling these opposites. However, there was no contradiction in the ultimate aim of the two doctrines. Zola said, "it is a matter above all of penetrating the mind and the flesh";[105] and Flaubert gave this superb emphasis to the predominance of talent over technique, whatever its theoretical base: "One must, by an effort of mind, carry oneself over into the characters and not draw them towards oneself. There at least is the method, which amounts to saying: 'Try to have plenty of talent, and even some genius if you can.' "[106]

Crackanthorpe's first stories were clearly written in submission to the French masters; as he noted in his paper on Barrès and Bourget: "It was with no small confidence that one followed the 'right' people, and echoed the 'right' things. Of such is the exuberance of extreme youth."[107] It is Flaubert in particular whose "bitter flavor,"[108] in Maupassant's phrase, and whose tone, "sometimes cruel, almost always dry,"[109] in that of Pellissier, can be sensed everywhere in *Wreckage*. And although Clarence Decker found that "the literary reputation of the Goncourt brothers in England was not, at this time widespread, and had little connection with the naturalist controversy,"[110] it is clear from Hubert's library and from his markings that he, at least, knew both their novels and their journals and had made some study of their techniques and subject matter. The Goncourts described themselves as the first *écrivains des nerfs,*[111] which recalls Blaikie Murdoch's description of the writing of the nineties as "art of nerves."[112] This particular derivation of Hubert's early fiction, and the sympathies it shows, give the work at times a rather transplanted air; the Goncourts perfectly described the formation of a literary personality in an aphorism that can neatly be applied to Hubert's career as a whole: "In literature, one starts off in search of one's originality laboriously, far from home, in the work of others . . . later one finds it naturally, in oneself . . . and quite close to oneself."[113] Flaubert's great liberating influence, from the point of view of a young English writer, was in the matter of morality in fiction; Maupassant preferred to "impersonality" the word "impassivity"[114] to describe Flaubert's position, and this preference was adopted by Zola who spoke of "our impassivity . . . in face of evil and in face of good."[115] Hubert was later to describe realism as being quite as ridiculous as any other literary creed;[116] but it is clear that he owed his enfranchisement from the implicit and long-standing obligation on the English novelist, which Hippolyte Taine defined as "Be moral . . . all your novels must be capable of being read by young ladies,"[117] to Flaubert as first and principal master. As early as 1885 George Moore, under the same influence, had reacted forcefully against Victorianism in his *Literature at Nurse*. No greater compliment could be paid to the best of Hubert's work than that offered by Frierson: "Crackanthorpe writes with the serene equitableness and the philosophical purity of Flaubert."[118]

The special respectability that Zola's theory seemed to give to the discipline of fiction must have had particular psychological value to a young man who had declined to follow in the academic footsteps of a scholastic father. Zola's critical work, borrowing from the physiological determinism then fashionable, accorded to the creative process of the imagination a new and, he hoped, intellectually impregnable status: "One day, physiology will probably explain to us the whole mechanism of thought and the passions; we will know how the individual human machine functions."[119] Zola spoke of experiments in fiction carried out on the same principles as those in medicine, and claimed that the literary experimenter would learn to master the phenomena of the world while the scholastic must end in sterility.[120] These experiments were likened to "operations" on the characters and the passions;[121]

elsewhere he spoke of "possessing the mechanism of man" and of "inquests on things and beings,"[122] while the Goncourts compared the literary process itself to an "autopsy on the movements of the heart."[123] For a time, such analogies were heady and exhilarating with their suggestion of power, influence, and limitless knowledge, the stuff to gratify any youthful ambition. Zola epitomized this grandiose view of the role of fiction in the closing words of his essay on Alphonse Daudet: "Today, the novel has become the tool of the century, the great investigation into man and nature."[124]

Of his appetite for novels at the beginning of his career, Hubert gave this account:

> At the outset, the novel seemed an introduction to life, an explanation of certain aspects of humanity . . . especially, perhaps, concerning women; one vaguely expected, through Literature, to learn about Life. . . . Later, and after a leisurely and lengthy fashion there came a certain awakening to the claims of one's private tastes.[125]

The last sentence suggests that the current between life and literature had been reversed, that the former had begun to make its proper contribution to the latter rather than depending on it for a vicarious instruction. Almost certainly it was sexual experience that released this counterflow. Edmond de Goncourt reported a dialogue on the subject of love in which Turgenev and Zola put respectively the ideal and the real concepts, the romantic and the analytic: Zola, who had led the conversation to this point, professed to believe that the phenomena noticeable in the state of love are equally found in the emotions of friendship and patriotism, and that what gives the sentiment of love its great intensity is simply *la perspective de la copulation*.[126] It was distinctly in this Zolaesque perspective that Hubert Crackanthorpe's early work was written and was meant to be read, and the frankness of the copulatory interest is appealing even when, at moments, the approach is rough. It is the writing of a very young man, innocent and urgent, but shadowed by a secret distemper, a melancholic cast, like an infection contracted and rooted in the being, though not yet manifest. It was as if he had, in Pater's disturbing image, "seen the snakes breeding" and was "uneasy for many days."[127]

3

Little Documents of Hell

Without forewarning the *Albemarle* ceased publication after the issue of September 1892; no doubt an agreed limit of funds had been reached. The periodical had been a notable success while it lasted: the *Speaker* described it as "the most promising of the new magazines," the *Guardian* as "a high-class review . . . very popular with a wide circle of readers," and the *Evening Standard* as an "aristocratically got-up magazine." Its demise brought Hubert's period of apprenticeship to a close, except that as a writer of fiction he was still practically unknown. He had published a variety of work in the *Albemarle,* in addition to the Zola and James pieces; his name at least had been made familiar to the literary public, and he had succeeded in associating it with those of some eminent men without excessive solemnity on his part. The editorial experience would no doubt be valuable if he should later wish to return to literary editorship, as in the event he was hoping to do at the time of his death. He must by now have been receiving from his father, as paternal acknowledgment of his status as writer, an allowance sufficient to live on and so to free him to prepare his first collection of stories. Like the Goncourts, he was financially independent of the sales of his work and was able to live and write as he chose, free at least from some of the endemic anxieties of authorship.

Hubert's movements between September and February of the following year are uncertain. However, he was definitely in London at some time in November 1892. After the success of the Ibsen production of that year, William Heinemann went to Norway to obtain the rights of a new play—*The Master Builder*—to be translated by William Archer and Edmund Gosse. Blanche Crackanthorpe's friend, the actress

Elizabeth Robins, described the eagerness and excitement that arose in anticipation of the new work and named some of the people who "came up and down those seventy-four steps for news from Norway"; among them were the Crackanthorpes and "their gifted and lovable son, Hubert."[1]

On Christmas Day 1892, Hubert received a copy of De Quincey's *Confessions of an English Opium-Eater* as a gift from Leila Macdonald, a handsome young woman of literary tastes, whom he was to marry on St. Valentine's Day 1893. This further extension of experience was one recommended to writers by Zola who, however, did not say whether bliss, mere assuagement of the flesh, or eventual tribulation was to be the most valuable part of it: "Marriage, in my opinion, is the school of the great contemporary producers."[2] Early marriage was also approved by Hubert's mother:

> Let life be simplified all round. When our sons and daughters come and tell us that they desire to "make their own experiment" in the shape of marriage upon what to our world would appear a minute income, let us be aiders and abettors of their midsummer madness.[3]

One reason for this encouragement was awareness of "the daily and nightly dangers to which our sons are exposed";[4] in this case it transpired in the end that the stable door of wedlock was shut too late, the nightly danger—that of infection—having probably claimed Hubert as victim. Moreover, if Blanche was the aider and abettor of the marriage she could not, with all her devotion from the "watchtower of her love," have done the beloved son a worse service. Physical accounts of the couple are enough to suggest contrast, if not actual incompatibility of temperament. Francis Jammes described Leila Macdonald as "a sort of hard-eyed Amazon,"[5] while Frank Harris gave this sketch of Hubert: "Just below medium height, slight and white-faced, with eyes like pale Parma violets and hesitating light voice growing confident and firm, however, in praise. . . . His judgement was curiously mature, too mature for his years."[6] The marriage took place quietly at St. Paul's Church in Knightsbridge; both man and wife were then aged twenty-two.

Leila's father had been given the traditional Macdonald names of Reginald and Somerled.[7] He belonged to a cadet branch of the great Highland family known as the "Lords of the Isles"; many accounts insist that Leila was a descendent of the famous Flora. Reginald Macdonald was an Etonian and Queen's Counsel, and he died in or about 1880. Leila's mother also died young; she was the daughter of a judge, Sir William Grove, who like Montague had intellectual interests outside the law, having published a number of scientific works that won him an international reputation in their field. He was a fellow of the Royal Society, vice-president of the Royal Institution, and a member of the academies of Rome and Turin.[8] After her parents' deaths, Leila was brought up by her grandfather and at the time of her marriage was living in his house at 115 Harley Street with her old nurse, who then became Sir William Grove's housekeeper. Leila dedicated her book of verse, *A Wanderer and Other Poems,* to the memory of this nurse, Mrs. Anne Gibbs. However precipitate, the marriage seems to have been accepted and approved. The couple had literary interests and ambitions in common, and both were, in material terms, well provided for; Leila's fortune was greatly augmented after the death of her grandfather in 1896.

After their marriage, Hubert took his wife to France, to the neighborhood of Orthez where he had stayed in 1889. Francis Jammes found them a house, the Villa Baron near Sallespisse, some nine kilometers from Orthez. Jammes left several accounts of his friendship with Hubert, including a poem called "Albion en Béarn," which appeared in the collection *Ma France poétique* and which gives a vivid impression of the newly married couple, well pleased with one another and with themselves:

> They had irises, and their English tobacco, and richly-bound books by their side, which they would read with eyelids half-closed against the pungent smoke. Their rooms—they were quite newly-married—had a smell compounded of Morocco leather, ambergris, and mackintosh. Cut glass bottles with gold tops, ivory brushes, and pieces of dark tortoiseshell with silver monograms were ranged meticulously on a piece of deal furniture of the inexpensive lodging. In the barn they housed their two nervous Tarbes mares, on which they looked so graceful and at ease.[9]

Jammes also told the story of the friendship in *L'Amour, les muses et la chasse,* which gives, together with some scattered references by Richard Le Gallienne, the best impression of the spirit, the "surface gaiety rising from a spring of melancholy,"[10] that seems to have been attractive to Hubert's friends and also of the impulse to praise noted by Frank Harris. Jammes's account of the early days of the marriage describes, however, a near-catastrophic accident, of a kind that in a fiction would be taken as inauspicious:

> I have spoken of that sort of warrioress whom my friend Hubert Crackanthorpe had married. . . . At the very start of their marriage, they came to the neighbourhood of Orthez and settled into a villa which I had taken for them. All four of us used to scour the countryside, I say all four because Charles Lacoste was with us. We gathered irises, we played with a goat which grazed on Virginian tobacco as if it were grass, we picknicked and, naturally, we had tea. Rather die than be without tea at five o'clock, wherever one might be, with one's kettle and spirit lamp. This last was almost the cause of a frightful accident. Hubert and I were about fifty meters away from his wife, on the bank of the Gave, when we saw her roll on the ground and heard a harrowing cry. Lacoste, who was with her, seemed to be going to her aid. We rushed over. The spirit had caused the lamp, which Mrs. Crackanthorpe was in the act of lighting, to explode and had burned her eyes horribly. Raising her eyelids, we could see only blood-stained orbs. . . . During the weeks following this accident, we often went to see our friends, nine kilometers from Orthez. When no more complications were to be feared for the young woman's eyes, our calm intimacy was resumed. In that sharp odor that is the exhalation of the English life, of leather and pale tobacco, we would read the poets: Shakespeare, Keats, La Fontaine, Mallarmé.[11]

It was at some time during the *calme intimité* of the spring of 1893 that Hubert, in alliance with other friends, persuaded Jammes to publish certain poems that had been omitted from his collections of 1891 and 1892. Jammes had held back work that was unconventional in treatment or theme, some of it the most beautiful and trenchant of his verse. Robert Mallet, in his biography of Jammes, spoke of these private poems, which Jammes had been writing since 1888:

What a passion of non-conformism accounted for these poems which he had been secretly writing for three years! He needed approval and encouragement to decide him to run the risk of scandal, in the venture on success. His old school companions, Charles Lacoste and Charles Veillet-Lavallée and most of all a young English writer staying at Orthez, Hubert Crackanthorpe, were, in 1893, the far-sighted and persuasive advisers whom he needed.[12]

And elsewhere Mallet remarks that "Crackanthorpe encouraged him to persevere in the direction of non-conformism."[13] The account given by the poet himself is even more flattering than this tribute:

Hubert Crackanthorpe wanted to take advantage of the great fuss that was being made of his first work, *Wreckage,* to get me known. He understood wonderfully well, and without the effort that certain Frenchmen, deformed by schoolmasters, have had to make, those poems which Lacoste and Clavand had already read, and which I had confided to him. He showed an absolute faith in my poetic future. He pressed me to the extent of overcoming my resistance up to a point: I authorised him to make a little choice from among my poems and, not to deliver them to a publisher as he would have liked, but to make a slim booklet of them, to be printed at Orthez . . . and limited to fifty copies, *hors commerce.*[14]

Jammes wrote of Hubert's great pleasure and exhilaration at having persuaded him to agree to the printing:

He was charmingly exultant, and I can still see him, in order to celebrate the little book, climbing like a squirrel in the oaks under which we were going to dine, to hang in them as many torches as the number of poems I had let him publish.[15]

The limited edition, entitled simply *Vers,* contained twenty-one poems; the garden of the Villa Baron was therefore lit by the number of candles symbolic of the coming of age, the advent to manhood. Jammes dedicated the volume to Charles Lacoste and to Hubert: "To you, Crackanthorpe, already well-known in your own country, and who have felt in yourself the inspiration of love and of human pity."[16] On his return to Paris, Hubert delivered copies of this collection to

Mallarmé, who liked and admired him, according to Jammes, and to André Gide and Henri de Régnier.

Jammes's mention of "love and human pity" is interesting because it implies an emotional experience less banal than that of a sensible, suitable marriage to a young woman of the sort described by Jammes himself in his references to Leila. Several of Hubert's stories, both in *Wreckage* and later, could suggest that he had as a youth been in love with a woman who was either a prostitute or a demimondaine; the realism in his personality could take him to prostitutes, while the idealism might expose him to the hazard of love. Jammes was possibly his closest friend at this time, and these allusions, though no more than suggestive, must have had some origin in conversation between them.

The stay at Sallespisse provided Hubert with the material for his *Set of Village Tales,* dated 1893–1895. In a letter to Selwyn Image, Hubert spoke of his way of life there:

> We have lazed through three hot weeks—reading, dozing, scribbling a little in some shady spot during the day and towards sunset, when the glare of the afternoon has given place to the cool of evening we ride or drive over this most fertile of lands. This is our life—an indolent, Southern life—a life of warmth and peace and half-formed thoughts.[17]

Wreckage appeared in March 1893, while Hubert was in France. He wrote to Image: "I have asked Mr. Heinemann to send you a copy of my little volume of stories. Will you please accept it as a token of my warm regard?"[18] Image sent a letter containing "two very sound criticisms," for which Hubert thanked him. There is no indication of what these criticisms were, but they were wholeheartedly accepted: "Yes, they are entirely true, both of them, and you may be sure I will remember them." News of the reception of his book had reached him in Spain, where he and Leila spent twelve days at the beginning of April. The post had come to him at Pamplona:

> Perched on a rock in the middle of a brown, sun-scorched plain there came to me reviews of *Wreckage,* and a charming letter from Lionel Johnson. As I sat on a bench in the white, bare plaza, reading them, it seemed so strange that far away

in London, people should be talking about one, thinking about one, writing about one; the letters, the reviews, all wore the unreality of a delightful dream.[19]

The letters to Image are a little self-conscious and literary, as to a kindly, approving tutor; but they are also outward-going and not defensive, showing no hint of uncomfortable self-doubt. Nor is there any sign of discord between the married couple:

> Then, there came over both of us a yearning, impatient and melancholy, for home, and a strange feeling of isolation in the midst of all this life in which we had no part. So back across the Pyrenees we hastened, driving far into the night in our eagerness to be home once more. In our absence the leaves had all burst their buds; the lilacs, the acacias, the honeysuckle and the laburnums were in bloom, and quantities of unknown flowers were carpeting the lawn—wild orchids with the shapes of grotesque insects, and purple orchises.[20]

It is impossible to know for how long the Villa Baron continued to be "home." But it was certainly at Sallespisse that Hubert heard from Heinemann of the progress of sales:

> Under the circumstances the book is, I hear, selling well: but W. H. Smith & Son, when they refused to have it on their bookstalls, blocked the best opening that exists for a book published at three and sixpence. One Arthur Waugh (do you know him) has said some most delightful things about it and me in the *Literary World;* so has William Archer in the *Westminster Gazette;* the *Daily Chronicle* gave me a column of "unwilling praise" as Johnson puts it; and besides, a mass of paragraphs have appeared elsewhere, good, bad and indifferent.[21]

William Heinemann was very proud of Hubert's first book; Grant Richards, in his *Memories of a Misspent Youth,* described a visit he had made one day in 1893 to Heinemann, the man "whose spiritual home was on the Seine" and who happened on that day to have received from the binders the first copy of *Wreckage.* "That was the sort of book he was then proud to publish. Crackanthorpe was, he said, to do great, great things."[22]

II

Wreckage contains seven "studies"; the title echoes that used by Baudelaire—*Les Épaves*—for the collection that included those poems that had been banned from the original publication of *Les Fleurs du mal*. The implication is that Hubert's mood and aim was to portray aspects of existence—"all the ugliness of life" in a Goncourt phrase[23]—that the conventional might think better left alone. The seven stories are indeed studies in ugliness, of one sort or another; of a world of physical or psychological degeneration, and of broken loves and shattered hopes. The use of the short-story form and of London settings reflects, as Henry James suggested, an emulation of the French:

> He was beset, . . . I gather, with a somewhat humiliated sense of the way Paris, cruel and tragic, Paris with its abounding life and death of every sort, has, as a subject, been royally ransacked, and of what experiments . . . might spring from our uglier and more brutal Bohemia.[24]

But it is also true that a passion for the summary and the emblematic—"a breath, a flame in the doorway, a feather in the wind" in Pater's words[25]—was characteristic of the English writers of the nineties; and Pater himself had drawn attention to the possibility that "Life in modern London . . . is stuff sufficient for the fresh imagination of youth to build its 'palace of art' of."[26]

The collection has for its epigraph a quotation from the Goncourts' *Germinie Lacerteux:* "Let the novel have as religion what in the last century they called by the broad and vast name, 'Humanity': that will be conscience enough for it; its right lies there."[27] The Goncourts had described that novel as *la clinique de l'amour,*[28] and they professed to follow Flaubert's axiom that in art there are neither beautiful nor ugly subjects; this, then, was the aegis under which Hubert made his first fictional experiments, examinations of drab, poverty-stricken existences and of psychological peculiarities, cases presented at the clinic of love, raw, contagious, and generally beyond cure. With such material, the self-effacement demanded by Flaubert requires great skill, and experience; in Hubert's early work there is some of the exaggeration of emphasis and of

language that is the result of strong compassionate feeling
being forced, for reasons of conformity to literary theory, to
express itself only through objective detail, often of a brutal
kind.

The first story in *Wreckage,* "Profiles," is divided into seventeen short, roughly equal sections. The opening is almost
lyrical, presenting a young engaged couple by a riverside on a
warm spring afternoon; the young man, an army officer on
leave, is asleep in the sun, while the girl, Lilly, fishes. Lilly is
the central figure and the story concerns her descent, through
a single sexual obsession, from angry innocence to corruption
and despair. She is at first lovingly described:

> Her body was thrust forward in a cramped position, as
> with both hands she held a long, clumsy looking fishing-
> rod. . . .
> She was bareheaded, and her crisp, auburn hair was
> riotously tumbling about her ears and neck.
> Quite pale was her skin, but pale, transparent, soft; ex-
> quisite was the modelling of her fresh, firm lips.
> There were great possibilities of beauty in the face.[29]

There is an echo of the description of Lucy in Meredith's *The
Ordeal of Richard Feverel,* hung "above green-flashing plunges
of a weir." Between the vernal freshness of this overture and
Lilly's final state, lies a total transformation difficult to estab-
lish in a short story without a degree of Zolaesque outrance
and overstraining. But Lilly's condition at the end is described
with simplicity and effective pathos:

> She grew careless of her dress and of her person and at last
> callous to all around her. She sank into the irretrievable
> morass of impersonal prostitution. . . .[30]
> For some time more she was seen at intervals in a little
> public-house at the back of Regent Street. Then she disap-
> peared. What had become of her no one knew and no one
> cared.[31]

Obviously the model for this drastic study of degeneration is
Germinie Lacerteux herself; it is ironic that the "impersonality" of prostitution should have been noted by the Goncourts:
"The great characteristic of the girl fallen into prostitution is
impersonality. She is no longer a person, no longer some-
one. . . . Consciousness and propriety of the ego are ef-

faced."[32] This is impersonality at its paradoxical extreme. As with Germinie, Lilly's degradation results not primarily from external events, but from a passionate development that is integral to her nature. An orphan, she lives at first with an aunt whom she hates with "an instinctive, imperious loathing."[33] Something of her temperament is revealed in the word *imperious*. She soon elopes to London with the young officer, and they stay together at a hotel: "it had seemed the more natural thing."[34]

Sexual consummation releases in Lilly impulses so strong that she seems to find herself driven to seek some more powerful experience, and gradually the couple become estranged without either of them knowing the reason: " 'I feel as if something strange were going to happen to me. I want to think about lots of things. That's why I want to be alone, quite alone.' "[35] The unrationalized and unspoken quarrel is communicated by the visual experience each has of the other:

> The moment of parting drew near and the tension became more and more painful.
>
> . . . of a sudden, he turned his face, contorted as in acute physical pain, and with a dryness in his voice, passionately implored her to return.
>
> But he did not touch her. Strange that she was observing him, curiously, for the first time conscious of distinct antipathy towards him. . . .
>
> But he did not press her any longer, for he dimly saw how it was.[36]

From his earliest fiction, Crackanthorpe shows an almost intuitive understanding of, and empathy with women, especially with women in pain; Pater had distinguished as "the only principle, always safe, a sympathy with the pain one actually sees."[37] Intuition here senses what is, in effect, an invisible unease, that of a woman aroused but unsatisfied, almost a sexual growing pain. Lilly is quickly taken on by another man, a traditional sexual villain of a kind familiar in Emily Brontë, a figure with "heavy black moustache and vermilion lips,"[38] and it is with him that she falls fatally in love. It is a first and last love; he discards her so quickly that she has no chance to moderate her passionate attachment. The description of the fate that overtakes her is melodramatic, an awful deterioration proceeding from a passionate nature:

> The seething turmoil of the great city, ruthless in its never-flagging lust, caught up the frailty of her helpless beauty, and playing with it, marred it, mutilated it. Like a flower, frostbitten in the hour of budding, she drooped and withered.[39]

This is like the description of the vice of Paris in Zola's *La Curée:* "that which brutal desire, and immediate satisfaction of instinct, toss down into the road, having broken and defiled it."[40] In Hubert's work the city is always seen as vicious and degrading, more an emotional and sexual slum than a "palace of art"; Lilly, unlike Zola's Nana, who became a force of nature "corrupting and upsetting all of Paris, between her snowy thighs,"[41] is quickly destroyed:

> Against the inevitable she made no continuous resistance. How could she? Only for a while; with the feeble struggles of a drowning creature she clung to the memory of her great love. . . .
>
> First, it was a dark-faced foreigner about Safford's build and height . . .
>
> . . . then it was any one who by some detail of his person recalled Safford to her . . .
>
> Fierce, fitful loves . . . born to die within an hour or two.[42]

Zola in *Les Romanciers naturalistes* described the fate of Germinie: "A slow moral degradation throws her into debauchery, once her lover leaves her. She needs love, as one needs the bread one eats."[43]

It is evident that "Profiles" owes much to the Goncourts, yet there is a freshness in the writing that makes the story the strongest in *Wreckage,* helping the reader to share the emotional experience of the author more than in any other in the collection. Although there is the apparent moral detachment prescribed by the canons of realism, the writer's sympathies are openly with Lilly, in her passion and in her plight as a victim of masculine society. Flaubert said: "I do not want to have love, hate, pity, or anger. As for sympathy, that is different; one can never have enough."[44] However, the stronger the author's subjective sympathy, the more likely it is to appear objectively in a disturbing intemperance of vocabulary. Flaubert may speak of Emma's laughter, "atroce, frénétique, désespéré,"[45] on her deathbed, but when Hubert describes a character as being convulsed by a "spasm of atrocious suffering"[46] the phrase does not convince. Passion and seriousness—as in the epicureanism of Marius—are beyond doubt but there is a certain monotony of hopelessness in the stories of *Wreckage,* from which the vivacious dialogue often comes as a relief.

The second story, "A Conflict of Egoisms," has claim to be the most depressing that Crackanthorpe ever wrote, calling to mind a critic's description of his work as "yellow and jaundiced" or Blaikie Murdoch's characterization of it as "steeped in inky blackness."[47] If "Profiles" stemmed from the Goncourts, this story has an obvious relation to Zola's *L'Oeuvre;* Zola's chief character is a painter while Hubert's is a writer, but both narratives deal with a woman's growing jealousy of her husband's work and the man's increasing emotional and sexual distraction. "A Conflict of Egoisms" presents the disastrous marriage of a middle-aged couple, each of whom have led isolated bachelor lives. They are at first drawn together by the woman's admiration of the man's literary work. She idolizes him and he, whose "whole view of human nature was a generalised, abstract view: he saw no detail, only the broad lights and shades,"[48] seems to marry almost inadvertently, like a somnambulist, with no clearer motive than to capture a domestic audience. In Zola, the sexual aspect is explicit: "O yes, he's at work," says the woman bitterly, "he has to get it all finished before he'll go back to a woman."[49] Hubert is less frank; his writer, Oswald, enters marriage with a very indefinite sexual attitude:

> In the interminable day-dreams, which had filled so many hours of his life, no woman's image had ever long occupied a place. It was the sex, abstract and generalised, that appealed to him; for he lived as it were too far off to distinguish particular members.[50]

After the marriage it is not made clear whether the desperate frustration of the woman is due to nonconsummation or simply to resentment of the man's encapsulation in himself, his inability to share his emotions or his creation with her day by day. The work becomes the focus of her anger, and of his efforts to retain his separateness, which grow more strenuous as his inner existence seems more threatened by this woman whom he has so unguardedly admitted into his life. Soon the capacity to write begins to fail:

> The effort required to seat himself each morning at his writing-table grew greater and greater, and the progress achieved each day was less. . . .
>
> And as time went on the thought of death began to haunt him till it became a constant obsession.[51]

Both Crackanthorpe's and Zola's women become almost frenzied with loneliness, jealousy, and hatred of the man's work. Oswald overhears his wife praying: "What is it that has taken you from me? Oh! I want you, I want your love. . . . My Oswald, I cannot live without it. Come back to me. . . . Oh! It is killing me. If only it could be."[52] Zola's Christine addresses the man directly: "Claude, listen to me . . . come back, oh! come back, if you don't want me to die of it, of being so cold and waiting for you."[53] Christine finally succeeds in getting the man to return to her in a scene of great erotic force in which he repudiates his obsession with the *oeuvre manquée;* in the morning, after a night of love, she finds him hanged in his studio before the unfinished canvas. Crackanthorpe is less emotionally forthright and less frank than Zola. There is no sexual reunion in "A Conflict of Egoisms." The writer's powers wither and the wife, like Hedda Gabler, destroys the envied manuscript; as a final ignominy, Oswald, although he fills his pockets with stones and makes for the river, actually collapses in the roadway before leaping and dies on the pavement. There is none of the "stirring character of a *dénouement*" that Marius expected of death.[54] For Oswald, suicide is unnecessary because his creativity, the only living part of him, has already been killed. Alone, he was complete and productive, having the "two genders of the mind"; the assumption of ordinary emotional responsibility toward another person has destroyed his capacity, not simply for work, since the period of his marriage is filled with a frenzy of work, but to foresee its equable, dependable continuance, the survival of powers. That both stories are allegories of castration is clear. But they are also studies of the psychological problem of the obsessed artist, and at that level Hubert's version is subtler though less forceful and less convincing than Zola's, and it is occasionally presented in a melodramatic language ill suited to the complexity of the theme. What the reader requires to know of such a situation is not the "how" but the "why," which Zola laid down should be of no more concern to the "experimental novel" than to experimental science.[55] Hubert Crackanthorpe's development was to be toward this *pourquoi,* toward the psychological account and away from the rather brutal dogma of naturalism to which at the time of *Wreckage* he still subscribed.

The shortest story in *Wreckage,* "The Struggle for Life," seems to have attracted particular critical attention. The story is a sketch, a "foreshortened picture" in Henry James's phrase,[56] of a young mother resorting to prostitution for a few necessary shillings. The reviewer in the *Athenaeum* praised its realistic method:

> There is a directness in his manner of telling a story and a sharpness in his brief delineations of character rarely to be found in English novel writers, and therewith an absence of all personal feeling which emphasizes the distinctness of the portraits. The little sketch, barely covering six pages, called "The Struggle for Life," exemplifies the last point best.[57]

The *Daily Chronicle* described "The Struggle for Life" as the masterpiece of the collection: "this art is not in one respect merely, but in all, the art of restraint, of reticence, of abstinence."[58] A first-person narrator is introduced into a dockside pub:

> Half a dozen gross gas-jets lit up the long low room, making a procession of queer-shaped shadows dance restlessly about the walls. . . .
> It was a Saturday night, so the place was quite full— bargemen with grimy furrows across their bronzed faces . . . riverside prostitutes. . . .
> It was hot, a foul, unhealthy heat; the very walls were sweating, and a bluish haze was filling the room.[59]

He sees a young woman approach a drunken mason, evidently her husband, and implore him to come away or to give her money; the man refuses, rejecting her violently, with a prostitute nestling on his knee. The narrator follows the girl out and onto the bridge, where she seems to hesitate at the parapet:

> It was a starless night, but the full moon had just risen from behind the thin, headless necks of a cluster of chimneys. . . .
> A cab was crawling up, its yellow lamps gleaming like the round eyes of some great night beetle.[60]

The woman is soon accosted: "the small, black figure of a man came slinking along under the wall." She resists at first, but is easily persuaded. The narrator hears her speak the closing words of the story: "half a crown then, and I can go home in an hour."[61] There is a most economically pointed contrast between the payment, and the painful duration of the service, a combination reminiscent of Hardy.

The impersonality of technique is actually increased by the use of a first-person narrator, who is shown as quite detached from the woman's fate; when he passes her on the bridge he sees her "tears . . . dripping onto the pavement,"[62] and he sits down on a bench a few yards away "to see the end of it."[63] This method adds sharpness to the narrative and focuses the characters; its disadvantage is that it seems, improbably, to identify the author with an inquisitive but uncompassionate bystander. Hubert was later to use this technique again, to beautiful effect, in his *Set of Village Tales* whose narrator has the readily engaged personality and warmth of the writer himself.

Wreckage contains two stories that deal with opposite extremes of male sexual experience. "Dissolving View" is a somewhat crude melodrama portraying sexual exploitation and betrayal in a conventional man of fashion who, on the eve of his marriage, is hugely relieved to learn of the deaths of his abandoned mistress and her child. That they died in misery in no way overshadows his relief with any sense of guilt. At the other extreme is "Embers," in which a deserted husband, an obvious sexual non-combatant but one in whom some glimmer of uxorious warmth—the embers of the title—still faintly glows, is haunted in his isolation by the return of his drunken wife and tormented by her demands for money. It is an interesting possibility that the story may have been suggested by the experience of Gissing, although the husband in "Embers" is certainly not intended in any other way to represent Gissing himself. There is another, literary, parallel, with the plight of Stephen Blackpool in Dickens's *Hard Times;* a significant difference is that Crackanthorpe treats the woman with much greater compassion than Dickens.

Many reviewers of *Wreckage* found, or purported to find in it evidence of discipleship to Maupassant. The critic in *Black and White* disapprovingly said: "A young English writer does ill to borrow his style and method from M. de Maupassant. The range of subject and literary methods . . . are too remote from English habits of thought to come well in English dress."[64] In later years both Arthur Symons and Henry James suggested that Crackanthorpe had been influenced by Maupassant, and James even spoke of "extravagant surrender."[65] But to return to the evidence of his library, Hubert seems to have possessed no work of Maupassant except his study of Flaubert in *Lettres de Gustave Flaubert à George Sand,* in which many passages have been marked. Hubert's early study took him to the sources of realism, the work of the men of an earlier generation, and it is likely that any parallelism with Maupassant would be the result of a parallel familiarity with their methods and material. One of the stories in *Wreckage,* "A Dead Woman," is a case in point. This tale depicts a reconciliation between a widower and his dead wife's lover after both have seen the futility of the quarrel that their first feelings had imposed on them. The theme was considered cynical, although Le Gallienne, a considerable philanderer, found nobility in this view of the possibility of friendship transcending adultery. Many commentators pointed out that Maupassant had treated a similar subject in "Inconsolables," and suggested that "A Dead Woman" was a variation on that story. But quite clearly this situation stems from Flaubert's *Madame Bovary,* if from no earlier source. After Emma's death Charles Bovary encounters Rodolphe at the market and they drink together; Rodolphe talks and Charles listens, his silent fury mounting but then dying away. At last he says, "I bear you no ill-will . . . no, I don't bear you ill-will any more."[66] Zola, too, had treated the theme in *L'Assommoir,* where the husband and late lover of Gervaise first exchange insults and then drink together in peace: "Men are men, aren't they? We are made to understand one another."[67] In all three cases, alcohol is the accepted solvent of hatred and sexual envy between men.

In spite of passages of overstatement and exaggeration of feelings, "A Dead Woman" is the only story in *Wreckage* not dominated by a sense of exasperated tension or depressive despair. The north country setting may in part account for this, giving an escape from the darkness of London and the degeneration that Hubert saw in urban experience. By contrast, in this story there is psychological growth, and the imagery in many scenes has a glow and color not to be found elsewhere in *Wreckage*. The placing of the tale in Hubert's own Cumbrian countryside gives an opening for his excellent rendering of the northern dialect, a difficult technical achievement whose success indicates an accurate ear and memory. And the abundance of the dialogue, in which he generally excelled, helps to produce a sense of relaxation, since in Hubert's early work it is in the narrative passages that strain is apt to appear. With dialogue he always seems at ease, capable of irony or humor and of leading himself toward unforced psychological delicacies. Early in the story the widower, an innkeeper, is talking with the farmer Jonathan, not yet aware that Jonathan had for years been the lover of the dead woman:

> "How's t' house doing, Richard?" asked Jonathan.
> "Middlin'."
> The other drank and sucked his moustache appreciatively.
> "Jonathan," Rushout began.
> "Well?"
> "It'll be a twelvemonth today."
> "Ay, sure, that it be," and he started all at once to puff vigorously at his pipe. . . . "Ye'll best be soon looking about ye, Richard. T' house can never prosper while there be no missus, and jest a look at that broomstick woman ye've got now is sufficient to drive even Mike over the way. I tell ye man, ye'll have to bestir yeself." . . .
> "Jonathan, it's a twelvemonth to-day. I'm goin' to drink to her soul." . . . The other stared at him in stolid astonishment; then mutely raised his glass. . . . The glances

of the two men met, and parted again hastily. It was as if the one had detected the other in some secret deed.[68]

The dead woman is symbolized by her white mare, which Richard has sold to the doctor though Jonathan had coveted her. At work in his fields, Jonathan hears "the stride of the white mare pounding down the road towards him. Ay, t'was she: many a time he had waited before, listening for her action along the road." The doctor stops to speak to him:

> [Jonathan] was surveying the mare—her legs, straight, slender, sinewy; her lithe and gracefully rounded body; her undersized head erect, neck arched, and ears cocked, while at regular intervals she shot out bars of breath from her quivering nostrils.[69]

The sensuality of the description brings into the story a sense of the dead woman's physical presence, and gives it substance.

> "Hold hard, doctor," broke in Jonathan. He pushed fiercely through the hedge and laid one hand on the mare's neck, pressing his cheek against her nose and speaking softly and soothingly to her. This for a few seconds, till she tossed up her head and he was forced to let her go.
> "Good day, doctor."
> "Good day to you, Hays."[70]

Here is the economy often absent in these early stories; the world *fiercely,* for example, sufficiently conveys the turmoil of feeling that cannot be openly expressed. The white mare haunts the story and is used at the end to mark the reconciliation between the two men.

Their quarrel, when Rushout discovers the truth, is never brought to a head because he collapses drunk in the snow, on his way by night to the agreed meeting place at which "something was to be settled between them."[71] Richard lies ill for several weeks, and Jonathan visits him. Each man thinks of the dead woman, and each has "a craving to hear the other mention her name." They draw together into a posthumous sharing that resolves loneliness, and softens deprivation:

> "Richard, she *was* a grand woman."
> "That she was—sich splendid hair."
> "Nay, but t'was her eyes that were the finest."

"Black—jet-black."
"Did you ever take notice of the lashes?"

Jonathan tells Richard that he has bought the mare from the doctor, who by driving her too hard has lamed her:

> Rushout reflected, then:
> "Jonathan, I'm powerful glad. I've always regretted ye didn't have her first."[72]

This story shows a maturity of understanding and for the most part avoids the melodrama that mars much of Hubert's novice work. The dialect, the effective symbolism, and the ease of the northern setting are carried forward to the later "Anthony Garstin's Courtship."

Wreckage was in general very flatteringly received, even where the attention was unfavorable. William Archer wrote in the *Westminster Gazette:* "The real excellence of Mr. Crackanthorpe's work . . . lies in the conciseness and concreteness of his style."[73] The reviewer in the *Daily Chronicle* was critical but perceptive:

> After this absolute passionlessness of delineation many writers have striven, but, in England at any rate, few have achieved the uncanny success granted to Mr. Crackanthorpe. . . . Of course, being the work of a singularly able man, *Wreckage* has the qualities of its defects.[74]

The French influence was noted: H. D. Traill in the *New Review* spoke of "deliberate crudities" and proposed the title of "the English Zola . . . for alike in subject and in treatment, Mr. Crackanthorpe is nothing if not Zolaesque";[75] while the *Sketch* discovered the connection with the Goncourt brothers: "Mr. Crackanthorpe is not ashamed to acknowledge his debt to masters who preceded Zola, for he sets in the forefront of his audacious little tales, a passage from the preface to *Germinie Lacerteux.*"[76] It is remarkable that these journalists showed themselves more perspicacious than Arthur Symons and Henry James in identifying the formative influences on Hubert's work, which his library confirms. Some reviewers attacked the book as decadent: the *Saturday Review* in a one-sentence note described it as "of the modern Ibsenistic school—pessimistic and unpalatable."[77] The two adjectives are quite apt, and Hubert would certainly have jibbed at neither of them. The effect of the stories when read as a whole is not unlike that described by Maupassant in speaking of Flaubert: "He fills the intelligent reader with a desolated sadness, in the face of life."[78]

In all, Hubert must have been gratified with the results of his first work. The book sold well, his publisher was enthusiastic, and much attention was drawn to his name; probably his father, certainly his mother, must have thought their own cleverness rewarded. His next fictional work did not appear until February 1894, which suggests that after *Wreckage* he paused, not only for marriage, but perhaps also to mark the close of a period of pupilage to masters of an earlier generation. In a copy of *Wreckage* inscribed to his wife he wrote, "To Leilin, the record of a phase."[79] This interval, like the period of introduction in Paris, the apprenticeship to Image, and the nine-month editorship of the *Albemarle,* appears as the application of logic and will to the steady building of a literary career—with audacity, as the *Sketch* had it. And Henry James, who in his "Appreciation" directed his critical genius, with such subtlety in some respects at least, onto these "few and broken experiments," also noted the brave initiative:

> What he had his fancy of attempting he had to work out for himself, in a public air but scantily charged with aids to any independence of conventions . . . and to work out as a point of honour, an act of artistic probity, an expression adjusted to his own free sense of life.[80]

III

There is no record to show how long Hubert and Leila were abroad after their marriage; probably they remained in France for months, and they may have visited Italy and Spain as well. By the end of 1893 they had moved into their new home in London at Chelsea Gardens, a block of Victorian flats overlooking the ground of Chelsea Hospital where the pleasure gardens of Ranelagh had once been. Hubert had taken a flat of eight rooms at five pounds a month; the block is unprepossessing, the rooms dark and small, the ambience decidedly proletarian. Chelsea Gardens belonged to a philanthropic body, the Improved Industrial Dwellings Company, and Hubert's neighbors there were authentic working men and their families. Leila may have found this setting uncongenial and the social mixture uncomfortable, but for Hubert they no doubt represented a necessary broadening of experience, new aspects of life somehow to be reconciled with the life of Newbiggin and of Rutland Gate. Rothenstein, perhaps naively, stated that Hubert was content to "live a quiet life in a workman's flat in Chelsea," but in reality there must have been poignant and stimulating contrast, between the "improved industrial dwelling" and the "fair old house."

From August 12, Hubert's parents and his brothers would certainly have been at Newbiggin for the great sporting event of the northern year, the opening of the grouse shooting. It seems likely that in this first year of marriage Hubert and his new wife were also there during some of the season, although in other years they seem to have withdrawn from Newbiggin and concentrated their lives in London, or Paris, or in traveling. A surviving photograph of Hubert shows a young man with a gun and two English setters, the breed used on the moors, and is a reminder that it was not only in Russia that nineteenth-century authors hunted and shot as part of native tradition, a natural activity of the countryside although in rather ironical contrast with their exploration, in cities, of the lives of the poor and vulnerable. Maupassant too, like Turgenev, was a keen sportsman who valued his shooting far above the métier of literature.

The grouse moor at Newbiggin lay high in the Pennines, on the bleak northeastern slope of Cross Fell, the summit of the Pennine chain. It was a young man's moor, reached only on foot or horseback by the Roman road called the "Maiden Way." For three or four days at a time the shooting party would live roughly, in the whitewashed stone lodge built near the sources of the rivers Tyne and Tees, the same building serving for shepherds in the winter. Even in August, sport at such an altitude can be as rigorous as the hills are lonely, doused in water or burned by a midsummer sun overhead, while underfoot the spongy peat holds an inexhaustible store of rain. By day, there would be the thrills and visual splendors of the mountain grouse drive; the skimming sweep, almost vertiginous in speed, of the packs of birds about the contours of the fell, over rolling slopes of heather whose interlocking lines would appear in a recession of blues or of deep green and purple in the capriciousness of the August light; and at night, peat fires, libations of claret and port, water drawn from the river running below the walls of the lodge, and meals of game and provisions brought up on horseback.

During the absence of the brothers, Leila must have made some efforts to come to terms with her husband's family, and particularly with her mother-in-law. Both tasks could have proved difficult. Close families held together partly by shared intellectual values, partly by a dominant maternal personality, can provoke a hostile reaction in those who marry into them. Solidarity, even if only intermittent, and conceit on the one hand, fear and envy on the other, play obvious parts. Leila seems on the whole to have made a not very favorable impression, but this was attributed, in the family, to upbringing rather than to intrinsic faults. After Hubert's disappearance in 1896, and before the discovery of his body in the Seine, Dayrell wrote a furious and comprehensive letter to Leila, an all-embracing indictment which is the source for both chronology and detail of the events before Hubert's death and for the character of his relations with his wife. Dayrell wrote:

> I will only lightly touch on this period of your married life: I wish to be as fair as I can towards you; nor will I blame you now for faults, which, as they appeared to us then, were faults of education rather than of heart.[81]

Blanche certainly had a personality to make her respected more than loved by those brought into first contact with her; she was undoubtedly loved by her sons—in their youth perhaps excessively, later with reservations—but her daughters-in-law must have had a hard time of it, despite Blanche's declared sympathies with the problems of young women. In her own family, she was redoutable; Leila was the first young daughter-in-law introduced into a family of sons to experience this, but in 1912 Dayrell wrote to his own wife:

> I fear my mother is now too old, her habit of mind too ingrained, for one to entertain any hope that she will modulate that sharp personal note in her relationship to you and others which I know is so jarring. Yet beneath it all I do

believe she wishes you well and that in any real trouble, you would find her a staunch and true friend.[82]

Twenty years earlier, before the loss of her much-loved elder son, Blanche may have been less sharp than this letter suggests; but Dayrell also implies that sharpness was a permanent ingredient in her character. And the fact that Leila had literary pretensions—in addition to her volume of poems she published work in both the *Yellow Book* and the *Savoy,* though in Ella D'Arcy's opinion it was Hubert's name that procured acceptance—is not likely to have helped, in the relationship with Blanche, if friction developed through differences of taste or values.

Residence at Chelsea Gardens was probably an aspect of what Le Gallienne referred to in writing of Hubert's "adventurous study of human life."[83] In any case, it was neither very prolonged nor constant, since both Hubert and Leila had the taste for travel and liberty to indulge it. William Rothenstein said that Hubert was "devoted to his wife,"[84] and perhaps for a year or two both man and wife continued in a more or less euphoric state, though if Dayrell is to be believed difficulties began almost at once. They remained intermittently at Chelsea Gardens for two years, before moving westward along the Thames to the handsome seventeenth-century surroundings of Lindsey House, which it was hoped would be their permanent home. On December 16, 1893, Leila wrote a draft of a will on a sheet of writing paper headed 36 Chelsea Gardens. After bequests of jewelry—of which she seems to have possessed a large amount—she made the following disposition:

> The sum of money that comes to me on the death of my Grandmother Macdonald I leave capital and interest to my husband . . . till his attaining the estate of Newbiggin . . . after which capital and interest bequeathed to Mrs. Josephine Butler to be used as she thinks fit in her work of female rescue from the streets.[85]

Inheritance from her grandparents made Leila an independent woman, free at a time when women were demanding freedoms; if she was unstable, as W. C. Frierson has suggested,[86] then this financial independence, more especially after the death of her grandfather in 1896, may well have gone to her head. The aphorism of Maurice Barrès—without money, there is no free man[87]—could have the rider—nor liberated woman—added to it. At this stage however, Leila still showed a wifely desire to benefit her husband, though with an afterthought, so characteristic of the period, for women on the streets. In Chelsea Gardens, the young couple must have begun to discover one another more thoroughly than was possible in France or at Newbiggin; in another part of Dayrell's long letter it is made clear that, in the family at least, it was not thought that the sharing of domestic responsibility had worked out to Hubert's advantage:

> I will merely say that during the whole of that period you persistently declined to perform, in any sense, those domestic duties which every husband, and especially a husband whose work requires concentration of thought and repose of mind, has a right to expect from his wife. You appeared to imagine that he could alike perform the duties of a housekeeper and pursue the career of a writer. To make up for your negligence of the former, he was, as you well know, obliged to sacrifice, in a great degree, the latter. Continuity of work and the quiet reflection so necessary to the artist became to him an impossibility, and in thrusting onto his shoulders the entire onus of domestic details, you marred, from the first, his literary prospects.

This charge, if true, is a heavy one. The younger brother's intense indignation and protectiveness, and what now seems a certain masculine bullying, an expectation of wifely virtue and fury at its absence, are unmistakable; the man who had so recently been a stammering boy composed his eloquent rebuke in the most contemptuous terms, hoping to wound and omitting nothing that could be painful or cutting.

It is not necessarily true, however, that Hubert's literary development was so much affected by the shortcomings of his marriage as Dayrell supposed, though perhaps his productivity was. During these early months of married life he was undoubtedly thinking about the technical process of fiction, leading himself away from dogmatisms, and enlarging the range of psychological study to which, obviously, his own experience must contribute. Zola's recommendation of marriage for literary production did not specify that the experience be a happy one; so Dayrell's conclusion founded in brotherly love was perhaps not the right one from the creative standpoint. A much more subtly undermining characteristic of Hubert's marriage and of his rash hopes for a sharing of the creative life, is powerfully expressed by the mysogynic Goncourts:

> What men like us need is a woman of not much breeding or education, but full of gaiety and natural spirit; because such a woman will delight and charm us just like an agreeable animal to which we could get attached. But a mistress with a smattering of society, of art, of literature, who wishes to keep up with us on an equal footing, with our thought, with our esthetic consciousness, and who has the ambition to make herself the partner of the book in gestation or the companion of our tastes, becomes as unbearable to us as an untuned piano—and very soon an object of antipathy.[88]

The last complex sentence is almost fiercely marked in Hubert's copy of the *Journal;* since there is so little evidence of the progress of the relationship between him and his wife until the events of 1896, these private markings take on a significance that might otherwise pass unnoticed. In a copy of his second book of stories, *Sentimental Studies,* Hubert wrote the following inscription to his wife: "*A petite âme,* this wretched book which one evening she wanted to take seriously."[89] Differences of esthetic and intellectual emphasis or of tastes, enjoyments, and choice of companions, could be as damaging to such a marriage as a writer's practical difficulties of time and repose such as Dayrell outlined. Frierson composed an imaginative account of the deterioration of Hubert's marriage, and it is impossible to know if Frierson, as the certainty of his tone suggests, had access to some surviving witness whom he did not name: "A well-born young writer and his wife drift apart. The wife finds no sympathy and understanding in the artistic circles where her husband moves."[90] There may be enough resemblance between this reconstruction and Dayrell's direct account to give each of them additional substance. But whatever the truth about the turn the relationship was taking, family fears were not due to any complaint by Hubert himself, not even to his brother: "He never spoke to us of his household worries: his was a proud nature and he loved his wife: in honour to her, his lips were closed, and it was not for us to open ours."

Hubert's first published work written after his marriage was the long story "A Commonplace Chapter," which appeared in February and March 1894 in the *New Review;* the second part of the story, "The Haseltons," was reproduced in the *Yellow Book* of April 1895. The story deals with an idealistic marriage that deteriorates slowly over a period of years, the sexually experienced and unfaithful husband tiring of a wife too young and simple for the sophisticated circles into which he introduces her. There is no substantial reason to relate the story directly to any detail of Hubert's own marriage, though the speculation has been made. It was written at a time when his relationship with his wife must have been still fresh; nevertheless the possibility of early, perhaps compulsive infidelities by Hubert is inevitably suggested by the detail of the story, which is also the first demonstration of his movement toward psychological exploration not dependant on any melodrama or outrance. Henry James defined the interest: "The possibilities of some phase, in especial, of a personal relation, a relation the better the more intimate and demanding, for objective intensity, some degree of composition and reduction."[91]

At about this time, J. T. Grein offered Hubert an opportunity to discuss in public his developing literary views. Hubert wrote to Edmund Gosse on January 23, 1894, from Chelsea Gardens:

> Dear Mr. Gosse,
>   You were so severe on me last time we met, at the National Club, that I fear you will perhaps cordially disapprove of the scheme which the enclosed prospectus attempts to expound in somewhat Continental English—& flatly refuse the little request I am about to make to you! Indeed, it is only after days of trepidation that I have at last decided to throw myself on your mercy.
>   As you will see, I have promised Grein to read a little paper on February 11th. I should be so proud if I could persuade you to act as my chairman.
>   Your duties would, of course, be nominal, and L am going to try to be very reasonable & temperate.
>   The thing begins at eight, & I will be over at ten, punctually.[92]

It is not easy to see what would have been the specific cause of Gosse's severity. He was an encourager of young writers and was sympathetic to the products of French naturalism, of which he wrote in his essay "The Limits of Realism in Fiction" that "it has cleared the air of a thousand follies, has pricked a whole fleet of oratorical bubbles . . . the public has eaten of the apple of knowledge, and will not be satisfied with mere marionettes."[93] As is implied in the title of the essay from which this rather confused array of metaphors comes, Gosse, like Moore and Gissing, valued Zola's example but believed that it lay in a direction where there was not much more room for development. Although Arthur Waugh complained of "a not infrequent luxuriance or audacity of expression" in Gosse's own work,[94] Gosse had perhaps criticized Hubert for resorting to Zolaesque exaggerations. In any case, by this time Hubert was moving away from Zola, and the disagreement between him and Gosse, if such it was, cannot have been a serious one since Gosse accepted the invitation and Hubert delivered his two-hour paper on the "Art of Fiction" at one of the Sunday Popular Debates. Conal O'Riordan mentioned this occasion in his foreword to *J. T. Grein:* speaking of Shaw, who at the time had his "Fabian fish to fry, and could not be induced to debate about esthetics in any form," O'Riordan said that "he was certainly not present when charming, ill-fated Hubert Crackanthorpe lectured . . . with Edmund Gosse in the chair: George Moore and I represented Ireland on that occasion."[95]

Moore's presence at the debate is interesting because he, Gissing, and Crackanthorpe were the writers in English who most used the newly won freedom to deal with sexuality in fiction more frankly, or more brutally. Frierson referred to "the relative liberty with which [Crackanthorpe] deals with sexuality"; and it was no doubt this comparative freedom in presenting the seamier side of sex that earned Hubert's early work much of its notoriety. Although an interest in sex and its accidents remained predominant in his work after *Wreckage,* it was a part only of the wide literary purpose described by Frierson: "The phases of Crackanthorpe's work . . . demonstrate with what seriousness he gave himself to the study of humanity and with what compassionate understanding he wrote about it."[96]

The essay "Reticence in Literature" which Hubert contributed to the second number of the *Yellow Book* in July 1894, though ostensibly a reply to Arthur Waugh's essay of the same title in the first issue, was probably an adaptation of the paper read in the Sunday debate; parts of it have a polemical tone, there is an admiring reference to Gosse, and the phrase "the art of fiction" appears in the opening sentence and repeatedly elsewhere. However, despite a lightness of tone characteristic of debate, the essay is a serious and suprisingly authoritative critical statement that points both the direction in which the twenty-four-year-old author was moving and to the real nature of his literary gift.

The piece is closely argued: its main theme, which reflects a special, rather obsessive concern of writers at the time, is the primacy of temperament in all forms of artistic production. As for reticence, in the sense of literary inhibition, Hubert believed that already the fight for freedom from it was practically won: "the roar of unthinking prejudice is dying away. . . . A new public has been created—appreciative, eager and determined."[97] The main goal of naturalism was therefore achieved: "Nowadays there is but scanty merit in the mere selection of any particular subject, however ingenious or daring it may appear at first sight."[98] Subjectivism reappears with the sanction of Zola's most often repeated formula almost directly translated: "A work of art can never be more than a corner of Nature, seen through the temperament of a single man."[99] Zola's definition seems to weaken the scientific pretension of his theory, although naturally he had attempted to forestall such a criticism:

> There is an abyss between the naturalist writer who proceeds from the known to the unknown, and the idealist who claims to go from the unknown to the known. . . . we will at least give you the truth of nature, seen through our own humanity.[100]

Crackanthorpe's conclusion is a simple one: "So then, the disparity between the so-called idealist and the so-called realist is a matter, not of aesthetic philosophy, but of individual temperament."[101] This is essentially the same conclusion as that expressed by Flaubert: "I cannot have a temperament other than mine, nor any other esthetic than that which is its consequence."[102]

The effect of temperament on literary art had been adumbrated repeatedly and elegantly by Pater, whose work was itself a specimen of the interaction of the two: "Literary art . . . is the representation of . . . fact as connected with soul, of a specific personality, in its preferences, its volition and power."[103] For the realist, the reintroduction of subjectivism brings back that most subjective of values, morality; Hubert's view was that the business of "the subtle, indirect morality of art is to . . . make of our human nature a more complete thing."[104] The writer should judge his right direction by the degree of resistance he meets, indicating where new ground lies to be won; and the organ, sense, or faculty that must process experience and transmogrify it into a humanizing literature is the temperament, the imponderable ego and its shadowy substructure. In a careful paraphrase of Bourget's judgment on Flaubert Hubert stated:

> Every piece of imaginative work must be a kind of autobiography of its creator—significant, if not of the actual facts of his existence, at least of the inner working of his soul. We are each of us conscious, not of the whole world, but of our own world; not of naked reality, but of that aspect of reality which our peculiar temperament enables us to appropriate.[105]

In this literary metaphysic, "vague but penetrating" to use a phrase of Crackanthorpe's from another context, Bourget had been anticipated by Pater in his famous "Conclusion" to *Studies in the History of the Renaissance:*

> Experience . . . is ringed round for each of us by that thick wall of personality through which no real voice has ever pierced on its way to us, or from us to that which we can only conjecture to be without. Every one of those impressions is the impression of the individual in his isolation, each mind keeping as a solitary prisoner its own dream of a world.[106]

From Pater to Bourget, and then to Crackanthorpe, there is a process of rendering the metaphysical concrete, and practicable from a fiction writer's point of view; in other words a progressive return to psychology as the focus of literary interest.

Hubert omitted this significant and Paterian sentence from Bourget's passage: "We only tell our dream of human life." Such a sentiment may have been too ethereal or subjective for his argument. However, his paraphrase of Bourget has both a biographical and a literary implication. Biographically, it allows, or at least gives probability to, inductions from the character of Hubert's work, including the annotations in his library, to his own character. The literary implication is summed up in the concluding words of "Reticence in Literature": "The essential is contained in the frank, fearless acceptance by every man of his entire artistic temperament, with its qualities and its flaws."[107] This self-acceptance owed much to the example of Pater, who had written of "an art in some degree peculiar and special to each individual; with the modification, that is, due to his peculiar constitution, and the circumstances of his growth, in as much as no one of us is 'like another, all in all.' "[108]

The argument put forward in "Reticence in Literature" represents a swing of the pendulum from an extreme of "impersonality" to a comparative subjectivity having the high purpose of enlarging human self-knowledge through analysis of emotion and mood. The purpose was nothing if not modern, and it was certainly in this direction that Crackanthorpe's literary individuality lay and would have developed, the derivativeness of early work being superseded by a sure recognition of his own appropriate sphere and the fellowship to which he must belong. The school of literary psychologists, which included Henry James who was a close friend of Bourget, traced its immediate ancestry to Stendhal, of whom Zola wrote: "Stendhal has taken only the head of man, in order to carry out a psychologist's experiments in it."[109] Zola concentrated on the physical life, the life of the organs; the novelists of psychology wished to treat the organs as reflected in the mind and the mind as expressing the organic life, for the interpreter capable of accepting the entire self, venom and all. This passage from Bourget's *Le Disciple* is heavily marked in Crackanthorpe's copy:

> What words could prevent this twenty-two year old head from being ravaged by pride and sensuality, by unhealthy curiosities and depraving paradoxes? Would one point out

to a viper, were it capable of reason, that it ought not to secrete its venom? "What am I a viper for?" it would reply. . . . To change no matter what in a being, is to check its very life.[110]

The movement of Hubert's attention and practice from one literary mode to another is illustrated in a contrast set out by Georges Pellissier:

> Some among our young novelists see nothing in human nature but blind instincts and impulses; their outspoken, sober narratives, marked with a strong and lively character and in simple, robust, raw language, depict in powerful relief characters whose activity is entirely physical.

In the margin next to this passage, Hubert has written the name of Maupassant; and next to the following that of Bourget:

> Others, on the contrary, bring to psychology that curiosity which is characteristic of our generation: followers of Stendhal, as the others are of Flaubert and Zola, they are interested only in "moods," "cases of conscience"; they produce "diagrams of moral anatomy."[111]

Most of Hubert's work after *Wreckage* belongs unmistakably to this second school; and although *Wreckage* in its day was thought novel and daring, a study of the later work shows that the literary act more in accord with Hubert's temperament and gift was in the apprehension of psychological complexities, often of a sexual kind, lying deep within the personalities he treated.

IV

The two parts of "A Commonplace Chapter," are perhaps the most ambitious of Crackanthrope's efforts in fiction. Taken together, they form the longest of his stories. But it is in method rather than in length that this work approaches the form of the novel and gives quite distinctly the impression that it was toward the novel that his talent was inclining. The technique used is more analytic than dramatic, more reactive than active, and the personalities are treated much more subjectively than in *Wreckage*. The rough forcefulness of the early work is replaced by insights studied at greater length: in "A Commonplace Chapter," the relationship of man and wife is rightly treated as one of great density and complexity, flowing from an emotionally intense beginning in a passionate idealism of love. To render this in the short form requires a narrative abruptness in contrast of moods and emotions that interferes with credibility. The "sequence of scenes, woven around a sequence of moods"—Symons's description of the method of *Marius*[112]—is inappropriate in such a context, though it may be at moments dramatically effective; and there are many touches in the story that are suggestive of the theater. However, some of the insights are startling, especially in light of the fact that they occurred to the writer in the early stages of his own marriage:

> She had come to disbelieve in Hillier; to discredit his clever attractiveness: she had become acutely sensitive to his instability, and, with a secret, instinctive obstinacy, to mistrust the world's praise of his work.[113]

In the original version, Hillier Haselton was a successful young barrister, but his profession was later changed to that of writer.

The construction of the story resembles a novel in miniature; it is made up of thirty-one short sections, some little more than a page in length. In this foreshortened picture of a complex and prolonged relationship, symbolic and picturesque episodes alternate with analytic passages; and precise focus on visual detail, which was one of Hubert's strengths, supports these techniques. A striking example occurs early in the story, on the eve of the marriage:

> The window was wide open, and the muslin curtains swaying in the breeze bulged towards her weirdly. She could see the orchard trees bathed in blackness, and above a square of sky, blue-grey, quivering with stifled light, flecked with a disorder of stars. . . . After a while, . . . she distinguished the forms of the trees. Slowly, monstrous, and sleek, the yellow moon was rising.
>
> She was no longer thinking of herself: she had forgotten that to-morrow was her wedding day: for a moment, quite impersonally, she watched the moonlight stealing through the trees.

> When recollection returned, it was wrapped . . . in a veil
> of unreality.[114]

The passage may owe something to Zola's *Une Page d'amour:*

> The two windows of the bedroom were wide open, and
> Paris, in the abyss hollowed out below the foot of the house
> . . . spread out its immense plain. . . . Hélène had had this
> distraction of the great city of Paris before her, for a week
> past. . . . The book slipped from her hand; she mused, lost
> in thought.[115]

If this were a tale of simple marital betrayal or of incompatibility, it would seem an undramatic treatment of a familiar theme. But there is a psychological element present that
locates the story in a region of emotional dilemma where
analysis is more important than drama. The emphasis is on
the fearful emotional discrepancies in the sex relation that
arise from illusion, from prior fantasy, or from egoistic hope
and longing that take no account of the needs or the truth of
the other person involved. "A Dead Woman" made the point
that love is safest when it is posthumous, the object of it dead
and buried; here there is no softening of that despairing view.
Among the living, sentiment is a passionate illusion creating
an unbridgable gulf between lovers. Bourget, speaking of
Flaubert's characters, claimed:

> The disproportion which causes them to suffer originates
> invariably in the fact that they have formed ideas in advance
> on the feelings they are going to experience. . . . So it is
> Thought . . . preceding experience, which condemns them
> to an assured unhappiness.[116]

No more succinct summary of the plight of many Crackanthorpe characters could well be imagined. And this narrowing
of the distinction between Flaubert and the novelists who saw
themselves as Stendhal's successors may explain the ease with
which Hubert passed from one influence to the other.

By having a writer as his central figure in "A Commonplace Chapter," Hubert was able to speculate on some of
the connections between literature, reality, and illusion. The
wife in this story, Ella, reads romantic fiction, "all glamor-
ous, sentimental felicity, at once vague and penetrating,"
which she contrasts with the "commonplace that was

hers."[117] Similarly Hélène, in *Une Page d'amour,* exclaims to herself: "How these novels lied! . . . Yet she remained beguiled . . . to love, to love! and this word, without her uttering it . . . vibrated in her of its own accord";[118] and Ella: "She let the book slip to the carpet. Love, she repeated to herself, a silken web, opal-tinted, veiling all life."[119] If Ella is deceived by novels, Hillier is deceived by himself; the disproportion between dream and destiny is quite as acute for the writer of fiction as for its reader. And in one way at least, the writer is worse off, being aware of his emotional disconnection from the start; the Goncourts' Charles Demailly described this state:

> The man of letters . . . analyzes himself when he is in love, and when he suffers he analyzes himself again. . . . Do you know how a man of letters attaches himself to a woman? In the same way as Vernet to the ship's mast . . . so as to study the tempest. . . . We only live in our books. . . . Other men say: "there is a woman!" We say: "there is a novel!"[120]

Haselton looks on his own life and on the lives of those about him as material to be digested for creative purposes. Reflecting on his discovery of the innocent and delectable Ella and on their engagement, he congratulates himself:

> The whole business was of a piece, he thought; picturesque, yet in no way cheap. . . .
> For her personality appeared to him abundant in possibilities; and it was on . . . these possibilities rather than on the obvious facts of her nature, that his imagination dwelt.
> . . . He took to describing the relation of sex as a great sacrament.[121]

Like Charles Demailly, he loves perhaps "more in the character of author, than in that of a man in love."[122] But his insincerity is not, at least at first, so much cynical as simply the product of his temperament and his calling. He sees his state before marriage as: " 'Only a sort of thin, relative contentedness. Because one didn't know any better. Not this sort of ultimate happiness.' And he reflected on the felicity of the new-found expression."[123]

Hillier's eloquence on the subject of love is only partly a technique of seduction. It is also the expression of a high and intense, if transitory, state of feeling. When, in a scene reminiscent of Maupassant's "Imprudence," he admits to Ella his earlier sexual relationships, she asks him:

"And *they,* were they all so beautiful?"
"Yes, every one," he replied with brutal pride.
"Much more than me? . . . I suppose you said to them all the fine phrases you have been saying to me. . . . No wonder they came so easily."[124]

But this first step in disillusionment is a small one only. There is an alternation in Ella of disillusion and exaltation linked to sexuality. After a day of disappointment and despair, she remembers in the end nothing but "his goodness, and the abandonment to the intoxication of his love."[125]

The great irony of the story is that the process of the wife's sexual awakening runs parallel to the decline of the husband's interest in her, and her consequent disillusion is the more painful.

She had begun, by a sort of classification of his sayings, to endeavour to arrive at the nature of his thoughts, to discover what was his faith. . . .
The passionateness of his love communicated itself irresistably to her. This had troubled her, she did not know whether it was right or wrong. . . .
Now, however, all these misgivings were merged in her aspiration to be worthy of him, to please him absolutely.[126]

There is here a distinct echo of Meredith's *The Egoist,* in the relationship of Sir Willoughby and Clara Middleton, who "became an attentive listener." But as usual, Crackanthorpe introduces a sexual element anchored in the woman's physical experience, an experience that he seems generally to suggest as being more powerful and profound than that of the man.

Characteristically enough, the husband's poetic fantasy of an ideal marriage soon begins to fade, and he manages the resultant dilemma with a new self-deception:

He entirely accepted the fact that he was tired of his wife. And, since he attributed this to some vague superiority in himself, . . . he was ready to blame her that she did not satisfy him. . . . and he clutched at this explanation as a justification for his recent vague dreamings concerning other women.[127]

This aspect of the story may owe something to a rather similar irony in Bourget's *Un Crime d'amour,* where the young lover of a married woman cannot believe himself to be her first, or even her only lover, for the sole reason of her sexual docility. It is as if disparities of feeling are inevitable and the notion of good faith in a sexual relationship hopelessly frail: "Hélène had no suspicion that, at this very minute, this man had found, in her absolute submission to his desires that had cost the poor woman so much, a reason not to believe in her."[128]

The second part of Crackanthorpe's story shows the marriage in the state of collapse and desiccation foreshadowed in the first. Hillier has achieved success and acclaim as a writer, while Ella feels often "a sting of quick regret that she had ever come to understand him and that she could not view him as they all viewed him."[129] Hillier embarks on an adultery that refreshes him and enables him to be kinder to his wife, and to regret the "lapses into roughness which had marred the first months of their marriage."[130] A crisis is brought about through the discovery of the adulterous situation by a cousin of Hillier's, a personality somewhat reminiscent of Thackeray's Dobbin, who is in love with Ella and who forces Hillier to make a melodramatic confession. However, this confession proves to be an anticlimax because the process of disillusionment in the wife is already almost complete:

> The scene seemed to have fallen flat. The tragedy . . . which he had been expecting, had proved unaccountably tame. . . . she . . . had not . . . appeared to regard his confession as an overwhelming shattering of her faith in him. . . .
> . . . he had caused her to suffer in a queer, inarticulate way, of which he was vaguely afraid.[131]

The reader of a Crackanthorpe story cannot expect any catharsis or resolving climax; in this one especially, concerned with "lying novels" and the soft misleading answers that literature may give to the unhappy, the aftertaste is bitter:

> She was even glad to see him as he really was . . . after all, his unfaithfulness was no unusual and terrible tragedy, but merely a commonplace chapter in the lives of smiling, chattering women, whom she met at dinners, evening parties, and balls.[132]

The justification for this examination of what Zola called an *adultère banal* must be, if anywhere, in the psychological treatment; and in fact the chief merit of the story is that it deals in a subtle, if inconclusive, way with Hillier's sexuality. A certain ambiguity in his sexual attitude to his wife is an expression of the conflict between the ideal and the real; in contrast to the "tense and cultured aspiration" of his love for her, he has a longing, which the narrative realizes, to "besmirch himself altogether in her eyes."[133] These contradictory attitudes must have a psychological origin. At Hillier's first appearance, his sexual character is stated: like Bourget's Adolphe who "understood that at college his imagination had been prematurely fouled,"[134] Hillier is aware that

> A precocious familiarity with the obscene had left upon his imagination a secret taint, which at moments had asserted itself irresistably. . . . in a sense, he was proud . . . of his personal charm; of his physical comeliness; . . . his conquests of women.[135]

The longing to besmirch himself evidently comes from a self-knowledge that cannot tolerate idolization, though it can stand a good deal of flattery:

> The innumerable small signs of her love for him, of her submission to him in all things, afforded his vanity a continual regalement such as it had never known before: beside no other woman had he experienced that sense of complete mastery. . . .
> Thus the best that was in him was brought to the surface.[136]

But he understands that it is not only the "best" that needs to find expression; his wife's idolizing and deluded view of him drives him to find in a mistress a contrasted and more comfortable attitude:

> The discretion of her cynical camaraderie . . . was sufficient to undermine all virtuous resolution. . . .
> There was something mannish . . . about her mind. . . . Her cynicism was both human and humorous.[137]

Hillier is an egoist, but not incapable of remorse. He regards his infidelity as unavoidable and healthy, but still has to try to reconcile it with certain uneasy intimations. The resulting tension produces one of the most vivid moments in the story, so natural and unexpected that it looks like a note of autobiography, more directly introduced than some of the nuances of Hillier's personality which might be the work of author's introspection. Hillier returns late one night from his mistress and finds Ella asleep in her chair, her breathing "soft and regular like a child's":

> He sat down noiselessly, awed by this vision of her. The cat, which had lain stretched on the hearth-rug, sprang into his lap, purring and caressing. He thought it strange that animals had no sense of human sinfulness, and recalled the devotion of the dog of a prostitute, whom he had known years and years ago.[138]

It is a notable moral and mental relaxation that makes possible the invention of such contrasts. That one should be able to know a prostitute, not merely use her, and then also remember her and her dog with an almost casual kindness argues a rather modern acceptance of humanity tending to support Le Gallienne's judgment on the fin de siècle:

> Here was not so much the ending of a century as the beginning of a new one. Those last ten years of the nineteenth century properly belong to the twentieth . . . and, far from being "decadent," . . . were years of an immense and multifarious renaissance.[139]

4

The Pursuit of Experience

I

The first number of the *Yellow Book,* published by John Lane, appeared in April 1894. Henry Harland, the editor, invited many well-established men of letters, Henry James, Edmund Gosse, and George Saintsbury among them, to contribute, but the dominant note was meant to be a youthful one, and experimental. James is known to have felt rather ill at ease in such a setting. In January 1924, in her memoirs of the three and a half "meteoric years" of the *Yellow Book,* Evelyn Sharp stated that "no literary youth of any epoch ever passed through a more entrancing nursery";[1] and Holbrook Jackson, writing in 1913, described the impact of the new quarterly:

> Nothing like *The Yellow Book* had been seen before. It was newness *in excelsis:* novelty naked and unashamed. People were puzzled and shocked and delighted, and yellow became the colour of the hour, the symbol of the time-spirit.[2]

The *Yellow Book* was an immediate sensation; among the first contributors were Max Beerbohm, Richard Le Gallienne, George Moore, Arthur Symons, Ella D'Arcy, John Davidson, Harland, and Crackanthorpe. The first edition sold out in five days, and another was produced, then a third. Reviews were in general hostile; the *Times* pronounced:

> On the whole, the New Art and the New Literature appear to us to compare in this singular volume far from favourably with the old and we doubt if the representatives of the latter will much relish the companionship, to say nothing of the cover, in which they find themselves."[3]

They were right so far as Henry James was concerned; he wrote to his brother, "I hate too much the horrid aspect and company. . . . It is for gold and to oblige the worshipful Harland."[4] The work of Symons, Aubrey Beardsley—who had provided the cover—and Crackanthorpe was severely condemned. The *Critic* spoke of Hubert's story "Modern Melodrama" as follows:

> The gutter is celebrated in prose by Mr Crackanthorpe, a young man who, when he writes of depravity, which he usually does, leaves nothing to the imagination. By the weak he is called "strong," by the strong—but what do the strong reck of Mr Crackanthorpe?[5]

At Oxford and Cambridge, although both *Isis* and *Granta* were condemnatory, undergraduates took pains to obtain copies; the *Oxford Magazine* noted, "We have even seen bold spirits reclining under trees regaling themselves with the *Yellow Book*."[6] And this boldness was outdone by Oscar Wilde who, despite his dislike of it, appeared with a copy of the *Yellow Book* under his arm, to take the witness stand at the hearing of his libel action against Lord Queensberry.

Hubert made five contributions in all; the first, "Modern Melodrama," portrays a demimondaine who, by sending a servant to eavesdrop on a conversation between her lover, or protector, and her doctor, learns that she is dying of a raging consumption. The presentation is crude and, as the title suggests, strains at dramatic effect. Like a one-act play, the story is set in one room, and relies on action offstage. The idea may have come from the Goncourt *Journal*:

> Doctor Simon will tell me in a moment whether our old Rose will live or die. I am waiting for him to ring, a sound which for me will be like that of an assize jury bringing in a verdict. . . . "It's finished, no hope, a matter of time." And one has to come back to the sick woman, pour out a little serenity towards her with one's smile.[7]

But in Hubert's little story there is no restoration of serenity; its whole point is that the girl insists on knowing the truth of her state and does not allow her lover any subterfuge or herself any consolation: "He hesitated, embarrassed by his own emotion. Presently he went up to her and put his hands round her cheeks. 'No,' she said, 'that's no good. I don't want that Get me something to drink. I feel bad.' "[8] The story belongs more to the phase of *Wreckage* than to that of *Sentimental Studies,* Hubert's second collection of stories.

Crackanthorpe was on friendly terms with Henry Harland, and the friendship flourished; he dedicated his second volume of stories "To Harry, in remembrance of much encouragement." They collaborated in writing a play, and it was probably with the "worshipful Harland" that Hubert joined forces in offering to Henry James the "token of esteem" in 1895 or 1896. The play, a farcical comedy called *The Light Sovereign,* was not published until 1917, twelve years after Harland's death and twenty-one after Hubert's. Their friendship had probably begun before the appearance of the yellow meteor; Harland had spent some years in Paris before 1889, so that he and Hubert could well have met there; or they could have been introduced by William Heinemann, who also published Harland's work, or by James, or by Gosse. The Crackanthorpes were among the regular Saturday evening guests who gathered around Harland at his house in the Cromwell Road, and K. L. Mix mentions that "for recreation they sometimes went with the Harlands to see the old-fashioned melodramas which fascinated the realist."[9] This suggests the possibility that "Modern Melodrama," with its surprising abruptness of dialogue and crude narrative, was a technical experiment under a theatrical influence.

On April 15, 1894, a dinner was held to celebrate the launching of the *Yellow Book,* but Hubert and Leila were already in France, on their way to Avignon, by the time the first issue was on sale. Hubert wrote to Selwyn Image on April 21, from Avignon:

> We have been remembering you, my dear Image, in this quaint home of your ancestors. They must have been very delightful people; practising a noble leisure. . . . We came all down the Rhône from Vienne in a funny little steamboat, and a most charming day we spent, sitting on deck in the boiling sun. The greens are, I think, the most wonderful here. You have every imaginable hue from the silver olives to the luscious yellow green of the mulberries. . . . So we are having a gorgeous time, as you may imagine, & London & English newspapers & the music-halls seem thousands of miles away. I haven't seen the *Yellow Book* yet; or heard what people are saying about it. I saw on the

journey out a reproduction of Beardsley's design for the
outside; & I have quite decided that that young man's work
is altogether offensive. But when you have a moment,
write & tell me what you think of it.[10]

The Beardsley design presents a candle-bearing Amazon in
domino, behind whom stands a masked faun wearing a las-
civious expression; paradigm, perhaps, of much that was
sexually bizarre in the fin de siècle. The dislike of Beardsley is
the more surprising in that Hubert's own work was often
attacked by critics who found in his frank portrayal of prostitutes, as much corrupting tendency as in Beardsley's exotic,
witty, and hedonistic designs. In "Reticence in Literature"
Hubert remarked how the different forms of the new art had
been condemned together, by those who disliked them: "And
a weird word has been invented to explain the whole business. Decadence, decadence: you are all decadent nowadays. . . . Ah, what a hideous spectacle. All whirling towards
one common end."[11]

The Crackanthorpes stayed abroad throughout the spring
and summer of 1894. A second letter to Image, undated but
probably belonging to that year, was written from Bagni di
Lucca in Tuscany. Hubert spoke of their intention of going on
to Florence "when the terrific heat abates" and of spending at
least a month there. Although no traveling companions are
named, they were evidently with friends; K. L. Mix has
suggested that Arthur Symons was in Italy with them in 1894.
The letter to Image seems to suggest a group of some kind:

> Simultaneously with this letter you will receive a tiny book
> setting forth the facts "of the prodigious appearance of the
> most holy Mary of Foce Colonia"—and you will be won-
> dering who on earth could have sent it to you & why. Well,
> this is how it happened. Last week a whole cavalcade of us
> started on donkeys at midnight to see, from a high place
> called "the field of flowers," the sunrise. On the way down
> we halted at a tiny mountain chapel hard by which, the
> guides told us, lived a hermit. And presently he
> appeared—a splendid old boy with a flowing white beard.
> We all stood looking at him & he at us for a whole minute,
> & then he began to address us—to our astonishment—in
> pure English. He took me into the little room where he
> lived, & asked me if I knew Mr. Mullins the sculptor. Then

it all came out—that he had worked for years & years in London as a sculptor's moulder—for Mullins, Thomas (of Capri), Onslow Ford & others. The old man was overcome with joy when I told him I knew Mullins slightly & he begged me to convey to him if I could, the little pamphlet which is concerned with the chapel where he lives. He scrawled his name on the back & I added the address, for he could write no more. He had lived for twenty years in the Euston Road, & now was ending his days in one of the most beautiful spots I have ever seen—a very wise old man—amid exquisitely modelled hill-slopes crowded with chestnut trees. . . . Have you ever been to the Appenines? I am sure they would fill you with delight. Here, none of the crudity of colour, the harshness of outline, the grandiose vulgarity of the Alps: there is a feminine gracefulness about these hills, & a sort of persuasive mysteriousness.[12]

In his letters to Image, mostly written from abroad, Hubert still shows himself a happy, exhilarated traveler, spontaneously enjoying himself and all about him. This cheerful and easily stimulated young man is not readily identified with the melancholic who, in *Vignettes: A Miniature Journal of Whim and Sentiment,* noted all the occasions of sadness and disillusion, the withering and fall of the leaf. These travel pieces, although ostensibly belonging to a single twelvemonth, almost certainly derive from journeys made over a period of several years. If a reference in *Vignettes* is to be relied on, Hubert was still in Florence in September 1894. In October, he joined the Harlands and the newly widowed Le Gallienne in Paris.

In Paris, he met Maurice Maeterlinck, who inscribed to him a copy of *Alladine et Palomides:* "A Hubert Crackanthorpe en souvenir d'une heure qui fut très douce. M. Maeterlinck. Octobre 1894." He also visited Edmönd de Goncourt; in his copy of the *Journal* for 1892–1895, published some months before the death of Edmond, and his own, Hubert wrote the following phrase next to the description of the famous *Grenier* in which the brothers held their assemblies: "Mise en scène que je vis en octobre 1894." In that month also, on the twenty-first, Francis Jammes inscribed a copy of *Un Jour* to "Leila et Hubert Crackanthorpe—leur jeune et vieil ami, Francis Jammes, Paris."

Another October entry in *Vignettes,* prefaced by Amiel's

saying, "all scenery is mood," describes the lake at Lausanne:

> Deep-blue, she lies plunged in silent meditation; . . . she
> has her grey days of gloom, and her dark days of despair:
> she has also her *jours de fête,* and her *jours de grande toilette*
> . . . often . . . she lies white, tranquil, statuesque, like a
> beautiful, sleeping woman: at times her humour is bewil-
> deringly capricious; the fleeting, furious rages of a spoilt
> child sweep across her; or, ink-coloured, she sulks during
> long hours, sullenly wrathful.[13]

The word *statuesque* seems to pick up an echo from Francis
Jammes's description of Leila as *amazone* and *guerrière;* the
immediate transition from the "beautiful, sleeping woman"
to images of spoilt rage and capricious sulking is suggestive.
Did Hubert have to contend with such tantrums in his domestic life? Leila's accident early in the marriage had left her with
painful difficulties of sight, for which treatment was sought
from specialists all over Europe; and the *monomanie des voyages*
attributed to Hubert by one of the Paris newspapers after his
death,[14] and which the journeys of 1894–1896 seem to sub-
stantiate, could well have been part of a policy to gratify,
mollify, and amuse a "spoilt child, sullenly wrathful," who
found physical tribulation hard to bear.

II

The third issue of the *Yellow Book,* that of October 1894,
included Crackanthorpe's "Study in Sentimentality," which
later appeared under the title "In Cumberland" in *Sentimental
Studies.* The difficulty with the word *sentimental* is that in
English it has taken on a pronounced element of mawkishness
that renders it ambiguous. In Flaubert's use of the word in
L'Éducation sentimentale this suggestion of insincerity and excess is absent; nor did the ambiguity attach to the word in the
eighteenth century when Sterne could employ it in its original
sense in *A Sentimental Journey.* Obviously it was in the Victorian age that the original sense was lost, and Hubert's intention clearly was, by an ironical use of the words *sentimental*
and *sentimentality,* to point to the degree of moral and emotional falseness with which the age had clouded the sexual
feeling. How, in so distorted a world, was the false to be

distinguished from the true and illusion from reality? In much of his work, unhappiness is a corollary of physical love, because physical love induces powerful and conflicting illusions and differing degrees or aims of desire. Hubert had stated in "Reticence in Literature" that "misery lends itself to artistic treatment twice as easily as joy";[15] easy or not, these *Sentimental Studies* seem to recognize no hope of happiness or of sexual congruence. Sentiment and love are studied like an illness for which the cure has yet to be found, recalling Thomas Hardy's phrase "the disease of feeling."

"Study in Sentimentality" illustrates most pessimistically a contrast between true and spurious sentiment, love and the pretense of love, producing at moments, like "A Commonplace Chapter," something approaching a parody of conventional "sentimental" treatment, but leaving a very bitter taste of frustration. This is a study of one of the recurring figures of Crackanthorpe's world, a lonely and sexually deprived man, a bleak personality in whom passion breaks out once and virulently, like an infection from another world. And indeed the protagonist, vicar of a remote valley parish, suffers the outbreak during the course of a serious illness by which the usual restraints on his imagination are loosened. At the height of his fever he is visited by a married woman to whom he was once engaged, briefly and in the distant past. From pity and because she thinks him dying, she lets him believe that she still loves him. During his slow recovery this fantasy of a shared and frustrated love takes possession of him to the exclusion of all reality:

> His prolonged isolation and his physical lassitude had quickened his emotions to an abnormal sensibility, and led him to a constant fingering, as it were, of his successive sentimental phases. . . .
> . . . After all, he loved as other men loved. . . .
> . . . Besides, he told himself exultantly, the sin, was it not already committed? "Whosoever looketh on a woman to lust after her, hath committed adultery with her already in his heart."[16]

The word *sentimental* is used here to refer to straightforward sexual feeling, and nothing about it can be intended as false, except the delusion that the feeling is reciprocated. Vulnerability to delusion in this most sensitive quarter is presented as the result of an unnatural life of chastity where adultery in the imagination is already a mortal offense. Bourget also pointed this out in *Mensonges*:

> This is a phenomenon of sentimental mirage, often found in chaste men, which delivers them like defenceless prey to the crassest of deceptions. This incapacity for judging their own sensations renders them even more incapable of judging the maneuvers of women who stir up in them all the accumulated treasures of a lifetime.[17]

The woman in "Study in Sentimentality" is superficially romantic and fundamentally hardheaded:

> It was like a chapter in a novel. His loving her silently all these years, and telling her about it on his deathbed. At the thought of it she thrilled with subtle pride: it illuminated the whole ordinariness of her life.[18]

When the vicar recovers his health—but not his wits—and presents himself with his absurd proposal of elopement, he is of course rebuffed with the greatest brutality. Despite a heaviness of touch—what Harland in a sympathetic and shrewd criticism of *Sentimental Studies* called "a trifle too much moral earnestness"[19]—the story conveys quite atmospherically a sense of overwhelming impulse in a character suffering from emotional hallucination as a result of libidinal damming-up, the distortion produced by concentrated feeling independent of the objective world. The fact that the ego is at the mercy of such feelings becomes more and more the focus of Crackanthorpe's attention in his developing work.

At some time during the autumn of 1894, Hubert and Leila returned to London. On December 26, Selwyn Image wrote: "Tonight after the theatre, Jan and I sup with the Crackanthorpes Oh! these nocturnal dissipations!";[20] and on January 25, 1895, Richard Le Gallienne wrote to his mother: "On Monday I had to work every minute and then the Crackanthorpes came to dinner and stayed till Tuesday."[21] What work Hubert himself was doing at this time can only be guessed; presumably he was still at work on the *Set of Village Tales,* which carries the date 1893–1895. He may also have been working on plays; his one-act pieces for Grein had been scheduled for production in September 1894, and although no plays, except *The Light Sovereign,* have survived, it is apparent that Hubert was interested in writing for the theater. There were some who thought him gifted for it; in *The Beardsley Period,* Osbert Burdett remarked, in admiration of the final, dramatic scene of "Anthony Garstin's Courtship," that "his dialogue, as this scene shows, can be splendid; and if he had not died so young, he should have written plays."[22]

1895 was another year of journeyings; if the chronological arrangement of *Vignettes* is any guide to Hubert's movements in this year, it was indeed restless. After two years of marriage, any fundamental discord must have been making itself felt; if Dayrell's accusation that Leila neglected household arrangements was just, then what Zola called "the rancor of domesticity" must have set in to a fair degree. This could be mitigated, at least temporarily, by travel, which might at the same time bring new material for work. *Vignettes* has as epigraph the anti-Paterian statement, "The pursuit of experience is the refuge of the unimaginative," suggesting the possibility that the spring of inventiveness was running dry; if so, the régime of Hubert's life may have been to blame. The Goncourts prescribed for the literary man as follows: "The emotions are adverse to the gestation of books. Those who imagine, should not live. One needs regular, calm, soothing days . . . to bring to light work that is seething and dramatic."[23] And Pater said of Marius that "it had always been his policy, through all his pursuit of 'experience,' to fly in time from any too disturbing passion, likely to quicken his pulses beyond the point at which the quiet work of life was practicable."[24] One is reminded of Oswald in "A Conflict of Egoisms" and his disastrous failure to "fly in time." In any case, Dayrell, though not an artist, understood that an essential, calm regularity was lacking in his brother's home. If there was sexual as well as temperamental incompatibility, the consequences would have been even more dire.

It is probable that in the spring of 1895 Hubert revisited the Béarn that he loved, and perhaps finished the *Set of Village Tales* there. In the early summer he and his wife were certainly in Normandy, first at Dieppe and then at Villerville, a few miles along the coast from the resort of Cabourg, part-original of Proust's Balbec. There was something of an English artistic colony at Dieppe in the summer of 1895; Walter Sickert was already living there and no doubt it was he who attracted the others: Ernest Dowson, Symons, Harland, and, according to Victor Plarr in his *Ernest Dowson,* "several artists and their wives, and others were then in the ancient town."[25] It is likely that it was in the summer of this year that Symons, John Lane, and Sickert saw Hubert set off with Sanger's Circus on its way to Le Havre; J. Lewis May gave an exact account of how this often misinterpreted adventure began:

> I never, so far as I remember, saw the gifted but ill-fated Crackanthorpe, who was, I believe, beloved by everyone. Lane used to relate an amusing story concerning him. Once, he [Lane], Harland, Walter Sickert, and Crackanthorpe were at Dieppe together. Sanger's Circus was also there and greatly handicapped by the fact that no one in the company could speak French. Hearing this, Crackanthorpe approached Lord George Sanger and offered his services as interpreter. . . . at five o'clock next morning—his friends having got up to see him off—Crackanthorpe departed on the back of an enormous elephant.[26]

Hubert was with the circus for four days and described the experience in diary form in "Bread and the Circus," which appeared in the *Yellow Book* in October 1895. This almost joyful account of random adventure is in the greatest possible contrast to the harsh stories of *Wreckage,* described by Le Gallienne as "those little documents of Hell." Hubert slept with the elephant keepers in the same tent with the beasts, and when the circus moved from town to town, traveling in darkness before dawn, he drove one of the wagons drawn by four horses: "Ahead, through the twilight, toiling up the hill, we could perceive the long train of lumbering waggons, each with a ragged petroleum flare swinging beneath the axle" and "the elephants, slouching silently along, and tearing up the corn by the roadside as they went." He found abundant scope for selective irony:

> It was a regular ceremony; it took place every morning behind the small horse-tent. The doctor sat on the steps of the harness waggon, and the tent-men lounged round him in groups. He would knock the ashes carefully from his

pipe, wipe his beery eyes, and clear his throat authorita-
tively before unfurling the *Standard*. He would begin at the
top right-hand column of the inside page, reading mechani-
cally almost right through the paper—the political
speeches, the police news, the foreign telegrams, the theatrical notices, and the sporting intelligence—till he had come
again to the advertisements. No one made any comment;
the tent-men just loitered and listened; and when he had
finished, they strolled away silently, as they had come. The
scene, in its droll solemnity, struck me as curiously pa-
thetic.[27]

Sentimental Studies & A Set of Village Tales was published by
Heinemann in July 1895. After parting from the circus at Le
Havre—"Strangely reluctant to leave, childishly eager to pro-
long indefinitely this short moment of departure"—Hubert
spent a few weeks at Villerville; then he and Leila traveled to
Wiesbaden from where he wrote to Image thanking him *de
tout coeur* for a letter that presumably contained an appreciation of the new work in *Sentimental Studies:* "I am very, very
grateful to you for that letter of yours." The reason for the
journey to Wiesbaden is given, and the explanation sounds a
slight but definite note of long-suffering:

> My wife, you know, has for a long time, had trouble with
> her eyes. And her London oculist—a man with a big
> enough reputation, & charging heavy enough fees—instead
> of doing her good, seemed only to be making matters
> worse. So at last, in desperation, we determined to come
> here, to consult Pogenstecker, who has the reputation of
> being the best oculist in Europe. . . . In three minutes he
> discovered the source of the trouble, that she is suffering
> from a sort of congestion of the eye-nerves, & that no
> spectacles could ever have helped her. She goes to him
> every morning at 8, & he massages round the eyes,
> straightening out the twisted nerves . . . today for the first
> time she is to do a little reading.[28]

Hubert went on to say that they hoped to return to London
within a few weeks; the passages in *Vignettes* that carry dates
in August and September are of London scenes and may be
evidence for his presence at home during those months of
1895, particularly as he was abroad all through the summer of
the previous year. Again using *Vignettes* as a tentative guide, it

seems that the travels were resumed in the autumn, with visits to France, Switzerland, Italy, and Spain.

III

Sentimental Studies contained two previously unpublished stories, "Battledore and Shuttlecock" and "Yew Trees and Peacocks." The second of these deals with a triangular love situation among middle-aged members of the English aristocracy. Like well-worn costumes from the theatrical outfitters, the characters are taken from stock and show signs not only of wear but of the slightly exaggerated stereotype that is one of the means of satire: there is Lord Sheire, complaisant husband; Colonel Hallam, honorable lover; and Lady Sheire, whose faded beauty like the "bed upon bed of damask roses, dying in gorgeous disorder . . . lavender, dull gold,"[29] gives off "an air of delicate, subdued sadness, as if the sensitive beauty of her soul had constrained her to long, intimate renouncements."[30] This sketch of frustrated female passion suggests that parody could have proved a fertile mode for Hubert. The story is presented through a symbolism of scenery and colors, of sky and garden. Holbrook Jackson remarked on the "acute colour sense of the period" often reflected in book titles—*The Green Carnation,* the *Yellow Book*—and added: "It would seem as though the Impressionist painters had made the world more conscious of the effects of light, and inspired writers with a desire to seek out colour visions for themselves."[31] As for "renouncement," this was a theme that preoccupied several of Hubert's contemporaries; Frank Wedmore gave the title *Renunciation* to one of his volumes of stories, while *Marius* is practically an epic of resignation, culminating in the self-immolation of Marius's death.

"Yew Trees and Peacocks" is an uneasy combination of experiment in style and satire on a certain literary convention of Victorianism. After Colonel Hallam's gentle announcement that he is about to take up an appointment in the East that will break his long and perhaps platonic attachment to Lady Sheire, she sees him walk away, arm in arm in friendship with her husband:

Behind the oaks the red sun dropped; . . . slowly the hues deepened, pouring themselves in a gorgeous flood over the sky—cornelian, saffron, gold—gradually, in flawless transition, cooling to thin yellow, and far away, across the park, dusky and indefinite, to chilly grey.

And there, where the furnace flared fiercest, . . . twisted and shrivelled, stiffened as if its life had been taken from it in the climax of its agony, lay the black, burnt carcase of a tortured cloud. The foliage of the yew-trees turned dark as pitch; from across the great park, all flushed, floated a faint lowing of cattle. . . .

Constance rose, shivering a little, and moved across the lawn towards the house.[32]

If the heavy alliteration—a little reminiscent of Pater's "perfumed juice of the find of fallen fruit"[33]—and the clumsy imagery show Crackanthorpe writing at his least prudent—and it never was his intention to write placidly—there remain virtues to offset the blunders. There is the eye of a colorist apparent in the first paragraph quoted; and there is a knack of psychological irony, shown in the dryness of the closing sentence. In the inhibited behavior of a civilized woman, to "shiver a little" is the only outward sign of an emotional drama, an "intimate renouncement" symbolized by the violent meteorological polychrome.

"Battledore and Shuttlecock" is a story of an unconsummated love affair between an ingenuous youth, one of Hubert's "chaste men," and a young prostitute of a superior kind, unharmed by her experiences and making her way back to an innocence she has never really lost. The story was admired by Henry James who said that in it Hubert reached "his safest limits in such a happy intelligence of the artistic essential."[34] The central irony of the story is at once obvious: the narration is from the youth's point of view and so, since the girl despite her profession insists that the relationship remain chaste, a particular frustration is conveyed. The girl, Midge, uses Ronald's ingenuous love as a stepping-stone by which she crosses from a life of prostitution to the safe shore of respectable marriage in a distant part of the country, where no one knows anything of her past. This reformation, and the capacity for it, may have been suggested by a remark of Paul Bourget's: "the easier a woman is, the more strength she has to pull herself together." In "Battledore and Shuttlecock," by a subtle paradox of psychology, the girl recovers from prostitution without giving herself to her rescuer, that is, through a love that is therapeutic because it is "pure." This is not to say that she is not attracted by the boy's innocence and even his timidity, in much the same way as the girl Suzanne in Bourget's *Mensonges:*

> She sensed in him a desire for her that was as passionate as it was fearful and respectful. And how it pleased her to be desired with such modesty! She was the better able to gauge the abyss separating her little René . . . from the bold and formidable pleasure-seekers who made up her usual world.[35]

Midge is much less cynical and, in the English manner, more roundabout, but the order of feeling is the same:

> "You somehow seemed to me quite different from all the rest. . . . You looked so young and shy and bewildered. And then, I was afraid . . . you wouldn't understand how it was I liked you. . . .
>
> . . . I always do things just as they come. It's my way—I can't help it. If I could, perhaps things would have been quite different. Now you know exactly what I am, don't you?"
>
> He flushed crimson: his whole being rose in revolt against the brutal thought she forced upon him.[36]

There is great delicacy here in that the revulsion is from the thought and not from the woman.

Midge is certainly Hubert's most affectionately realized female subject; she is sexually enticing and has a genuinely autonomous personality that makes her mistress of herself as well as of others. Ironically, Ronald feels "a great compassion for the frailty of women" though the real vulnerability is in himself, since it is he who is the virgin. Midge, on the other hand, has rewarding memories of her sexual experiences: "No bitterness flavoured her musings. . . . She had found men pleasant, affectionate, generous. So she recalled each one, without rancour: and of one she thought almost tenderly, for he was now dead."[37] Clearly, she is a very different sort of prostitute from Lilly in "Profiles," who passed in increasing despair from man to man, hating each in succession more because she had loved only the first. Midge's appearance shows no mark of decay or corruption: "She was in black; a sleeveless dress, just betraying her breasts, banded at the waist with vivid crimson. Her smooth hair hung low over her nape, as was the fashion, in a dark, heavy coil."[38] This entirely unapologetic portrayal of a prostitute who has not been maimed or maltreated by men—perhaps the mistress of the dog remembered in "A Commonplace Chapter" was her original—and who can discreetly return to marriage and motherhood, is convincing partly because of the verisimilitude of the presentation and partly because the girl, like her creator, sees her position from a morally neutral standpoint. She feels "no savagely revolting realisation of the part she had played."[39] Although the language suggests a degree of Victorian sexual shame the author comes no nearer than this to disapproval. The impression is that it is Midge herself who knows what is best for her and who controls the affair with Ronald, ending it at the moment dictated to her by her own intuition and insight. The success of the creation is the reward of an almost strict Flaubertian impersonalism.

The story traces the progress of Ronald's inevitable frustration. At first he does not realize that Midge is a prostitute and therefore, in the easy and obvious sense, to be had. By the time he becomes aware of this, he is in love in an idealistic way—Crackanthorpe's short cut to permanent misery: "She stood, a white and dazzling figure, blocking the centre of his imagination. . . . Ignorance simplified his whole prospect: blind jealousy of the male, unpricked by the goad of sexual vision, drowsed on."[40] The pathos of Ronald's case, expressed in the somewhat Shakespearean image of the last sentence, is not just in the inexperience that prevents him from knowing how to deal with this girl, but also in the isolation of his love. Because Midge has been a prostitute, she can be introduced neither to his family nor to his friends. At the same time, he cannot reach her because her experience puts a great space between them, which she makes no effort to cross. Midge's journey to innocence is counterbalanced by Ronald's toward sexual maturity:

She saw scarcely any one but Ronald now; . . . living entirely in the present, she thoughtlessly accepted the chastity of their relations as irrevocable. . . . sometimes she mused indolently concerning the past, wondering whether certain memories had not after all been left her by dreams.[41]

In these circumstances, Ronald's sexuality can only be expressed symbolically, and this is achieved by means of an admirably dramatized episode of a drive on a stormy night in a "double phaeton, the horses plunging between the bars of light from the carriage lamps." Ronald, driving the phaeton, behaves with a bravado and boldness not seen in him before, a show of skill and forcefulness that is clearly a sublimation of the obstructed sexual longing:

> He twisted the rein round his wrist by the buckle, and with a steady wrench from the shoulder hauled the horses on to their haunches. Her grip was on his arm—so tight that he almost cried out.
> Then they swung round the corner. . . .
> "I think this is splendid—dashing through the night, with the wind and the rain. I shouldn't mind a scrap if we were to smash up. I'd rather like to be killed with you, Ron," she laughed nervously.[42]

Midge, however, recognizes the significance of the drive. Sexual abstinence can no longer be imposed on Ronald; marriage is precluded, and a fully sexual relationship could only be, for her, a return to the position of a woman kept in secret. She ends the liaison with a letter which is as painful to the man as the frustration has been:

> "It came to me quite suddenly that it could never go on like that. . . . Something would have happened. I feel quite sure of it. So . . . quite suddenly I made up my mind to go back home. . . . I am quite *certain* I'm doing what's best. . . . No one down there knows anything about what I've been doing in London. . . . I shall . . . become very good and steady."[43]

There is a drily ironical postscript to the story. Twelve years later Ronald sees Midge again, now married to an innkeeper at Huntingdon and the mother of three children: "She knew him at once; but because of her husband, refrained from betraying it. And he just glanced carelessly at her and never recognised her."[44] The oddly negative character of so much of Hubert's work, even that which is not absolutely pessimistic by intention, seems to come partly from a misanthropic tendency, inclining him toward somber ironies; but also from inner disposition, as though the introspective vision was heavily shadowed by a sense of loss, an awareness of the evanescence of love and the mutability of desire. W. C. Frierson noted this, in differentiating him from Maupassant: "The scorn, the emotion, the irony that flash from his pages . . . are the very structure of his narrative, and the logical emanation of his thought."[45] In *Vignettes* there is a reflection on the apparent incomprehensibility of caprice in the emotions, which makes an apt footnote for "Battledore and Shuttlecock":

> There are women whom we worshipped years ago, who would certainly fail to move us to-day; books that enthralled us in our childhood, which we hesitate to open again; places we had read of with delight, and for that reason shrink from surveying.[46]

This preoccupation with the intermittency of the heart, a theme to be exhaustively analyzed by Proust, seems almost a hallmark of the fin de siècle.

IV

At the end of *Sentimental Studies,* in a separate section, is the *Set of Village Tales,* six in number. These little stories set in the Béarn have a character quite distinct from Crackanthorpe's other work; they are lighter, more concentrated, more moderate, and without strain. Henry James described them as "the half-dozen vivid little chapters . . . each of the briefest, but each, by studied compression . . . a small, sharp, bright picture."[47] In *The Romantic Nineties,* written many years later, Richard Le Gallienne wished that the dryness and hardness of Hubert's work had been relieved by "some suffusion of his austerely suppressed self . . . that self . . . strangely different from his work, so gentle, and chivalric, and romantic."[48] The *Set of Village Tales,* in which the author appears in his own identity, demonstrates how right Le Gallienne was. The technique probably owes something to Robert Louis Stevenson's *Travels with a Donkey in the Cevennes* but more to

Alphonse Daudet and his *Lettres de mon moulin;* and it is, of course, a departure from what Wendell Harris called "the adroit analysis of personality"[49] as practiced by Henry James and Maurice Barrès. Here, the element of direct observation embraces a first-person narrator who is observant, sensitive, and humorous, but not on the whole analytic, and whose acceptance by the village community is a guarantee of his consistency as a storyteller. And this role of affectionately engaged observer is one particularly well suited to Hubert's talent for dialogue. These stories show another side of him, both as a writer and as a man—the capacity for tender irony, not unlike that of Turgenev in *A Sportsman's Sketches,* worlds away from the almost factitious pessimism of *Wreckage.* Moreover, the use of a first-person narrator avoids a certain suspicion sometimes aroused by Hubert's earlier work that the author is no more than half concealed behind the impersonal technique, and can be seen taking aim at some chosen emotional or social problem.

The first of the tales, "Lisa-la-Folle," concerns a traditional figure of village life, the local madwoman; in this case one with an exotic history, and whose madness is used to sound a note of poetic myth. Frierson remarked that "it was Flaubert who inspired him with the ideal of becoming the master stylist that he shows himself to be in Lisa-la-Folle";[50] and Wendell Harris has suggested that the symbolism of this story shows Hubert's vision that "there had been in the infinite past, somewhere amongst the roots of the world, a great betrayal."[51]

Lisa's past is recounted to the narrator by the village elder and gossip, old Cauhapé: how, many years earlier, the soldiers had come to "gallop about the valley . . . in their great plumed hats, and red cloaks reaching below the heels," and had taken Lisa away to Paris and set her up with "carriages and horses and servants, and a gorgeous mansion, where . . . so old Cauhapé had heard tell . . . many a shameful deed was done."[52] Then one day she had returned, barefoot and in rags, "chattering and laughing to herself . . . about things which had no sense":

> Everywhere the land was cracking with thirst; for there had fallen no rain through the summer. . . .

> That evening the rain had come . . . and Monsieur le curé had found her in the lane behind his house, sitting drenched to the skin, still laughing to herself at her own thoughts.[53]

The community had dealt with her with a hardheaded charity: "They set her to mend the roads. . . . Four kilometres of the road to Hagetmau they allotted her."[54]

One day the narrator is out riding and Lisa (like Jonathan Hays with the doctor and the white mare) steps forward from the roadside to stop him. She proposes to impart to him "something that I have never told to any of them, . . . you can tell it to the people of the land from which you come."[55] Her allegorical tale concerns the love of the sun and moon; she says she has "lived with the great sun many a long year . . . in the old time." She describes the moon's love, "a clinging love—a love surpassing the deepest love of woman," and speaks of the moon's act of betrayal from "spirit of wantonness" and of the sun's "red wrath": "And now, while the great sun sleeps . . . the moon walks the heavens alone, wan and thin and wasted." This is the allegory in which Harris saw a vision of cosmic betrayal, but it is more probable that it is simply a metaphor of sexual betrayal and of a consequent eternal penance. A peculiar irony, perhaps unconscious but nonetheless bitter, is added to the story by one of Lisa's reasons for confiding in the narrator: "You are a stranger . . . you are young, and you have a beautiful wife."[56]

Francis Jammes, although he does not figure in these tales, seems never far away from them, since a return to the values of the peasant community was the essence of *Jammisme.* For Hubert, the great interest was the stability of a society and a way of life basically adequate—in contrast with the life of cities—to its people's needs. Although subject to laws of climate and the land, and to certain sexual laws, often broken, the rural community was not the victim of the great metropolitan oppression and its delusive freedom that was the context of much of his other work. But the shortest of the *Village Tales,* "The White Maize," nevertheless shows how painful the agrarian disaster can be: "Old Cauhapé said it was the end of the world. For eight days and nights, the ceaseless hiss of the rain."[57] On the eighth day, there is a "sickly glimmer of light from the west," and the acacia bloom, washed from the branches, lies on the road "thick like sodden snow."[58] The image effectively conveys the season's treachery of winter-in-spring, like the terrible fall of hail in Zola's *La Terre:* "One could see nothing on the ground but the thick bed of hailstones, a whitened sheet."[59] The narrator walks toward the house of his neighbor:

> Eudore . . . looked up at me . . . but he gave me no greeting, nor moved his hand to his béret, military-wise, as was his habit.
> . . . but . . . just held his open palm towards me. In it lay a young maize-sprout, fresh-plucked.
> I understood. . . .
> The maize had come up white. The fields were all dotted with thousand and thousands of rotten sprouts, and Eudore was altogether ruined.
> At the Toussaint he was sold up.[60]

The story "Saint-Pé" concerns another neighbor, an indigent whose high-sounding, made-up name is the title of the story and whom Eudore hates for his idleness and sponging: "Saint-Pé . . . and the curé, and the officier de santé and I represented the classes at Sallespisse; but Saint-Pé alone *vivait en rentier.* For from sunrise to sunset he was idle; he had not done a day's work since the war."[61] Saint-Pé possesses two assets; one is his dog Pluton, loathed by Eudore as a stealer of ducks, the other is his house, described in a manner worthy of Hardy:

> He lived in a ramshackle, one-roomed, mud-floored building, from one corner of which at night, through the broken tiles he could lie and watch the stars. But the house was his own property, and every Tuesday, Thursday, and Saturday morning he shuffled out of it in his clumsy sabots to beg around the neighbourhood.[62]

One day Eudore catches the dog Pluton among his ducklings and shoots him:

> [Saint-Pé] led me behind his house, and lifting his coat, all plastered with patches, uncovered poor Pluton's corpse, with his tail stretched behind him, stark and straight, as I had never seen it while he lived. "Et maintenant," said

Saint-Pé proudly, pointing to the half-dug grave, "et main-
tenant, monsieur, je travaille."

The digging of the grave is completed by Eudore, Saint-Pé
being old: "Stop a minute; I will dig for you." This conclusion has been described by William Peden as "an epiphanal
incident which anticipates Joyce or Anderson at their best."[63]

He pushed his way through a gap in the hedge, and
taking the spade, dug out the grave. And when he had
finished, Saint-Pé lifted the stiff carcass tenderly and placed
it inside; then shovelled the earth over it with his clumsy
sabots.[64]

The tale of "The Little Priest" is recounted to the narrator
by old Cauhapé, with sardonic glee at the sexual downfall of a
cleric. It is the story of a young priest who had been employed
in the local château as tutor, and had fallen in love with the
daughter of the family: " 'His beard had not yet started to
grow. I remember he had a grave look on his little face, and
large, dark eyes. I never liked the look of them; it seemed as if
it was with them that he did all his thinking.' "[65] The little
priest had run away, and put on ordinary clothes "like a
young man of the town," and later disappeared: " 'That is
why I always say,' old Cauhapé concluded, 'that none but old
men should be priests. A young man in the soutane is an
abomination.' "[66]

Two of the tales are more dramatized than the sketches of
Eudore and Saint-Pé and more direct than the allegory of Lisa;
both are short stories told with the utmost skill and with a
compression that serves the irony. "Etienne Mattou" is an
admirably biting drama of retribution in which the detested
local moneylender, who has destroyed Eudore and others and
amassed great wealth in the process, is cheated of his entire
fortune by his young wife, more stony-hearted even than
Mattou himself:

It was the fair at Amou. On the ox-market, under the
plane-trees, a sea of blue bérets; an incoherent waving of
ox-goads; hundreds of sleek, fawn-coloured backs and
curved bristling horns.
Etienne Mattou had been found murdered.[67]

The body has been discovered on the railway line, the head crushed by the train wheels; unrecognizable except by the markings of the clothes. The narrator drives the widow home from the market:

> Jeanne never spoke a word; she sat quite still, her hands folded loosely on her lap. . . .
>   . . . There was something brutal about the silence of this drive . . . I struggled to find . . . some good word for the dead man. But I could not.[68]

The murderer is never found, though Cauhapé "for a whole week grew quite garrulous over the mysterious crime."[69] Nor does the narrator ever see Jeanne again. She lives on in the dilapidated château, "richer than ever now, for Etienne's life had been insured for eighty thousand francs. And people began to speak of her more kindly."[70] The narrator, on his way back to England, enters a café in Le Havre and hears a familiar voice: "In a flash it came upon me. It was Etienne Mattou . . . that trick . . . of pressing the ball of his thumb under his nose, as he meditated. . . . yet . . . Etienne had been dead nearly a year."[71] Mattou had evidently been waiting at Le Havre for Jeanne to join him with the insurance money, added to their accumulated fortune—the body on the line dressed in Mattou's clothes being that of some beggar whom they had murdered. Mattou tells the narrator that he is going back, "to see after Jeanne—to give her a little surprise."[72] The story concludes with a splendid irony:

> I do not think he ever returned to give Jeanne that little surprise. At least, no one out there ever saw him. Jeanne still lives in the country. She has made over all her money to the convent of the Sacré-coeur at Navarrenx, and now she is a cloistered nun, and will never come out till the end of her days.[73]

The sixth and last story of the set, "Gaston Lalanne's Child," is more complex and serious than any of the others. Neither Hubert nor Cauhapé figures in the story, and the tone of the narrative is deliberate and detached, within a straightforward convention. The wife of Gaston Lalanne is expecting a child; they are a fine couple:

> Gaston had the strength of a heifer, and the burliest shoulders in all the village; and Jacqueline was so tall that she seemed made to match him. . . .
>   . . . And if they asked him for news of little ones he would smile and wink, and looking proudly at his wife, would answer, "Nous en ferons des tambour-majors."[74]

Gaston's character demands that he excel in all things: "Ever since he was a boy—the biggest boy in the communale school, of course—it had been his habit to do things better, on a bigger scale, than the rest."[75] Naturally, this extends to the matter of paternity; the child, when it arrives, must testify to its father's prowess: "he was very eager that the baby should be fine and strong."[76]

The husband of Jacqueline's sister Marthe is a rolling stone; he farms the land adjoining that of Gaston but is often away, and in his absence Gaston drives Marthe to market: "Anna, Eudore's wife, began to hint again that Jacqueline had better look to that hulking husband of hers; but no one else thought there could be wrong between them, because Gaston was married to Marthe's sister."[77] This presumption of innocence turns out to be oversanguine:

> Though no harm had ever passed between them, Gaston was quite aware how things stood with her. It was hard on her, certainly, he thought with easy pity, that she was left so much alone, and that he could not console her, being under obligations to her husband.[78]

It is not long before the sense of obligation gives way in the face of a temptation rendered additionally subtle by the flavors both of incest and of the vanity so neatly suggested by the phrase "easy pity":

> Every Tuesday morning . . . after they had done their business, they met at the Café Laborde, off the ox-market, and came home together in the cool of the late afternoon. Marthe was smartly dressed in a flaming red dress . . . and the red looked beautiful against the brown of her skin.[79]

Jacqueline, when six months' pregnant, trips and falls one day in the vineyard; her baby is stillborn and she herself dies the same night. When Marthe attempts to console Gaston by telling him that she too is carrying his child and adds, "mine, I tell you, mine will live," his first reaction is to disburden himself of guilt by laying the blame for the double death onto the woman: " 'Marthe,' he said . . . in a whisper, 'it is you that have killed Jacqueline; it is you that have killed my child. . . . Quick, I say, get out of the house—quick—the sight of you makes me mad.' "[80] But a little later, with a peasant's fatalism and practical view of conception, gestation, birth—all in sum more important than legitimacy—he relents:

> Twenty minutes later he went down-stairs, and finding Marthe standing in the doorway, gazing stupidly before her, touched her shoulder, saying—
> "Come and hold the lantern for me, I must see to the Breton cow who is in calf."[81]

Throughout the *Village Tales* Crackanthorpe displays a growing confidence, a surer touch with irony, and an increasingly adroit economy of method and vocabulary. The material is more distanced because there is less emphasis on disaster. Most of all, there is a sense of enjoyment and affection in the writing. In comparing the *Village Tales* to *Dubliners* and other works, Peden remarks that the techniques used "give the reader a sense of identification with a place, its people, and their way of life more commonly associated with the novel than with the shorter fictional forms."[82] In *Vignettes* Hubert wrote of his "steadfast" love of the Béarn:

> The melancholy of its wide plains, burnt to dun colour by the Southern sun; the desolate silence of those dark, endless pine forests that lie beyond; the hesitating contours of wooded slopes . . . and the Gave, spurting over the rocks.[83]

For him it was perhaps the equivalent to the remedy for despair prescribed by Pierre Loti who, like Jammes, wrote about the Basque country:

> However wretched you may be, make sure of always having a little corner of yourself which you don't allow the pain to invade, and which can reason about it: this little corner will be your medicine chest.—*Amen.*[84]

V

Reviews of *Sentimental Studies* were respectful, but critical. Writing in the *Yellow Book* under the pseudonym of "the Yellow Dwarf," Henry Harland was cool:

> In dealing with Mr. Crackanthorpe's book, my prize critics will kindly give attention to the actuality of his subjects, the clearness of his psychological insight, the intensity of his realisation, the convincingness of his presentation, and the sincerity and dignity of his manner. At the same time, they will point out that Mr. Crackanthorpe often says too much, that he is reluctant to leave anything to his reader's imagination, his reader's experience. . . . Mr. Crackanthorpe strains a little too hard, a little too visibly, for the *mot juste*.[85]

The ambivalence of this criticism appears in others; the *Saturday Review* decided that Hubert had "toppled over into a flood of psychological analysis. He . . . wishes to exercise all his cleverness upon analysis. Mr. Crackanthorpe" the critic added, "seems to have devoted more attention to Mr. Henry James than is wise. . . . A writer of less promise would not be worth so much anxiety."[86] In the *Academy,* Lionel Johnson was the critic: "His stories bite and grip, they are fearless and uncompromising; but they are full of beauty, the more beautiful for being free from all facile sentimentality and moralising."[87] Comparing the new collection to *Wreckage,* he went on:

> In *Sentimental Studies* . . . the treatment is more elaborate, less incisive, more spacious, less concise. . . . The elements that go to the making of great creations are discernible in his present work, but they are not in proper fusion, proportion, combination. Mr. Crackanthorpe is excellent in psychological analysis, in pictorial description, and in dramatic narrative. It is strong work, sometimes, as is natural, over violent and daring.

Hubert wrote appreciatively to Johnson in the same spirit as he had written to Image:

> I needn't tell you of the pleasure that your generous praise gives me; but it is for your stimulating criticism that I am especially grateful. You have formulated certain faults, of

which, for some time past, I had been feeling obscurely conscious. I feel that you have done me an immense service. . . . Other critics may be kind: you make me eager for work.[88]

These reviews were the last that Hubert lived to read; had his emotional life been happy, this respectful attention and Johnson's generosity would certainly have been encouraging. As it was, much of the pleasure and self-esteem were probably dimmed by what Bourget called the "irritability which is the most unquestionable sign of a decline of love."[89]

The autumnal journeys recorded in *Vignettes* seem to belong to this year. A note of disenchantment, and of something more deeply troubled is apparent in these pieces. The vocabulary is replete with terms of withering and fading: "At the Certosa di Val d'Ema" records a visit to a monastery last seen the year before, "on that mellow September afternoon all garnished with soft light, all fragrant with . . . pleasant, prosperous peace"; but now the sky darkens and the rain clouds gather, "A sombre, swelling herd." Hubert sets out from Florence

> rattling through the dust in the face of the coming storm. By the roadside, the grey olives matched the sky; all around, the vines hung delicately dying, drooping in tired curves their fragile garlands . . . like lingering traces of some bygone *fête*.[90]

At Perugia, he watches the people gathering for the day of the dead: "Before the red gate of the Campo Santo the crowd surges; within, every alley is black with the press of people. . . . To visit the dead all the town is come."[91] In many of these pieces there is a Pater-like tension and melancholy. Holbrook Jackson, in a discussion of the frequency of images of whiteness in the writing of the nineties, which he traced to the influence of the chapter entitled "White Nights" in *Marius the Epicurean,* remarked that "*Vignettes* has a reference to some white thing on almost every page." In passing, the Christian name of Hubert's mother—Blanche—may be remembered: Jackson associated this whiteness both with the "mystery of white innocence" and with images of sensuality, quoting W. B. Yeats's phrase, "the white breast of the dim sea."[92] However, innocence and sensuality may in their turn be lost and polluted, while white remains one of the shades of mourning.

Vignettes outlines an itinerary from Tuscany to Naples, and then a voyage across the Mediterranean, through the Strait of Gibraltar, and round Cape Trafalgar. Dayrell was in Spain in 1895 and wrote to his mother from Seville, at the beginning of December: "I have received a lordly intimation from Bertie that he is coming here 'just to look me up'!"[93] In the piece dated November 30 and entitled "In the Bay of Salerno," the author speaks of "strange meanings of life and love and death," and of love being "but a passionate illusion."[94] The note is ominous. Dayrell did not mention Leila in his letter, but it can be presumed that she accompanied Hubert on these journeys; had she not, this would have been one of the indictments of Dayrell's denunciation of November 1896. It is not certain however; she could have returned to London from Italy, leaving Hubert to make the journey home by sea and to visit his brother without her.

In Seville, there were dancing girls to be seen:

> Amid volleys of harsh, frenzied plaudits la Manolita dances . . . with a tense, exasperated restraint; supple as a serpent; . . . curling and uncurling her bare white arms.
> Out in the cold night air, as I hasten home through the narrow, sleeping streets, her soft, girlish frame still sways before my eyes.[95]

But the piece directly following this erotically tinged passage seems to hint at deep melancholy and self-questioning:

> To ride alone beneath the stars . . . to break, with a sudden clattering of hoofs, the gloomy stillness of distant village-streets . . .
> . . . to unlearn the past . . .
> To elude desire; to disdain the thrill of hate; to forget the long aching of love.

Pater, too, had spoken of Marius's "resolve . . . to exclude regret and desire."[96]

Upon his return to London in December 1895, Hubert moved from Chelsea Gardens, where his flat was to be taken over by Julie Norregard, Le Gallienne's mistress and later his second wife. The Crackanthorpes' new home, at 96 Cheyne Walk in Chelsea, faced south across a garden to the Thames, and comprised the eastern wing of the suburban mansion of Lindsey House, built in 1674; from a literary point of view the interest of the site lay in the fact that the house stood on the ground of Thomas More's farm. Number ninety-six had been the home of the painter Whistler until 1878; it was a few doors from Turner's house, and next to that of the engineer Isambard Brunel. Lindsey House had been divided into several sections in the eighteenth century, but with its hipped mansard roof and segmental-headed windows it kept the unified aspect of a modest French country-house slightly inflated in scale, and now encroached upon by English eighteenth-century town houses. After Hubert died, it became the home of his uncle Sir Charles Cookson until his death in 1906.[97] Inside, there were rooms of noble proportions, especially on the first floor, which contained a double drawing room with long windows overlooking gardens both to north and south. Hubert, in Dayrell's words to Leila, "spent large sums in getting up the Cheyne Walk house to suit you": the interior was decorated by Roger Fry, another pupil of Selwyn Image, in a starkly simple, rather odd and anachronistic scheme of black and white. Fry and Hubert seem to have had divergent views on the sacrosanctity of a designer's effects: "I fence with Hubert Crackanthorpe," Fry wrote on March 15, 1896, "whose house I have decorated with infinite care. Alas! he has proceeded to furnish it and therewith to destroy all my schemes of colour or at all events to mar them; fancy hanging photographs in a room where I had given him white walls and black wood dados. Oh, the pity of it."[98] Photography was naturally a great interest of the time; the last issue of the *Albemarle* had carried an article by the artist W. B. Richmond entitled "The Influence of Photography on Art," which discussed the work of Eadweard Muybridge, the inventor of a technique for photographing animals, and later humans, in motion.

The domestic ventures suggest that a determined effort was being made to shore up a marriage that was perhaps already shaky; and obviously these arrangements were made in an expectation of permanence. The house in Cheyne Walk would have provided a handsome setting for a young literary couple who meant to live and to entertain on a generous scale; and another reason for the move was that Leila was pregnant at the end of 1895. In the spring of 1896, according to Dayrell, she suddenly made up her mind to go to Italy, and she did not return to London. It is clear that at some moment between the New Year and her departure, she had miscarried, but her behavior was not accounted for by that alone: "as for my brother, since your *fausse couche* . . . you had, to use his own words to his mother, 'conceived a physical repulsion to him.' Yet he was patient."[99] Beyond all doubt, the marriage itself was now in process of aborting, and a subsequent part of the letter gives a likely cause. Meanwhile both man and wife became susceptible to new attractions which may have overwhelmed them.

The first number of the *Savoy* appeared in January 1896, edited by Symons and Beardsley and published by Leonard Smithers; the second issue, that of April, included Leila's poem in dramatic form, "The Love of the Poor." Dowson wrote to Smithers on April 25, "I see you have a dialogue by Mrs. Crackanthorpe. Why do you not get a story from Hubert her husband?"[100] The July issue carried Hubert's most cogent story, "Anthony Garstin's Courtship," which was the last of his stories to be published in his lifetime and was included in the posthumously published *Last Studies*. Symons, perspicacious but hesitant, said of it, "I seemed to feel . . . when it came into my hands in the summer of 1896, for publication in the *Savoy*, something almost like a reaching out in more or less a new direction."[101]

Hubert lived on alone in Cheyne Walk until August, in the funerary and marriage colors of its great black and white spaces. There is nothing in either his writing or his reading to suggest that he considered chastity a possible ideal, and evidently at some time during this lonely period he became involved with Le Gallienne's sister, Sissie Welch. Meanwhile, at Viareggio on the Tuscan coast, Leila had, according to Dayrell, "made the acquaintance of a French adventurer of the name d'Artaux. From the time you made this man's acquaintance your letters to my brother grew colder & farther apart."

The last of Hubert's letters to Selwyn Image was written early in May 1896:

My dear Image,
    I am giving after dinner on Tuesday a little birthday
party, & should be so awfully pleased if you would manage
to look in.
    Always yours

Younger and more entertaining company was invited for the
earlier part of the evening. A week before the party, Hubert
wrote to Ethel Clifford, the daughter of Henry James's friend
the novelist Mrs. W. K. Clifford:

Dear Ethel,
    I'm getting up a little bicycling expedition for the even-
ing of the 12th to celebrate the melancholy fact of my 26th
birthday. We propose to start from here at 8 & come back
to supper. Will you honour us. I'd be awfully pleased if you
would. I could call for you about 7.30 & bring you over
here.
    Always yours, Bertie.[102]

Leila's absence was evidently not being taken tragically; Dayrell stated that to the last moment Hubert continued to trust
his wife and to believe that their marriage could be preserved.
Dayrell's letter, however, is not free from whitewashing, and
this statement is difficult to reconcile with Hubert's own
activities in these months. Le Gallienne's biographers,
Richard Whittington-Egan and Geoffrey Smerdon, had access
to surviving members of the Gallienne family, and concluded
that Hubert had "fallen hopelessly in love with Sissie and
there is no doubt that, whether or not she had given him any
physical encouragement, she had allowed him to become
dangerously entangled with her emotionally."[103]

    On August 4, Hubert and his father attended the funeral of
Leila's grandfather Sir William Grove; Leila was not present,
although his death made her a comparatively rich woman. In
the aftermath of her miscarriage, her behavior showed that
she was determined to exploit her independence without re-
gard to discretion. Hubert was not very discreet either. On
August 11, Julie Norregard saw Le Gallienne off at Holborn
Station on his way to Switzerland; on the channel boat Le
Gallienne was met by his sister and Hubert, who were quite
openly traveling together to Paris. The three crossed to
Calais, and Le Gallienne described the incident in a letter to
Julie:

Crackie stood us lunch with champagne! . . . Crackie was a perfect dear—got my luggage through the customs, changed my small fortune at the bureau, and generally did everything for me—for which I was the more grateful as my asthma rendered me rather helpless—and here *is a great secret*. I must tell you a still sweeter thing about him. I'm not supposed to know—but Siss couldn't resist telling me and I cannot resist telling you—do you know that to get £40 for me, *he pawned a whole lot of their silver, at Atten-borough's*. He must be somewhat of a brick to do that, don't you think?[104]

At Calais, Le Gallienne parted from them, and his sister and Hubert went on to Paris, where they remained together until the day of Hubert's death.

5

Fears of a Deeper Color

I

Mary Elizabeth Gallienne, always referred to by her brother as Sissie, was the eldest of his sisters and the closest to him in temperament and interests. She was born in 1868 and so was two years younger than Richard and two years older than Hubert. Like Le Gallienne, she was strikingly handsome, a flamboyant dresser, an independent spirit, and susceptible to love affairs of which that with Hubert was the first but not the last. Grant Richards said that from her first arrival she "became at once a personage in literary London and remained so until her death. An almost beautiful woman, she had much of her brother's taste in books."[1] Their literary interests had developed side by side; Le Gallienne dedicated *English Poems* to her, reminding her of "those old mornings when we rose with the lark, and, while the earliest sunlight slanted through the sleeping house, stole to the . . . study to read . . . you, perhaps, Mary Wollstonecraft, and I, Livy."[2]

In 1887 Richard Le Gallienne rebelled against a tyrannical paternal régime, with the support of his sister who, however, could not leave home until her marriage. Richard made his way by gradual stages toward a fully-fledged literary life in London. In 1891 he moved into rooms in Staple Inn with his old friend James Welch, then a member of the Wilson Barrett theater company and working in London. Welch married Sissie Gallienne on January 3, 1893, a few weeks before Hubert's marriage to Leila; in the same year he appeared as Lickcheese in the Independent Theatre's production of Shaw's *Widowers' Houses*. Le Gallienne described him as "well known for his wit in the nineties" and as the most persistent of all the early Shaw enthusiasts, who "long before Mr. Shaw came into his own . . . tried manfully to win him a London public."[3] Grant Richards said of the Welch ménage that it was "for a time refreshing and beautiful—books and more books."[4] It is hard to see how the refreshing and beautiful atmosphere could have survived Sissie's three-month stay with Hubert in Paris, but at the end of that time, and in dramatic enough circumstances, she returned to her husband, and the marriage continued nine more years. This dubious result was made possible by a conspiracy of silence, directed by Dayrell, after his brother's death.

There must have been many in literary circles in London and Paris who knew of the liaison with Sissie Welch, but Hubert's mysterious, supposedly suicidal death was generally attributed to despair at his wife's desertion; and Dayrell allowed news of the desertion to be judiciously propagated at the time of the recovery of the body. Hubert's alleged devotion to his wife was stressed, and later repeated in more or less well-known accounts such as that by William Rothenstein; while silence—the most becoming form of mourning—was preserved about Hubert's own conduct. Nevertheless, he and Sissie were repeatedly seen together in Paris between early August and the final, drastic scenes at the beginning of November; but apart from a single newspaper insinuation on December 14, 1896, it was not until 1928, with the appearance of Frierson's "Realism in the Eighteen Nineties and the Maupassant School in England," that public reference was made to what Frierson called "a liaison with the gifted and daring wife of a friend"[5] whom he did not name; Richard Whittington-Egan and Geoffrey Smerdon were the first to do so.[6]

Letters, of course, were another matter; after Sissie's death in 1907, Le Gallienne wrote to his wife who was then living in Paris: "Her death seemed to mark the end of my youth. . . . and there in Paris, how often you must think of her and Bertie. I often think of them together buying old silver in a heaven that looks like Paris." To his sister Margaret he wrote: "Darling, beautiful Siss. There has never been anyone quite like her. She was so much her own victorious, radiant, wise-hearted self."[7] Some months later he again mentioned the relationship between his sister and Hubert, saying that although he had wanted to write to his old friend and late brother-in-law James Welch, he feared that Welch might not want to hear from him: "I often think . . . that that affair with Bertie, some years ago, sank deeper in than any of us knew."[8] Welch, with reason, must have blamed Le Gallienne for complicity in the affair, particularly if Le Gallienne met his sister and Hubert in Paris on his return journey from Switzerland, as the remark in the first letter suggests. Le Gallienne reached London on August 22, 1896, having spent two nights in Paris on the way; unless Hubert, Sissie, and he had been together in Paris at some other time, this must have been the occasion when he saw them buying French silver.

During August, they stayed at hotels; the Paris papers later named several at which Hubert was alleged to have stopped. But at the beginning of September Leila arrived from Italy, still in the company of d'Artaux, and the Crackanthorpes took an apartment at 18 avenue Kléber. Af first, Sissie remained at a hotel while Hubert formally rejoined his wife; but before long, at Leila's invitation, Sissie joined the others in the avenue Kléber. For two months, they lived in a strange *ménage à quatre,* which Dayrell described: d'Artaux painted a portrait of Leila in bed; Hubert's room adjoined that of Sissie, and he went everywhere with her, day and night. When the quartet was together there were card-games and, according to Dayrell, Hubert was generally made to take the bank. "On the few occasions on which my brother won . . . the Frenchman showed unwillingness to pay." Relations between Leila and Hubert deteriorated rapidly in this impossible situation; the two women must have seemed in striking contrast with each other: Leila the *amazone,* preparing her acrid charges, and Sissie, described by her brother in *The Lonely Dancer* as "silent, as was her wont," and as "such a dewy marvel of a girl,/Warm as the sun, and ivory as the moon." Any unbalance in Leila's temperament certainly now came to the fore:

> From the day of Mrs. Welch's arrival your behaviour to my brother underwent a complete change: you were even offensive and told him he must see after her and take her everywhere. He was only too glad to have a friend to talk to, while you were still more free to stay out with d'Artaux.

Dayrell's letter, which shows at moments a quite uncharacteristic degree of hypocrisy, was the second of two written to Leila after his brother's disappearance. The hypocrisy may be accounted for by pain, which is also manifest throughout this sad document. A draft of the second letter shows that the final version, for all its harshness, had been somewhat softened; for example, it is only in the draft that the painful reminder of Leila's miscarriage appears. The fair copy of the final version had the approval of Montague Crackanthorpe, for the initials "M. C." appear by the side of Dayrell's own signature. It is clear that by November 25 the results of private inquiries into the events preceding Hubert's disappearance had been assimilated. In his earlier letter, which has not survived, Dayrell had attempted to appeal to "the kindlier feelings I still believed you to possess, and to beg you to make matters no worse than you had already made them, and I was willing to look upon your conduct, disgraceful as it had been, as the paroxysm of a foolishly jealous woman." But by now Dayrell and his parents feared that Hubert was no longer alive. The second letter constituted a violent accusation against Leila, a rebuttal of accusations against Hubert, and a pretence of ignorance of the affair with Sissie:

> Things have come to light in the course of the last few weeks which exhibit you in a very different light. . . . You proceeded to make my brother's life a misery to him: I can only conceive that you were actuated in this by the desire to drive him to "desert" you.

The last sentence must refer to the "physical repulsion," or, in Bourget's phrase, "physiological divorce."[9]

It is possible, though unlikely, that Dayrell was genuinely unaware that before Leila's arrival in Paris, his brother and Sissie had been together there for four weeks; or he may have thought that the behavior of a husband in his wife's absence was nobody's business but his own, even if the conduct of the wife should come to be investigated. Some of the newspapers, however, were inquisitive; the *Daily Mail* of December 14 suggested that Hubert might have left Paris with a lady seen in his company not long before his disappearance. They had been several times to the Hôtel Cambon together, to visit the Grant Allens. Hubert's companion was described as re-markably attractive:

> She was an Englishwoman, and appeared to be on very affectionate terms with Mr. Crackanthorpe. She passed as a friend of Mr. Crackanthorpe and as such was introduced to Mr. Grant Allen. . . . I have received a description of her to the effect that she was slim, petite, exceedingly pretty and dressed somewhat loudly. After that visit of October 20th, neither Mr. Crackanthorpe nor his companion was seen again.[10]

But four days later, the *Daily Mail* rather disingenuously protected itself by stating that shortly after October 20, the lady in question had left Paris to "rejoin her husband in London, where she has remained. It was not until November 5th or subsequent to the lady's departure from Paris that Mr. Crackanthorpe disappeared." Sissie in fact returned to London on the morning of November 5. Grant Allen's reply to the earlier report appeared on December 15: "The lady who called on my wife, about October 15th, was well known to both of us. . . . She was visiting Mrs. Hubert Crackanthorpe at the time."[11] The process of judicious shuffling and adjustment of dates and facts was under way. A number of Paris newspapers also spoke of Hubert's being seen "en joyeuse compagnie,"[12] "en compagnie d'une jeune femme,"[13] and "en compagnie d'une femme galante,"[14] but as these remarks could hurt no one, they were ignored.

The writer Grant Allen was the uncle of Grant Richards, who in October 1896 spent several weeks in Paris and saw a good deal of Hubert. Richards stated in *Memories of a Misspent Youth* that the "society in which Crackanthorpe was living in Paris included Sissie Welch, Le Gallienne's sister, whom I knew well and whose relations with the Grant Allens were also old and very friendly."[15] This is the only contemporary reference to the affair, guarded as it is. The seriousness with which Hubert took his literary life is demonstrated by the fact that in the midst of this immensely uncomfortable marital tangle, and torn as he was between instincts probably conservative and loyal, tending to protect his marriage, and a new and passionate alliance, he yet tried to engage Grant Richards in a literary initiative. Richards was about to start his career as

publisher on his own account; the *Savoy,* in the hands of
Leonard Smithers and Arthur Symons, was failing, and Symons had let Hubert know the state of affairs. On the last
evening of Richards's stay in Paris, he was invited to meet
Hubert at the Café de la Paix at midnight. Hubert, he said,
"was always a little mysterious, and also more than a little
smart and elegant. Nothing Bohemian about his appearance."[16] This remark suggests that Grant Richards knew
something of the strange experiment in luxurious bohe-
mianism being conducted with such unhappiness in the
avenue Kléber. On the occasion of the midnight meeting,
according to Richards, there was a serious discussion of the
possibility of taking over the *Savoy,* with Hubert as editor.
Richards's account gives the impression that Hubert had great
hopes of reviving the periodical and overcoming the reaction
against "decadence" and the supposed excesses of Beardsley.
The two men agreed to meet again in Paris within a few
weeks. On October 30, five days before his disappearance,
Hubert wrote optimistically:

> My dear Grant Richards,
>   I have just heard from Arthur Symons that the *Savoy* is to
> cease in December. Would you be disposed to consider the
> idea of taking it over then with me as editor? I do not know
> under what conditions Smithers would be willing to cede
> the title: but I imagine that an advantageous arrangement
> might easily be arrived at. The sum you mentioned that
> you might be prepared to risk (£250) would, I expect, be
> sufficient to continue a monthly magazine which already
> has secured a certain *clientèle* and had a certain *succès d'estime.*
> I believe without vanity that my name (for certain reasons
> which I need not specify) would be more valuable than
> Symons', & certainly yours would be an improvement on
> that of Smithers. . . . We should make a fresh start; break
> away from the "Beardsley tradition" & have, I think, a
> very fair chance of success.[17]

The scandalous distractions of Beardsley's more daring work
(the original design for the first issue had displayed John Bull
in what Shaw described as a state of "strained" sexual arousal
and was suppressed only on the combined advice of Shaw,
Selwyn Image, and Herbert Horne) were evidently felt to

have cost the *Savoy* some of its literary interest; in any case, Grant Richards soon decided that his capital was insufficient, that the reaction against the magazine had not spent itself, and that Crackanthorpe could not save it. The project was evidently an exciting one for Hubert, and no doubt he could have recruited another publisher and found another source of capital; but all his schemes, whether literary or amorous, were about to be swallowed up by events. No rescuer came forward for the *Savoy* and as Holbrook Jackson remarked: "With the passing of that excellent but short-lived quarterly the decadence in England may be said to have passed away."[18]

II

Toward the end of October, *Vignettes* was published by John Lane; the reviews that appeared in November and December were on the whole unwelcoming. The critic in the *Saturday Review* of December 26, the day after Hubert's death was announced in the press, complained:

> Mr. Crackanthorpe's book, like most experiments in writing prose as if one were writing sonnets, is but a collection of notes, whose only value is that they may some day be worked into the substance of a story or an essay. . . . We have turned over page after page of clever, ingenious summarizing of separate detail, but we have found nowhere a page of pure beauty; all is broken, jagged, troubled.[19]

The most troubled and prescient pages of *Vignettes* describe a ride in the "great, parched plain" of the Landes:

> Since sunrise I had been travelling—along the straight-stretching roads, white with summer sand . . . and on towards the desolate silence of the flowerless pine-forests.
>   And there the night fell. . . . The road grew narrow as a footpath, and the mare slackening her pace, uneasily strained her white neck ahead.
>   Out of the darkness a figure sprang beside me. A shout rang out—words of an uncouth *patois* that I did not understand. And the mare, terrified, galloped forward, snorting, and swerving from side to side.
>   And a strange, superstitious fear crept over me—a dreamy dread of the future; a helpless presentiment of evil days to come; a sense, too, of the ruthless nullity of life, of

the futile deception of effort, of bitter revolt against the extinction of death.[20]

It is worth noting that the phrase "a vague fear of evil," not unlike the "presentiment of evil days" appears at least twice in *Marius the Epicurean*. What Hubert had referred to in "A Commonplace Chapter" as "mere literary melancholy" was perhaps beginning to take a painfully real form, expressing itself in a literary echo.

During the last days of October and the first week of November the rivers of France were in flood, after a tremendous and incessant rainfall. In Paris the level of the water was higher than it had been for thirty years. On November 1, the *Times* gave an account:

> The spectacle [of the Seine in Paris] is extremely picturesque, for the river is at most points double its usual width and is dotted with partially-submerged trees and with flotsam of all kinds. . . . Steamers have ceased to ply . . . being unable to pass under the bridges, and since yesterday the river has risen 18 inches, while a further rise is apprehended. The plot of ground below the Pont Neuf is entirely submerged, and the water even reaches the lower branches of the trees.[21]

The Paris newspapers put less emphasis on the picturesque aspect: *Le Matin* on November 1 described the water as yellowish and murky, saying that the Seine had never presented so horrible a sight; the river was full of driftwood and tree trunks, and the water, having entirely submerged the *quais,* was level with the top steps of the stone stairs leading from them. On the same day *Le Journal* described the wreckage of every kind, dancing and spinning on the swell of water.

In the Crackanthorpes' apartment in the avenue Kléber there was equally a pressure of events and feelings no longer to be contained within ordinary channels. At the beginning of November, Leila took the hardheaded precaution of sending to London for her solicitor, John Hills, who arrived in Paris on November 4. Meanwhile, the floods continued: on November 2, *Le Journal* described the current as alarmingly rapid, the Seine roaring along with a frightening noise. An account in *Le Matin* on the same day mentioned a frequent type of accident:

In Paris, throughout the day a vast crowd has been stationed on the bridges and along the length of the *quais*. A number of accidents have occurred . . . two boatmen trying to retrieve their barge were carried away in the flood. Their bodies have not yet been found.[22]

Dayrell Crackanthorpe's letter gives an impression of what was going on in his brother's household:

This life which you had instituted, proceeded on these lines for some weeks, & it seems that, at the end of this period, you or d'Artaux or both of you decided to bring matters to a head. My mother was to arrive shortly to stay with you, & no time was to be lost: you appear to have laid your plans coolly and most deliberately. Whether you had previously been poisoned by your own thoughts, or by the insinuations of your *protégé,* I know not, but certain it is that you never did what any self-respecting woman would have done—have a frank explanation with my brother. On Wednesday November 4th you entered Mrs. Welch's room early in the afternoon while she was putting on her dress to go to the photographer, & saw there my brother. He retired from the room as you entered it. Here was your chance: and forgetting your own frightful indiscretions with d'Artaux . . . you turned this incident into a case for separation, and without giving either my brother or Mrs. Welch the vaguest idea of what you proposed to do, you, in the company of the man d'Artaux, left him.

It is apparent that Leila was acting on the advice of her solicitor, who must have pointed out that the evidence necessary for divorce charges could not, in the circumstances, have been difficult to obtain. Dayrell spoke of "the nasty-minded testimony of your *femme de chambre* whose mind & tongue seem to have been alike befouled by what she termed 'son expérience de la vie conjugale.' "

On November 4 and 5, the level of the flood subsided by about a foot; the *bateaux-omnibus* did not resume service until November 9, on which day the flood was still running, though it had abated. Leila's discovery of her husband in Sissie's room, the latter half-dressed in the middle of the afternoon, was the immediate pretext for her flight from the avenue Kléber and brought about the final rupture of the marriage:

So well laid were your plans that in a few words spoken shortly after this incident to Mrs. Welch on the subject of the visit to the photographer, you left your guest in absolute ignorance of the misconstruction you had placed on my brother's presence in her room. You then went off to drive and to dine with d'Artaux. When Mrs. Welch & my brother returned to tea, and when you and your *protégé* did not appear to dinner, my brother expressed no surprise at your absence as your dining out with d'Artaux had been no infrequent occurrence. My brother & Mrs. Welch then went to the opera & on coming home at 11.30 found your curt note lying on the table. He was in despair: he told Mrs. Welch to go to bed & rushed out to try & find you. He failed that evening to trace you & then returned, exhausted in mind & body, & flung himself on the sofa. He told Mrs. Welch that in any case her name & her husband's must not be besmirched & the next morning, having sent her off by the first train, traced you to the Hôtel Mirabeau. It was then that he sought an explanation with you and you threatened him with the police. He sent for his father, and the latter being unable to come that day, his mother started instead.

Several reputations would have been upset in the consequent ugly divorce actions; the advent of Leila's solicitor, Hills, was the guarantee that the quarrel was too well developed and fundamental to be settled by explanations. Sissie being gone, Hubert was alone—like the dying Marius after his quixotic dismissal of Cornelius—until the arrival of his mother later that day; she took rooms at the Hotel de France on the quai Voltaire, where Hubert joined her. Dayrell continued:

He gave her a full account of all that had happened. He did not allege that you were d'Artaux's mistress, but said that you had become infatuated with the man & that he [d'Artaux] wanted your money. I mention this as a striking instance of the generosity of his character as compared with yours. He was quite cool & collected in the evening, & made up his mind to return next day to defend Mrs. Welch's name . . . I am firmly convinced that it was his absolute intention to return. So determined was he that the solicitor whom you had already summoned was sent for to formulate his charges.

This summoning of Hills was catalytic in its effect. However selective may have been the story Hubert told his mother, and whatever Dayrell's protestations, it is obvious that evidence of adultery could not have been lacking. If Hills's charges had been limited to adultery, nothing worse than an unpleasant episode, a relatively commonplace chapter, would have resulted. The radiant Sissie, so calm in her brother's descriptions, might eventually have taken the place of the unbalanced Leila. However, adultery was not the only, nor the most important charge; Leila also accused Hubert of communicating to her an unspecified venereal infection, the marital offence known euphemistically as legal cruelty. Dayrell's fury in speaking of this is reminiscent of the disgust that Ibsen's *Ghosts* had evoked in London critics, the horror being in proportion to the familiarity of the risk:

> Hills began by founding his case for a divorce on the slender evidence of the bedroom scene and the testimony of the *femme de chambre* . . . and then it was that your solicitor formulated the foul & beastly charge technically known as "legal cruelty." I dare not trust myself to speak all my thoughts on this last dastardly outrage on the sanctity of married life.

Here is a reflection of Montague's exalted view of matrimony. Dayrell's next sentence, however, rather reduces the force of the rebuttal: "I can only say that there are many women on the street who would recoil in horror from making such an accusation." The implication is that a wife venereally infected by her husband should show the same tolerance as would a prostitute. If Dayrell knew as much as this about the behavior of women on the street, it would be naive to suppose that Hubert knew less.

Poor Dayrell: his love for his brother shines through the concealments, the double standards, the rage of his letter.

> To a pure minded man such an accusation from a woman for whom he had sacrificed everything must have meant despair: and whatever step he took that evening is wholly & entirely attributable to that hideous charge. If my brother should be dead, it is *this* that has killed him. For my own part, I would sooner my brother was at the bottom of the Seine than again under the influence of a woman such as you.

Dayrell's vehemence suggests that at the back of his mind he may have recognized the likelier cause of despair to be, not the falseness, but the probable truth of the accusation. And Hills could scarcely have made the charge without first assuring himself that there was some medical evidence to support it; Dayrell himself referred to a course of treatment that Leila was undergoing in Paris. If Hubert was the source of the infection, and if it was a grave one, it would explain much; Leila's sudden departure after her miscarriage, the "physical repulsion," and the ominous tone of the autumnal pieces in *Vignettes*. Above all it would account for despair, since there would now be the danger of infecting a second woman or even another generation. Love would have come to seem almost synonymous with sickness and disaster.

After the conference on the evening of November 5, Hubert left his mother's hotel and walked some way along the quai Voltaire with Hills; the two men parted there, and Hubert was not seen again alive. He had arranged to return with his mother to London by the night train, but she was left to travel alone. In the days following, the anxiety at Rutland Gate must have been intense as all efforts to trace Hubert failed. Sissie Welch, who had returned to her husband, albeit under the protection of her brother, must certainly have been in painful doubt. Le Gallienne wrote in a letter:

> Siss and I have been talking and talking all evening. Dear girl, she is of course very upset, but wonderfully brave too—the more I think of it, the more I think it may not be the worst, but that he has simply gone right away from some wild notion of honour. . . . there is no further news and it is now midnight.[23]

As part of the family inquiries made after Hubert's disappearance, Dayrell undoubtedly had conversations with Sissie, who would have had to be extremely guarded; nonetheless, the matter of the infection was evidently broached because Dayrell's letter to Leila mentioned "the explanation of your ailment afforded by you yourself to Mrs. Welch," though he did not say what that explanation had been. From the time of his meetings with Sissie, Dayrell seems to have taken on the responsibility for protecting her from scandal, assuming a tenderness for his brother's mistress that perhaps augmented his dislike of the widow.

It is evident that by November 25, the family was almost convinced that Hubert was already dead, his body washing to and fro on the bed of the Seine or crushed against a pier of one of the many bridges in that sinuous double curve, trapped by silt and other waste of the flood; or carried off by the strength of the flow to cleaner stretches of the river, and the open sea. There was no particular reason to think that his remains would ever be found. Dayrell was now in a peculiarly painful position, not only because of his affection for his brother. To the end of his life he would dream from time to time that Hubert returned, an ever youthful figure, in effect to disinherit him by reclaiming the elder brother's rights. The feeling that Hubert's death—if Hubert was indeed dead—had put him next in line of inheritance is reflected in Dayrell's letter to Leila, with its whitewashing, its heated denials, and its very apparent aim of projecting onto her all the guilt for the breakdown of the marriage; and more important, for the possible suicide, the almost certain death: "I would sooner my brother was at the bottom of the Seine."

III

Early in December, Aubrey Beardsley wrote to Smithers, "I hear tragic things of Hubert Crackanthorpe."[24] Many rumors must have been in circulation during these weeks. In Paris, Hubert had been heard to speak of going to Biarritz, or to Spain, in search of peace: Biarritz would have been the disembarkation point for the Béarn, of which he had said in *Vignettes:* "The old, penetrating charm of this tiny corner of the earth returns, and the old longing to bind myself to it, to have my place in its life, always, through the years to come."[25] During the time of tensions, described tactfully in the French press as *chagrins de ménage* and *chagrins intimes,* he perhaps longed to escape with Sissie to the calm villages under "the distant Pyrenees, a long, ragged, snow-capped wall." It could have been jealousy that prevented his taking that sensible course, perhaps a cerebral jealousy of the sort described by Bourget, which has as its mainspring "not the vision of physical caresses, but the certainty that one has not sufficed for the happiness of the woman one has loved."[26]

It must have been in jealous anger and in the dilemma felt by the husband in Meredith's "Modern Love"—"Can I love one, and yet be jealous of another?"[27]—that Hubert went out in search of his wife on the night of November 4. Several of the Paris newspapers described his having taken a carriage to various parts of Paris, late at night, and having finally engaged in a furious argument with his coachman which had had to be settled by the police. When he found Leila the next day he may well have threatened her, and possibly it was in response to threats or even violence that she in turn thought of calling in the police. The Paris newspapers concluded that only Hubert's family could possess the key to his disappearance, a conclusion that Dayrell was soon to put to advantage. *Le Matin* found the part played by Montague surprising, and alleged that he had known for some weeks that his son was dead; the paper added that the Paris police had no idea how he had arrived at this certainty.[28] The private investigation had evidently convinced him. He departed early in December to Egypt in company, according to *Le Matin,* with several members of both houses of Parliament. This seems to have been a preexisting plan in connection with some legal or political study, a project that was not abandoned because Montague had no further doubt that Hubert was already dead. He was still away when his son's body was found, and so he was not responsible for the subsequent dealings with the press, which were evidently the work of Dayrell.

The body was discovered by a waterman on Christmas Eve 1896, near the Pont d'Alma, a few hundred yards downstream from the quai Voltaire where Hubert had last been seen. The remains were now in an advanced state of decomposition, the head and face unrecognizable. It was apparently the common conclusion among the English colony in Paris that Hubert had committed suicide following his wife's threat of divorce action, and there was much talk in the newspapers of a letter, said to have been found on the body, that testified to this. However, a letter found in Hubert's pocket would scarcely have been legible, any more than the face itself, dimmed and erased by two months' immersion in the sewage and winter surge of the Seine. On the other hand, Dayrell had mentioned Leila's "curt note," which Hubert must have shown or given to his mother just before his disappearance. The likely conclusion is that Dayrell, who arrived in Paris on Christmas Eve, had hinted to the press that a letter existed by which all was explained. Part of his purpose must have been to silence Leila, and in this he seems to have been entirely successful. Meanwhile, some of Hubert's English friends had gone to the Morgue—the *funèbre établissement* of the quai de l'Archevêché, behind Notre-Dame—to view the wretched piece of human wreckage exposed on its marble slab. They found it unrecognizable. But on Christmas Day, Dayrell and Oliver identified their brother by his signet ring, cuff links, and certain medals that he habitually carried in his pocket. They reclaimed the corpse, had it inclosed in a triple coffin, and returned with it to London, sealed from sight, on December 26.

On Christmas Day the *Times* and other London papers announced Hubert's death and gave an account of his disappearance some two months before. Some of the London papers showed signs of not accepting the assurance of the Paris police that there was no question of violence or murder. The detective in charge of the case was reported to have said that he had regarded it as one of suicide from the first; but no kind of inquest or judicial inquiry was ever held, which suggests that Dayrell fully agreed with the police that the more quietly and the sooner his brother's remains were removed, the better, since the chief actor and sufferer was already beyond reach within his threefold shell. And Dayrell's instinct may have been right; by silencing speculation and throwing the whole responsibility for what had happened onto Leila and her desertion, he was able to protect Sissie from public unpleasantness. What is more, Dayrell had a strong personal reason to wish to silence gossip and forestall any scandal; he was then in a junior position at the Foreign Office, having entered the diplomatic service in 1895, and was about to leave for his first foreign posting. Perhaps it seemed to him that newspaper speculation, painful and useless, might also injure his career at its outset; certainly, public discussion of Hubert's venereal disease, if it should come to that, could do Dayrell no good in Whitehall. The result was that a presumption of suicide, tacit, unquestioning, and quite possibly correct, but not based on any open inquiry, was fostered, and has been repeated ever since. The tone and emphasis of the repetitions have varied from the comparative sensitivity of Vincent Starrett, who said in *Buried Caesars: Essays in Literary Appreciation,* that Hubert killed himself for "the love of a woman," and because he "could no longer bear to go on living,"[29] to the prattle of Rothenstein in *Men and Memories:*

> Poor Crackanthorpe . . . was devoted to his wife. It was rather she who was free from prejudice. Forty years ago a man felt it more of a disgrace when his wife took the reins into her own hands and drove away with another man on the box seat, than he would to-day. But when poor Crackanthorpe put an end to his life, it was said to be the judgment of God for adoring French idols.[30]

Despite Dayrell's efforts, conjecture about the manner of Hubert's death continued for some days in the Paris press. Both *Le Figaro* and *Le Journal* mentioned mysterious details that hinted that Hubert might have been attacked: "Possibly he may have been thrown into the Seine following a scuffle,"[31] suggested *Le Journal.* On Christmas Day itself, the *Daily News* in London received a long letter from Robert Sherard, written from the Authors' Club in London, giving voice to the doubts of a number of Hubert's friends. Sherard was a friend of Le Gallienne; of Ernest Dowson, who died in his house; and of Oscar Wilde, whose biography he wrote. He had been for many years the Paris correspondent of an American newspaper and was well known in Parisian society and journalism. He also happened to be a great-grandson of Wordsworth, and he confessed to feeling a special interest in Hubert's fate. The *Daily News* published the letter on December 26:

> Sir, I trust that the relations and many friends of Mr. Hubert Crackanthorpe will not be satisfied with the ingenuous "Perhaps he fell off a bridge" of the French police, to say nothing of the abominable alternative which is blandly suggested. I never met Crackanthorpe, though he was my kinsman, but for all I know of him, I can give the lie to the theory of suicide. Men like Hubert Crackanthorpe do not commit suicide. . . . Nor do people fall off bridges, and the gentlemen of the quai des Orfèvres are well aware of this. They are all the more aware of it, that they know

among their parishioners there are several industrials who make a speciality of helping strangers over the Paris bridges, after emptying their pockets. This speciality is known in Parisian *argot* as *foutre le pante à la flotte* and is intermittently practiced—especially on winter nights. . . . It is a horrible thought that a gentle and frolic poet like Crackanthorpe may have been done away with by the ruffians of the Latin Quarter, and it is intolerable that we, his relatives, friends, admirers and countrymen are to be told, without any proof in support, that he killed himself.[32]

It is odd that not even Sherard mentioned the great flood of the Seine in the first week of November, which would certainly have eased the work of anyone making an assault of the kind he described, around midnight on November 5. Sherard's letter gives the impression that he was writing as spokesman for others more closely involved, but who preferred to stay behind the scenes. Le Gallienne, who continued to express doubt and surprise, would be the likeliest of Hubert's friends to wish, on his own and his sister's behalf, to protest discreetly against the presumption of suicide that was clearly emanating from family sources.

Sherard urged a private inquiry in the Latin Quarter, saying that the Paris police had motives for inactivity. But the family had their own reasons for silence, a silence that, so far as Dayrell was concerned, was to lie upon memories of his brother, in Wordsworth's phrase, "with a weight, heavy as frost, and deep almost as life." He never relaxed his vigilance: on December 22, 1946, under the heading "Extracts from our Files of Fifty Years ago," the *Cumberland and Westmorland Herald* reprinted an account of Hubert's disappearance and of the recovery of the body, and Dayrell, having cut out the item, wrote acidly beside it, "Why rake up this tragedy to satisfy local curiosity?" The instinct not to satisfy gratuitous curiosity was one of the surest in his temperament and it accounts for the speciousness of the following notice, which appeared in a number of English newspapers on December 28, 1896:

> We are requested by Mr. and Mrs. Crackanthorpe to state that, according to the medical evidence, there is no doubt that Mr. Hubert Crackanthorpe met with his death on the evening of Thursday, November 5th. He had been

with his mother until 11.30 that evening, when he went for a walk, and was last seen at 11.50 p.m. on the quai Voltaire within 300 yards of which place his body was found seven weeks after.

For the last months of his life he was living in Paris; during that period he never left it for a single day, and the circumstances of every day of his life there are perfectly well-known to his family.

Mr. and Mrs. Crackanthorpe, having been much pained by numerous statements in the Press, for which there is no foundation, earnestly request that this statement may be accepted as final, and that the Press will generally abstain from further reference to a subject so deeply painful to them.

Montague, being in Egypt, could not have drafted this notice of which Dayrell was the probable author. The presumption that Hubert's heart had been broken by his wife's desertion, and that he had taken his life in consequence, was never again seriously questioned.

The body in its stoutly built French coffin was incinerated without delay at Woking, and a funeral service, conducted by Edward Lyttelton, Hubert's Eton tutor, was held at All Saints' Church in Knightsbridge on January 1, 1897. Among the congregation was Ethel Clifford, the young poetess who had been invited to the bicycling party on Hubert's birthday the year before. She preserved Hubert's small, neat letter of invitation, with her own account of the funeral service written that night:

The Service was so sad, so pitiful. On New Year's Eve we danced, and I, for one, saw nothing heartless in so doing. That Bertie lived was firmly my conviction. Even the news that his brothers had identified the body as his, brought no sorrow for death, only grief that one we loved so much should keep us so long in suspense. When, in the church I read the prayer they had made for him, and lifting wet eyes, saw the white draped altar and the flowers, there, for the first time I realised that it was finished, he would not come again. . . . Even now, I do not feel he sleeps, if spirits come, his will, I think. And all day long I hear the splashing of the water under the boat—where he was found.[33]

A prayer, specially printed and distributed at the service, included this passage: "Grant that his life (so troubled here) may unfold itself in Thy sight. . . . and if there be ways in which he may come, grant us a sense of his nearness in such degree as Thy laws permit." This suggests that Blanche, who developed spiritualist interests in later life and filled a room with photographs of the vanished elder son who had been, in a special though not a diminishing sense, her creation, was the author of the prayer. She perhaps hoped to bestow a last endowment: what Pater called the "secondary sort of life which we can give to the dead, in our intensely realised memory of them—the 'subjective immortality,' as some now call it."[34] Blanche wrote to Ethel Clifford: *"Don't forget him.* Everything, everybody, are so soon forgotten. Keep one chamber of your memory his—he was so loyal, so loving, so brave."[35]

Immediately after the service, the ashes were taken to Newbiggin and placed in a marble urn of classical outline, standing on a tall plinth in the little chapel that connects the church and the house. In 1922 Francis Jammes wrote of the spirited friend whom he remembered from their adolescence:

> His identity was established by a strange stone which he wore on his finger, and which he had shown me. His arms were engraved on it. He said it was unique; he too was unique, and I regret him deeply! His ashes were placed in the funerary crypt of his family château, a crypt which I had described to him from having seen it in a dream, two years before his death.[36]

The crypt in question, a veritable "township of the deceased" crowded with antecedents and their numerous families, had however been sealed up by law before the end of the nineteenth century, since its opening was inside the church, and no addition to the numbers within was now allowed.

On January 2, the *Star* carried on its front page a tribute written by Le Gallienne, who had apparently been persuaded, rather against his will, of the possibility of suicide:

> We ask no longer why and how he died. . . . That he has left us thus of his free will, without a word of adieu, without a wave of the hand, is hard to think. . . . He loved life so well, and it was so good a sight to see him alive so

eagerly, so passionately, and with so vast and sympathetic a humanity.[37]

He also claimed that "perhaps no other writer of his generation had so thoroughly equipped himself for his calling of novelist by so adventurous a study of human life." This study of life was the very thing most condemned by Jeannette Gilder in the *Critic,* on the same day:

> I am not at all surprised at the tragic death of Mr. Hubert Crackanthorpe. No young man, or old one for that matter, could write such morbid, loathsome stories as he wrote and have a sane mind. He was the most pronounced type of decadent. According to the stories that are told of him, he was searching for material after the manner of Mr. Stephen Crane, and much the same sort of material. There is, after all, a good deal of truth in some of Nordau's theories. A man must have a diseased mind who finds pleasure in writing of diseased morals.[38]

Lionel Johnson wrote a few lines of memorial verse, dated 1897, but which did not appear until January 1950 in the *Poetry Review:*

> Ours is the darkness, thine the light:
> And yet the haunting thought of thee,
> O fair and cordial friend! makes bright
> The darkness; and we surely see
> Thyself, thy very form and face,
> Filled with a fresh perfecting grace.[39]

IV

In 1926 Richard Le Gallienne again referred to Hubert, in *The Romantic '90s:* he spoke of his "lovable and boyish presence . . . unforgettably dear" to those who still remembered him and of his tragic death, "mysteriously self-sought." Premature mortality removed many of the men whom Le Gallienne described as "the brief and brilliant figures of the time," including Beardsley, Dowson, Johnson, and John Davidson. "Early death," in Le Gallienne's gothic image, "seemed to be a *macabre* shadow taking part in the joyous spring-dance of the *fin de siècle* renaissance." Precocious flowering and early withering have come to be associated with the arts of the nineties; but, as Le Gallienne pointed out, the group of men most closely identified with the "yellowness" of the period was "only accidentally a group, and, being all of them strikingly independent individuals, had really very little in common."[40] If more of these artists had lived on into the maturity of their powers, the progressive character of their early work would have been remembered and the supposed decadence forgotten; this seems especially true of Hubert, whose last work shows, in Holbrook Jackson's phrase, "an approximation to a more English tradition."[41] And if a main characteristic of decadence in literature is a vocabulary and choice of expression that are *faisandé*, "gamy," it is hard to find any example in his work.

Crackanthorpe's was the first and most publicized of these early deaths, and it seems to have been regarded symbolically: "His life was as short as one of his stories," pronounced Rothenstein, while Starrett, hardly more intelligibly, described the death as "the perfect conclusion, the consummate touch necessary to round out a brief and tragic existence, leaving its fame a thing of slight and sinister beauty."[42] If indeed Hubert entered of his own will into the yellowish flood sweeping past the quai Voltaire with a terrifying roar— and it can never be certain that he did so—then Starrett was right in emphasizing problems of literary temperament, especially as the evidence of Hubert's library proves irrefutably that his own was one of marked melancholy. Some of the themes of his work—his preoccupation with the delusions of love, and of human effort, and even with the nullity of life itself, or what Amiel called "the bitter sense of the inanity of life, and of the transitoriness of things,"[43]—exposed him to charges of morbidity, but these themes are, after all, common in any literature. As Henry James pointed out, it was a question of degree and emphasis:

> Suddenly, in the light of his death, the whole proportion and perspective appeared so to alter that friendly remembrance, moving backward, dropped the mere explanation of juvenility of posture and left it to merge itself, with compunction, in the thought of instincts and fears of a deeper colour.[44]

Although a retrospective review on an assumption of suicide cannot be reliable evidence of the nature of the man, nevertheless Hubert's markings in his volumes of Amiel's journal provide material evidence for the "fears of a deeper colour" at which James merely guessed. Amiel then seems to loom over Crackanthorpe's shoulder, misanthropic, hopeless, eloquent, and minatory. What is most noticeable is a terror of age; countless passages of melancholic rumination connected with the inexorable incidence of birthdays are marked, passages expressing "disgust and weariness of life, mortal sadness,"[45] and giving the sense of a feverish interest in death. Suicide was almost constantly in Amiel's mind, as was the paradoxical but characteristic anguish of the melancholic in face of the evanescence of the human personality: "Even the dragon-fly is not a frail enough symbol; it is the soap-bubble which best translates . . . that fugitive appearance of the little ego that we are."[46]

It is arguable that the marked passages signify no more than what Hubert himself had called a "mere literary melancholy," the state of mind described by the Goncourts: "We are like people who have nothing between them and suicide, except a truce, for certain work to be done."[47] Hubert, reading the literary evidence, noting the growth of despair in those he most admired and seeing with a realist's eye the prospect of emotional and physical misery brought on by age—and probably under the pressure of a hateful physical distemper of his own—may at a moment of strain have chosen to "give life the slip," thus expressing in action what to Amiel, indecisive, guilty, and long-lived, remained no more than a metaphor: "I go gently into the coffin, in my own lifetime. I experience a kind of indefinable peace of annihilation, the quietude of Nirvana; I feel the rapid river of time flow before me, in me."[48] But it is almost equally possible that an accident of some kind, a fall, a false step in the darkness, or an assault could have plunged him into the Seine like many others who lost their lives in the flood of that year.

V

Ernest Dowson wrote on June 10, 1897 to Conal O'Riordan:

"Crackanthorpe's ghost is calling to me from the other side of Styx."[49] In fact, Hubert's voice was not yet quite silenced on this side, since two of his stories remained unpublished. With "Anthony Garstin's Courtship," they appeared as *Last Studies* in 1897. The book was dedicated by Blanche "To the loyal friends of my beloved son, who saw in the unfolding flower of his manhood a renewal of the bright promise of his early youth." Stopford Brooke furnished a graceful poem of which the last stanza is:

> Too rough his sea, too dark its angry tides!
> Things of a day are we; shadows that move
> The lands of shadow; but where he abides,
> Time is no more; and that great substance, Love,
> Is shadowless.

Henry James supplied an "Appreciation," which has been variously described as "cautious," "ambiguous," and "resentful." It contains clever and even generous criticism, chilled by what Frierson called "la froideur et l'équanimité" of James's temperament and by an inevitable condescension, a little disguised in circumlocutions. In a letter to Blanche, Stopford Brooke did not conceal his dislike of it:

> I have read Henry James' preface and, to tell you the plain truth, I do not understand half of it. I do understand that he intends to say pleasant and true things, and that he has been at some pains to analyse and describe his impressions of your son's character and work, and that those impressions are such as you would like, but he has now arrived at so involved and tormented a style that I find the greatest difficulty in discovering what he means.[50]

James spoke of the "joy" of most of Hubert's pages but also of "the predominance of the consciousness of cruelty of life, the expression, from volume to volume, of the deep insecurity of things." He saluted Hubert's sincerity:

> Reality and romance rose before him equally as, in fact, in their essence, unmuffled and undomesticated; above all as latent in the question, always a challenge for a keen literary spirit, of difficulty of execution. He had an almost precocious glimpse of the charm of the technical problem.[51]

The three stories in *Last Studies* deal with psychological problems of considerable depth and difficulty. Their common element is the theme of emotional mutilation, or of resistance against it; and the stories, completely unlike in other ways, fit together quite neatly in this sense, although the neatness may be accidental. The first, "Anthony Garstin's Courtship," treats a son's struggle to escape his mother's domination and to get a wife of his own, a project long delayed since he is well into middle age. The third, "The Turn of the Wheel," is an approach to the subject of the *femme froide* considered in the context of her emotional relations with her father. And between these two is "Trevor Perkins," a brief study of an almost neutered figure, a young man who has rejected his parents and isolated himself, finding all emotional connection impossible.

It is obvious that Hubert's psychological inquisitiveness, one of his most marked literary characteristics, was leading him to trace a more and more direct line of influence between the vicissitudes of love, even the capacity for it, and early emotional memories and ties. With a few more years of literary exploration he would certainly have been ready for the theories of Freud. An interest in the structure of the mind appears quite early in his work, pressures from the unconscious being often noted, and emotions shown as arranged in layers, one over the other: "the consciousness of her pride filled her with joy."[52] Sometimes there is fusion, and emotional reinforcement as in this example, but more usually the result is inner division, conflict, and a sense of paralysis.

There is no such paralysis in "Anthony Garstin's Courtship." This story is set in Cumberland and repeats, on a grander scale, the technical success of "A Dead Woman," using much dialogue which is conveyed in a consistent and cleverly rendered Cumbrian dialect. There is, too, some powerful scenic description employing semipoetic, Paterian prose rhythms: "A stampede of huddled sheep, wildly scampering over the slaty shingle, emerged from the leaden mist that muffled the fell-top, and a shrill shepherd's whistle broke the damp stillness of the air."[53] The vocal and visual elements place this work, like the *Set of Village Tales,* within a locality; in this case in a beautifully realized Cumbrian microcosm, where Crackanthorpe could well have won the same enviable literary prerogative as that of Daudet in Provence, or Hardy in Wessex. Indeed, many commentators have cited Hardy in connection with this story. Bernard Muddiman wrote: "It is a little masterpiece conceived almost in the hopeless bitterness of Hardy at his darkest."[54] Muddiman added that to find elsewhere in English literature this "unsavoury cruelty of humanity" one must come to James Joyce. Although this story does not share the hopelessness of *Jude the Obscure,* which was published in 1895, there is a certain affinity between Anthony and Jude, both in their sexual irregularities and in what Pater described as "that inward tacitness of mind," a quality he related to the "partly puritanic awe, the power of which Wordsworth noted and valued so highly in a northern peasantry."[55]

This story of a dour mother and her grim, lonely son who longs for a woman but has never till now had the spirit to set out and get one, is indeed, if anything in Crackanthorpe's curtailed work deserves the description, a masterpiece; it is strongly dramatized, narrated without excess, and free from what Henry James delicately referred to as "the touch *beside* the matter."[56] Drama is allowed to do its own work, neither impeded nor driven, distance and selection being exactly right:

> There glowed within him a stolid pride in himself: he thought of the others who had courted her, and the means by which he had won her seemed to him a fine stroke of cleverness.
>
> . . . And when, at intervals, the brusque realisation that, after all, he was to possess her swept over him, he gripped the stones, and swung them almost fiercely into their places.[57]

Mrs. Garstin's hold over her son is maintained through a combination of emotional blackmail and freeholder's right:

> She would remind him that the farm belonged to her, that he would have to wait till her death before he could bring the hussy to Houtsey; he would retort that as soon as the girl would have him, he intended taking a small holding over at Scarsdale. Then she would give way, and for a while piteously upbraid him with her old age, and with the

memory of all the years she and he had spent together, and he would comfort her with a display of brusque, evasive remorse.[58]

The personality of Anthony, an idealist and a romantic lover beneath the stolidity of a hill farmer, is at the heart of the story, and is expressed as much by his silences as in his speech. He is admirable and redoubtable, but not lovable; the girl with whom he has fallen in love can only express such affection as she feels for him through the medium of the dog who is his shadow. As a result Anthony, though of all Crackanthorpe's creations perhaps the most alive, makes a rather harsh impression:

> Henry Sisson asked if he'd started his courting; Jacob Sowerby cried that Tony'd been too slow in getting to work, for that the girl had been seen spooning in Crosby Shaws with Curbison the auctioneer, and the others (there were half-a-dozen of them lounging round the hay-waggon) burst into a boisterous guffaw. Anthony flushed dully, looking hesitatingly from one to the other; then slowly put down his beer-can, and of a sudden, seizing Jacob by the neck, swung him heavily on the grass. He fell against the waggon-wheel, and when he rose the blood was streaming from an ugly cut in his forehead. And henceforth Tony Garstin's courtship was the common jest of all the parish.[59]

Anthony's love for the girl Rosa has a paternal as well as a sensual character; he has passed directly to this from a filial relation with his mother, until now the only woman in his life. He wins Rosa by accepting the illegitimate child she is carrying as his, though it is not; she is saved from disaster, and Anthony's mother, believing the child to be her son's, is forced to take her in. Such bitter ironies may recall both Zola and Hardy. Anthony himself soon comes "to ignore the irregularity of the whole business: almost to assume, in the exaltation of his pride, that he had won her honestly; and to discard, stolidly, all thought . . . of the coming child that was to pass for his own."[60] The atmospheric unity of the story is supported by a succession of images of light against the northern darkness; of light failing, in an engulfing winter world:

> The air was very still; below him a white filmy mist hung

across the valley: the fell sides, vaguely grouped, resembled hulking masses of sombre shadow; and, as he looked back, three squares of glimmering gold revealed the lighted windows of the square-towered church.[61]

In the ferocious closing irony, Mrs. Garstin accepts the girl whom she has for so long refused to receive, and in the same breath she disinherits Anthony of the land that is his living. The mother's revenge is that of a woman rejected for another woman, irreversible and without compromise:

> "Ye've brought shame and bitterness on yer ould mother in her ould age. Ye've made me despise t' varra seet o' ye. Ye can stop on here, but ye shall niver touch a penny of my money; every shillin' of 't shall go t' yer child, or to your child's children. . . . 'For them that hev sinned without t' law, shall also perish without t' law.' "[62]

Despite this matriarchal curse and although the girl does not love Anthony, there remains a persistent if almost unwilling optimism in the story, overlooked by Muddiman, because of a sense of sexual congruence, extremely rare in Crackanthorpe's work, that seems embedded in the texture of the narrative and the dialogue.

"Trevor Perkins," which Lionel Johnson described in the *Academy* as "masterly" and "almost intolerably successful in its method,"[63] is a satirical view, or sketch, of a fin de siècle personality, an isolated and feeble young man who, though widely read, is narrowly educated and who sees decadence in the state though really it is in himself:

> "When a man does some violence to his own nature in adhering to the parent bulk; when its character and aspirations are not repeated in him . . . then of the State it may be said . . . that nature is no longer in it . . ."
> The words . . . sang in his ears as he stirred his tea. . . .
> Yes, the curse of decadence lay over the land.[64]

Perkins is "eternally haunted by the habit of introspection" of the complete egoist; he has discarded his family and in his sterility can reach neither men nor women. His physique is unprepossessing and his face wears "the pale placidity of a thoughtful mind."[65] Hubert's intention was to mock certain fashionable attitudes by demonstrating their appeal to a personality intrinsically ridiculous:

A new generation had arisen . . . old before its time—
"Venue trop tard dans un siècle trop vieux" . . . incapable
of faith, groaning beneath an accumulation of precocious
experience. . . .
Yes, and in his own case how true it all was![66]

However, the story develops a much greater psychological
interest than the satire at first suggests. The germ of the idea
seems to come from Barrès who, in both *Un Homme libre* and
Sous l'oeil des barbares, spoke of the "cult of the ego . . . we
must defend it daily, and each day create it afresh."[67] This is
precisely Perkins's position: "After all, Life was more important than Literature, and . . . an assiduous cultivation of self,
by means of a cunning management of experience, represented the last word of a *fin-de-siècle* philosophy."[68] Once
again there is a very distinct echo of Pater: "What we have to do
is to be for ever curiously testing new opinions and courting
new impressions . . . gathering all we are into one desperate
effort to see and touch."[69]

Perkins, who more than once in the story has recourse to
desperate effort, decides to seek out a girl—a waitress in a
cafe, like the girl loved by Dowson—whom he has known in
a slight, flirtatious way for some time. But now his purpose is
more serious and more calculated:

> He had felt . . . that where his fellow-men failed to com-
> prehend his secluded attitude, a woman might succeed; and
> that a woman might appreciate him for that very sensitivity
> of his which was so apt to excite the coarser sex to active
> hostility.[70]

This delightfully ironical psychological observation is followed by dialogue between the two that is among the best
that Hubert ever wrote:

> "Well, Miss Hammond, and what have you been doing
> with yourself?" he began, with a forced jauntiness.
> "Oh, nothing wonderful. Just jogging along—same
> song, same tune."
> "Do you know, I've been intending to come round to
> look you up for ever so long?"
> He looked up at her quickly: he fancied he detected a note
> of resentment in her voice, and he added hastily—
> "I suppose you thought I'd forgotten all about you?"

"Perhaps I didn't think anything at all about it."

He smiled indulgently.

"Come, don't be angry," he continued.

"Angry! I'm sure I don't known what you mean."

"But you're offended with me, I can see."

"What a funny man you are, to be sure, Mr. Perkins!" she retorted.

He felt reassured: they were friends again once more. "Don't go," he went on insinuatingly; "I want to ask you something."

She paused, leaning her wrists on the table: her lips were expectantly parted.[71]

There is an inspired banality in this, and an irrational sequence of speech and thought that are the marrow of creative invention, the dialogue of the inadequate in finely ironic contrast to Perkins's intellectual pretension.

In the second part of the story Perkins walks in Hyde Park with Emily and discovers, though the excitement of the physical contact, what he calls the "tragic aridity of his heart."[72] The park is full of ordinary lovers, and it is by comparing the easy sexual communication of the multitude with his own reaction, that he realizes he has "no heart to give":

How fresh and sweet and simple she looked in the pale moonlight! Could he not, during one short, mad hour, escape from himself?

. . .The heavy breath of human love seemed to float through the warm, still, night air.[73]

He kisses Emily with "a fierce and feverish desperation," the last word demonstrating, as in Pater, the basic hopelessness of any attempt at escape. "Even in this wild moment of ecstasy, he retained a vivid consciousness of the relativeness of things."[74]

The story leaves the mouth dry with futility and frustration; it is certainly a very clever technical achievement and show of intuition, a cunning caricature of several kinds of impotence. Perkins's egoism and conceit are essentially defensive, and the experience with Emily is used to illustrate his problem because it is in sex that self-possession should be most surrendered. But he is incapable of the liberating change of state that sexuality may afford; for him, to be in contact is to suffer an alien invasion of the *moi* and to feel the need to repel it: "All at once he felt strangely cool—master of himself: he realized that he had definitely reconquered his personality."[75] William Peden has described Perkins as the "lonely prototype of a thousand literary descendents."[76]

A sense of restricted emotional freedom, caused by conflicts within the personality, is another of the great disappointments that reality may bring: "A being is independent only in certain very broad realities fixed by the centuries," pronounced J. H. Rosny in *L'Impérieuse Bonté*.[77] The aphorism expresses a paradox, a reversal of the obvious order, of the sort that attracted Hubert; but it is also a reminder that emotional restriction and inhibition originate within the individual life-span rather than in history's perspective. Many of Hubert's characters are in a state of division within themselves, and it was his tentative discovery that the division can result in emotional paralysis. His last story, "The Turn of the Wheel," is an illustration of this outcome.

The story has all the characteristics of a novel in miniature, and the psychological complexities of the theme certainly call for the ampler space of the novel form. It is written in a poised, cautious, somewhat Jamesian style. The young woman so passionately in love with her father is a privileged only child, living in several homes and surrounded by all the trappings of wealth. She has long since rejected her mother, with impatience, and finds relations with men other than her father almost impossibly unreal. She is unaware, however, that the father has had a succession of mistresses throughout his married life. The mother is therefore in the position of the wife in "A Commonplace Chapter," after twenty years of systematic and humiliating infidelities; but she also has to bear the bitterness of her daughter's attitude to her, a contempt that is clearly the product of the girl's attachment to her father: "Hilda had altogether supplanted her, driven her into the background, transformed her into a person of no consequence."[78] Hilda judges herself "insensitive to the ordinary agitations of love,"[79] but she allows herself to become engaged to a successful and smooth young man of whom her father approves; her frigidity with the former contrasts with the heat of her feelings for the latter: "A score of intimate tokens of his love for her flitted through her mind: she felt

hotly ashamed that she had not requited him more wor-
thily."[80]

The disillusionment of the girl, though not her release, is
brought about, first by an aunt who reveals to Hilda that her
father is a womanizing and faithless husband; and then by his
delirium in illness in which he calls for some of these women
by name. The father dies, and his daughter's horror and anger
at the betrayal—not of her mother but of herself—deprive her
of the capacity to mourn:

> Since his death, she had never cried; she felt no grief; she
> was only embittered against the humiliation. . . .
> . . .how she had worshipped him, reverenced him, jeal-
> ously excluded others from any share in her affection.[81]

Finally she is shown as reconciled to marriage with a steady,
dull, faithful fellow who would "prove in no way exacting
. . . she would be able, without difficulty, to conceal from
him that she did not care for him." Her life of feeling is closed
because, though the father is both discredited and dead, it is
with him that her love remains:

> She fondly fancied that, in time, perhaps she would change.
> . . .
> He came nearer to her, as if to kiss her: she drew back
> hastily, exclaiming—
> "We must go down. The horses will be getting chilled,
> and Hodges will be wondering what has happened."[82]

So once more, and for the last time, the reader of a Crackanthorpe story is denied any semblance of a happy ending,
and the author's vision of "the pitifulness of human love, its
crude, primitive basis, the curiously blinding glamour of its
endless elaboration"[83] is reasserted.

VI

Abruptly and prematurely, Hubert disappeared from the
literary scene at a moment when, in the words of Holbrook
Jackson, "keen observers of literary phenomena felt that he
was already ripe for fuller and truer expression."[84] Jackson
followed Rothenstein in likening Hubert's career, in its brev-
ity, to one of his own stories; the real resemblance lies in the

aftereffect of frustration that is common to the life and the work. Lionel Johnson, in the *Academy* of November 20, 1897, presented a farewell review, quoting the letter Hubert had sent him after his praise of *Sentimental Studies:*

> "Eager for work!" Saddening words to read now, but then most true; and I quote them because they sound the note of his literary character. He took his literary life, as he took travel, movement, the open air, with an eager animation and delighted energy. It was a buoyant passion, virile and rejoicing.[85]

The *Speaker* of December 24, 1897, described the "beautiful young face, sensitive, refined, and thoughtful," and exclaimed sadly, "So much promise, and so little time for adequate performance! . . . Hubert Crackanthorpe's was an interesting individuality even to those who merely guessed at it."[86] On January 8, 1898, Arthur Symons's review of Hubert's work as a whole appeared in the *Saturday Review:*

> Few have gone further in the direction of bare, hard persistent realism, the deliberately unsympathetic record of sordid things. . . . With Crackanthorpe there was always a revolt, the revolt of the impersonal artist to whom evil things had certainly no attraction but a cold, intellectual one, against those English conventions which make it difficult to be quite frank in English. . . . And the hardest thing that can be said of him is that he misses beauty in his desire to come closer than beauty will let men come to truth. . . . After all has been said, what I call Crackanthorpe's heroism remains . . . he was one of those who fight well, who fight unselfishly, the knights errant of the idea.[87]

The last point was also made by Henry James, who spoke of "the undeliberating gallantry that was discernibly latent in him,"[88] though James's remark was directed more at the personality than the work.

Frierson expressed the opinion that had Crackanthorpe lived, he would have become "one of the masters of the English novel."[89] And the *Athenaeum,* in a review of *Last Studies,* also saw a movement toward the novel: "The third story . . . shows great tenderness of observation, and, though not so striking as the shorter sketches, suggests that Crackanthorpe would not have proved inadequate to a sustained picture of life."[90] But the question of potential development, quite speculative as it must be, is more a question about temperament and will than about gifts, as Lionel Johnson seemed to suggest in two phrases describing Hubert's literary temper as it appeared to him: "The pity of it! The pity of it! *That* was always the unspoken yet audible burden of his art."[91] This must be the outgoing and imaginative compassion that is a mainspring of literature. The second phrase, however, adumbrates a less dynamic form of pity, one that is deflected inwardly, on the self: "A kind of haunting melancholy set at the heart of things."

If this deep inner melancholy really was the ruling element in Crackanthorpe's nature, and his work merely its expression, then one could conclude that by the time of his death the melancholy had eroded him—pressure of flood on river bank, in an adverse season—and that the death itself, apparently so dramatized a gesture, was intended as a literary *finis* translated into action. On the other hand, if the talent, the diligence, and the intuitive empathy rose from a self-renewing source, a creative spring running from the depth of the personality, then the loss to literature was a real one, while all the rather factitious mystery surrounding his death dissolves in a simple, deep regret. Amiel's prophecy of his own fate would then apply to Hubert's: "Extremely subjective in feeling and objective in thought . . . you will die without ever having really unpacked your baggage."[92]

In this light, all of Crackanthorpe's careful work, produced nonetheless with youthful dash, can be seen as an early experimentation of the kind recommended by Zola, that of a finely gifted literary technician aiming at strenuous achievement, and lit, moreover, by the nimbus of an unfailing probity—often the least requited of literary virtues. But the flower would have unfolded, to borrow Blanche's image; concentration and growth of forces, assiduous development of gifts, would have allowed the mature artist a sure expression and an extended range. Instead, and pitifully, there echoes and re-echoes across interrupted work what Henry James called Hubert's "troubled individual note," a note sounding also in his life, and too soon extinguished, in Pater's famous phrase, by "sleep before evening."

Notes

Chapter 1

1. Richard Le Gallienne, *The Romantic '90s,* p. 179.
2. Wordsworth's maternal grandmother, Dorothy Crackanthorpe, was the daughter of Richard Crackanthorpe of Newbiggin (1687-1752). Wordsworth was therefore a first cousin of Hubert Crackanthorpe's grandfather.
3. William Wordsworth, *The Excursion,* bk. 6, lines 553–55.
4. Montague Crackanthorpe to Blanche Holt, December 21, 1868, in the author's possession.
5. Ibid., December 22, 1868.
6. Montague Crackanthorpe, *Population and Progress,* p. 42.
7. Sir Bernard Burke, *Burke's Genealogical and Heraldic History of the Landed Gentry of Great Britain,* 11th ed., pp. 364–66.
8. William Wordsworth and Dorothy Wordsworth, *The Early Letters of William and Dorothy Wordsworth,* p. 63.
9. John F. Curwen, *Castles and Towers of Cumberland and Westmorland,* p. 386.
10. John Ruskin, *The Seven Lamps of Architecture,* rev. ed. (London: George Allen, 1903), p. 357.
11. Hugh Montgomery-Massingberd, ed., *Burke's Genealogical and Heraldic History of the Landed Gentry,* 18th ed., 3:218–19.
12. Mary Moorman, *William Wordsworth, the Early Years: 1770-1803,* p. 88.
13. John Fisher, later Bishop of Salisbury and then a fellow preceptor with Cookson, wrote to him on March 30, 1787 from Windsor: "It is by order of the King I write to you: tell Cookson from me, said his Majesty yesterday, that by sending Hughes to Worcester I have now made his Road to Windsor perfectly smooth: I have a great regard for him, & will have him in my own Church here," in the author's possession.
14. William Cookson to Dorothy Cowper, March 21, 1786, in the author's possession.
15. Ibid., July 1787.
16. Wordsworth and Wordsworth, *Early Letters of Wordsworth,* p. 37.
17. Ibid., p. 51.
18. Ibid., p. 61.

19. Ibid., p. 98.

20. Ibid., p. 96.

21. William Wordsworth and Dorothy Wordsworth, *The Letters of William and Dorothy Wordworth: The Middle Years,* 1:398.

22. Blanche Crackanthorpe to Edgar Cookson, 1913, in the author's possession.

23. Ibid.

24. "Obituary: Mr. Crackanthorpe, K. C.," *Times* (London).

25. Ibid.

26. Crackanthorpe, *Population and Progress,* p. 50.

27. Ibid., p. 14.

28. Ibid., pp. 9–10.

29. "Obituary: Mr. Montague Crackanthorpe K. C." *Eugenics Review.*

30 Crackanthorpe, *Population and Progress,* pp. 18–19.

31. Interview with Elizabeth Countess of Iddesleigh. Lady Iddesleigh's mother was Marie Belloc Lowndes, sister of Hilaire Belloc and for many years a close friend of Blanche Crackanthorpe, with whom she founded a literary women's luncheon club called "The Thirty."

32. Crackanthorpe, *Population and Progress,* p. 113.

33. Blanche Crackanthorpe to Dayrell Crackanthorpe, December 1, 1913, in the author's possession.

34. Ibid.

35. Sir Paul Harvey and J. E. Heseltine, eds., *The Oxford Companion to French Literature* (Oxford: Oxford University Press, 1959), s.v., "Rabelais, François."

36. Trustees of the British Museum, *The Art of Drawing* (London: 1972), p. 62.

37. Anthony Richard Wagner, *English Genealogy* (Oxford: Oxford University Press, 1972), p. 235. "[The Marquis de] Ruvigny guessed in 1911 that the number of Edward III's descendents then living might total some 80,000 or 100,000 persons."

38. "Obituary: Mrs. Crackanthorpe," *Times* (London).

39. Marie Belloc Lowndes, *The Merry Wives of Westminster,* p. 66.

40. Florence Emily Hardy, *The Later Years of Thomas Hardy, 1892-1928* (London: Macmillan, 1930), p. 46.

41. F. O. Matthieson and K. B. Murdoch, eds., *The Notebooks of Henry James* (New York: Oxford University Press, 1947), p. 150.

42. Belloc Lowndes, *Merry Wives of Westminster,* pp. 67–68.

43. Ibid., p. 66.

44. Lawrence P. Jacks, *Life and Letters of Stopford Brooke,* 2:479.

45. Ibid., p. 523.

46. Blanche Crackanthorpe, "The Revolt of the Daughters," pp. 25, 425.

47. Ibid., p. 30.

48. Jacks, *Stopford Brooke,* 2:610.

49. Blanche Crackanthorpe, *Letters of Diana, Lady Chesterfield, to her Daughter and Sister,* p. 13.

50. Ibid., p. 43.

51. Ibid., p. 55.

52. Ibid., p. 6.

53. Blanche Crackanthorpe, "Sex in Modern Literature," p. 616.

54. Ibid., pp. 607–8.

55. Ibid., p. 615.

56. Crackanthorpe, *Letters of Diana, Lady Chesterfield,* p. 115.

57. William Crackanthorpe, "A Westmorland Gentleman's Record of the Grand Tour, 1812–1815," *Penrith Observer,* June–October 1891.

58. Michael-Waistell Taylor, *Manorial Halls in Westmorland* (Kendal, Eng.: Titus Wilson, 1892), pp. 33–41.

Chapter 2

1. Blanche Crackanthorpe to Edgar Cookson, 1913, in the author's possession.

2. Dayrell Crackanthorpe to Blanche Crackanthorpe, 1880–1883, in the author's possession.

3. Hubert and Dayrell Crackanthorpe, *Mayes Gazette,* August 26, 1882; *Howtownian,* August 20, 1883, August 27, 1883, August 18, 1884, September 2, 1884, April 6, 1885, August 31, 1885; *Sedbergh Gazette,* August 14, 1887, August 22, 1887; in the author's possession.

4. Algernon Gissing and Ellen Gissing, *Letters of George Gissing to Members of his Family,* pp. 144–45.

5. Henry James, "Hubert Crackanthorpe," pp. xvi–xvii.

6. Eric Parker, *Eton in the Eighties,* p. 236. Parker wrote: "We all . . . recognised [Francis Tarver] as the best teacher of French we had." Tarver was responsible for the adaptation, annotation, and editing of many French classical plays—in particular those of Mòliere—and translations, which he published in series for school use. It is quite possible that Hubert was sent to Tarver's house because of his special interest in French and that Tarver encouraged him. The Eton records show that Hubert did many extra hours in both French and German, especially during his last year *(Eton Calender* [1888]; *Eton Chronicle* nos. 461–65 [1888], Eton: R. Ingleton Drake at the Eton School Press, 1888).

7. Parker, *Eton in the Eighties,* p. 323.

8. Wasey Sterry, *Annals of the King's College of Our Lady of Eton Beside Windsor* (London: Methuen, 1898), p. 209.

9. Montague Crackanthorpe, *Population and Progress,* p. 21.

10. Hubert Crackanthorpe, *Sentimental Studies,* p. 9.

11. Dayrell Crackanthorpe to Blanche Crackanthorpe, November 12, 1886, in the author's possession.

12. Paul Bourget, *Un Crime d'amour,* p. 38.

Que d'ignominies et de bassesses dans ce monde où les plus âgés avaient dix-neuf ans, où les plus jeunes en avaient huit! . . . il n'était question que d'infames amours entre ces grands et ces petits.

13. Ibid., p. 39.

Alfred et lui avaient été du petit nombre de ceux que la contagion n'avaient pas atteints. Mais le plus grand avantage de ce dégoût avait été, pour lui du moins, de le conduire tout jeune à la poursuite des filles, et son initiation aux plaisirs naturels eu lieu dans la plus basse prostitution.

14. Katherine Lyon Mix, *A Study in Yellow,* p. 183.

15. "Mr. Hubert Crackanthorpe," *Kendal Mercury and Times.*

16. William C. Frierson, "Realism in the Eighteen-Nineties and the Maupassant School in England," pp. 38–39.

17. Ibid.

18. James, "Hubert Crackanthorpe," pp. xvii–xxiii.

19. William C. Frierson, *L'Influence du naturalisme français sur les romanciers anglais de 1885 à 1900,* p. 122.

20. Richard F. Niebling, "The Early Career of George Gissing" (Ph.D. diss., Yale University, 1943), p. 22.

21. Austin Harrison, "George Gissing."

22. Royal A. Gettman, *George Gissing and H. G. Wells: Their Friendship and Correspondence* (London: Hart-Davis, 1961), pp. 231—33.

23. Gissing and Gissing, *Letters of George Gissing,* pp. 144–45.

24. A. C. Gissing, ed., *Selections Autobiographical and Imaginative from the Works of George Gissing* (London: Cape, 1921), pp. 218–19.

25. Francis Jammes, *Mémoires,* p. 158.

Un jeune Anglais fort distingué vint à cette époque villégiaturer à Orthez et donner à mon existence une distraction inattendue. Il se nommait Hubert Crackanthorpe . . . [et] devait conquérir, à la fleur de l'âge, une bruyante renommée. Son premier livre, tout d'amertume et de scepticisme hautain, *Wreckage,* scandalisa mais séduisit. Ce misanthrope est resté mon ami jusqu'à sa fin tragique. Mais, en 1889, il n'était encore qu'un garçon élégant, nerveux et racé, qui décevait un peu sa famille par sa volonté de n'en point hériter les séculaires traditions. . . . Il me fut présenté au *Cercle* par M. Vidal, l'homme aux favoris de coton, qui ne savait trop que faire de ce gentleman au regard byronien qui, d'un ton glacial débitait . . . les propos les plus affolants.

26. Dayrell Crackanthorpe to Ida Crackanthorpe, July 19, 1912, in the author's possession.

27. Ibid., July 26, 1912.

28. Edmond de Goncourt and Jules de Goncourt, *Charles Demailly,* p. 73.

Cette sensivité nerveuse, cette secousse continue des impressions . . .avait fait de Charles un mélancolique. . . . il était mélancolique comme un homme d'esprit, avec du savoir-vivre.

29. Jammes, *Mémoires*, p. 158.

Hubert Crackanthorpe connaissait à peine la langue française quand nous nous rencontrâmes. Deux ou trois mois après, il la parlait couramment et même avec charme.

30. Blanche Crackanthorpe, "The Revolt of the Daughters," p. 27.

31. Hubert Crackanthorpe and W. H. Wilkins, "Editorial," *Albemarle*, September 1892.

32. R. H. Sherard, *Twenty Years in Paris* (London: Hutchinson, 1905), p. 387.

33. There exist seven letters to Image, written between 1892 and 1896, in the possession of the author.

34. Richard Le Gallienne, *The Romantic '90s*, p. 79.

35. Bernard Muddiman, *The Men of the Ninties*, p. 135.

36. Walter Pater, *Marius the Epicurean*, 1:104, 111.

37. Selwyn Image, *Selwyn Image Letters*, p. 64.

38. Edgar Jepson, *Memories of a Victorian*, p. 211.

39. W. G. Blaikie Murdoch, *The Renaissance of the Nineties*, p. 54.

40. Ernest Dowson, *The Letters of Ernest Dowson*, p. 132.

41. Rothenstein, *Men & Memories*, 1:239. According to Rothenstein, this group was responsible for the entire design of the Savoy Hotel in London. Image, Mackmurdo, and Horne were all men of independent means; Horne spent his later years in Florence and wrote an authoritative biography of Botticelli.

42. Victor Plarr, *Ernest Dowson, 1888–97*, p. 67.

43. Ibid., pp. 67-68.

44. Dowson, *Letters*, p. 46.

45. Joseph Hone, *W. B. Yeats, 1865–1939* (London: Macmillan, 1942), p. 79. Hone includes both Image and Horne as members of the Rhymers' Club, although neither of them contributed to either of the Rhymers' Club's books of verse.

46. Grant Richards, *Memories of a Misspent Youth*, p. 339.

47. Mark Longaker, *Ernest Dowson*, pp. 60-61.

48. "Ibsen's New Drama," *Daily Telegraph*, March 14, 1891.

49. Conal O'Riordan, "Foreword," p. 11.

50. Hubert Crackanthorpe, "Realism in France and England," p. 41.

51. Michael Orme, *J. T. Grein*, p. 115.

52. Crackanthorpe, "Realism in France and England," p. 41.

53. Murdoch, *Renaissance of the Nineties*, p. ix.

54. Hubert Crackanthorpe, "Reticence in Literature," p. 262.

55. Ibid., p. 267.

56. Pater, *Marius*, 2:103.

57. James, "Hubert Crackanthorpe," p. xv.

58. Mix, *Study in Yellow*, p. 185.

59. Paul Bourget, *Mensonges*, pp. 491–92.

Ecrire, . . . c'est se transformer soi-même en champ d'expériences, . . . ce que Claude Bernard faisait avec ses chiens, ce que Pasteur fait avec ses lapins, nous devons le faire, nous, avec notre coeur, et lui injecter tous les virus de l'âme humaine. . . . Et voila une belle page de plus à joindre au patrimonie littéraire.

60. This library is in the author's possession.

61. Henri-Frédéric Amiel, *Fragments d'un journal intime,* 1:216.

Minuit sonne. Encore un pas fait vers le tombeau.

62. Gustave Flaubert, *Lettres de Gustave Flaubert à George Sand,* p. 14.

Chacun de nous porte en soi sa nécropole.

63. Paul Bourget, *Essais de psychologie contemporaine,* 1:119.

La façon d'écrire se mêle à la façon de sentir.

64. Amiel, *Journal intime,* 1:111.

65. Georges Pellissier, *Le Mouvement littéraire au XIXe siècle,* p. 129.

66. Paul Verlaine, *Choix de poésies* (Paris: Charpentier, 1892) p. 306.

67. Bourget, *Un Crime d'amour,* pp. 103-4.

Des jeunes gens timides ont un battement de coeur presque into-lérable, même en franchissant le seuil des maisons où il se vend du plaisir tout préparé.

68. Edmond de Goncourt and Jules de Goncourt, *Journal des Goncourt,* 1:98.

Heureux garçons! — moins analystes que nous: de grosses natures qui se grisaient régulièrement de plaisir sans effort. . . . l'âme en rut.

69. Amiel, *Journal intime,* 1:160, 165.

Ma croix c'est l'action. . . . Par l'analyse je me suis annulé.

70. Ibid., 2:242.

71. Edmond Scherer, "Introduction," in *Fragments d'un journal intime,* by Amiel, l:lxix.

Amiel . . . est la victime d'une constitution psychologique très particulière. . . . Ame tendre et pudique, il se débat entre l'amour qui tend à la possession et la satisfaction qui profane.

72. Amiel, *Journal intime,* 1:22.

L'idéal m'empoisonne toute possession imparfaite.

73. Ibid., 2:155.

La peur de ce que j'aime est ma fatalité.

74. Goncourt and Goncourt, *Journal,* 3:22.

L'amour moderne, ce n'est plus l'amour sain, presque hygénique du bon temps. Nous avons bâti sur la femme comme un idéal de toutes nos aspirations. . . . . en elle et par elle, nous voulons satisfaire l'insatiable et l'effréné qui est en nous. Nous ne savons plus tout bêtement et simplement être heureux avec une femme.

75. Sherard, *Twenty Years in Paris,* p. 348.

76. Amiel, *Journal intime,* 2:140.

Je suis . . . partagé, perplexe.

77. Ibid., 1:199.

Il y a deux formes de l'automne: le type vaporeux et rêveur, le type coloré et vif; presque la différence des deux sexes. . . . chaque saison serait-elle bissexuelle à sa façon? Chacune aurait-elle sa gamme mineure et sa gamme majeure, ses deux côtés de lumière et d'ombre, de douceur et de force? C'est possible. Tout ce qui est complet est double.

78. Le Gallienne, *George Meredith* (London: John Lane, 1900), p. 87.

79. Pater, *Marius,* 2:31.

80. W. H. Wilkins, "The Divorce of Catherine of Aragon," *Albemarle,* January 1892, pp. 32-33.

81. "More Opinions of the Press," *Albemarle,* July 1892, p. 43.

82. G. B. Shaw, "Shaming the Devil about Shelley."

83. Crackanthorpe, "Realism in France and England," p. 43.

84. Charles W. Furse, "Modern French Art and its Critics."

85. D. S. MacColl, "The Logic of Painting."

86. Flaubert, *Lettres à George Sand,* p. 273.

Dans l'idéal que j'ai de l'art, je crois qu'on ne doit rien montrer des siennes, et que l'artiste ne doit pas plus apparaître dans son oeuvre que Dieu dans la nature.

87. James, "Hubert Crackanthorpe," p. xi.

88. Hubert Crackanthorpe, "Notes for a Paper on Barrès and Bourget," p. 84.

89. Hubert Crackanthorpe, "Mr. Henry James as a Playwright."

90. Wendell Harris, "Hubert Crackanthorpe as Realist," p. 87.

91. Frierson, *L'Influence du naturalisme français,* p. 122.

La froideur et l'équanimité de son tempérament le rendaient peu apte à faire écho à la rudesse et à la chaleur des personnages . . . il n'a pu qu'imparfaitement s'expliquer l'insistance de Crackanthorpe à considérer la sexualité comme un facteur important pour la compréhension de la nature humaine.

92. Crackanthorpe, "Realism in France and England," p. 40.

93. Ibid., p. 39.

Les parvenus se meublent toujours le salon qu'ils ont ambitionné autrefois dans leur souhaits de jeunes gens pauvres. . . . L'ameublement trahit l'homme.

94. Ibid.

95. Emile Zola, *L'Oeuvre,* p. 483.

Oui, notre génération a trempé jusqu'au ventre dans le romantisme, et . . . toutes les lessives du monde n'en ôteront pas l'odeur.

96. Hubert Crackanthorpe, "Reticence in Literature," p. 262.

97. "M. Zola at the Authors' Club," *Times* (London), September 29, 1893, p. 8.

98. Crackanthorpe, "Realism in France and England," p. 40.

99. Ibid., p. 41.

100. Ibid., p. 42.

101. Ibid., pp. 41, 43.

102. George Moore, *Confessions of a Young Man* (London: William Heinemann, 1926), p. 75.

103. Goncourt, *Journal,* 5:314.

Eh! mon Dieu, je me moque comme vous de ce mot *naturalisme,* et cependant, je le répéterai, parce qu'il faut un baptême aux choses, pour que le public les croie neuves.

104. Emile Zola, *Mes haines,* p. 26.

Vous n'avez donc pas compris que l'art est la libre expression d'un coeur et d'une intelligence, et qu'il est d'autant plus grand qu'il est plus personnel.

105. Ibid., p. 99.

Il s'agit, avant tout, . . . de pénétrer l'esprit et la chair.

106. Flaubert, *Lettres à George Sand,* p. 41.

Il faut, par un effort d'esprit, se transporter dans les personnages et non les attirer à soi. Voilà du moins la méthode; ce qui arrive à dire: Tâchez d'avoir beaucoup de talent et même de génie si vous pouvez.

107. Crackanthorpe, "Notes on Barrès and Bourget," p. 83.

108. Guy de Maupassant, "Gustave Flaubert," in *Lettres à George Sand,* by Flaubert, p. lxxvi.

109. Pellissier, *Mouvement littéraire,* p. 325.

110. Clarence R. Decker, "Zola's Literary Reputation in England," PMLA 49:1149.

111. Goncourt and Goncourt, *Journal,* 3:248.

112. Murdoch, *Renaissance of the Nineties,* p. 26.

113. Goncourt and Goncourt, *Journal,* 2:187.

En littérature, on commence à chercher son originalité laborieusement chez les autres, et très loin de soi, plus tard on la trouve naturellement en soi, et tout près de soi.

114. Maupassant, "Gustave Flaubert," p. xiii.

115. Emile Zola, *Le Roman expérimental,* p. 126.

Notre impassibilité . . . devant le mal et devant le bien.

116. Crackanthorpe, "Reticence in Literature," p. 261.

117. Hippolyte Taine, *Histoire de la littérature anglaise* (Paris: Hachette, 1892), 5:39.

Soyez moral. Il faut que tous vos romans puissent être lus par les jeunes filles.

118. Frierson, *L'Influence du naturalisme français,* p. 122.

Crackanthorpe écrit avec la séreine équité et la philosophique chasteté de Flaubert.

119. Zola, *Roman expérimental,* pp. 18-19.

Un jour, la physiologie nous expliquera sans doute le mécanisme de la pensée et des passions; nous saurons comment fonctionne la machine individuelle de l'homme.

120. Ibid., pp. 24-25.

121. Ibid., p. 16.

122. Ibid., p. 155.

123. Goncourt and Goncourt, *Journal,* 2:15.

124. Emile Zola, *Les Romanciers naturalistes,* p. 331.

Aujourd'hui, le roman est devenu l'outil du siècle, la grande enquête sur l'homme et sur la nature.

125. Crackanthorpe, "Notes on Barrès and Bourget," p. 83.

126. Goncourt, *Journal,* 5:328.

127. Pater, *Marius,* 1:25.

Chapter 3

1. Elizabeth Robins, *Theatre and Friendship,* p. 78.

2. Emile Zola, *Les Romanciers naturalistes,* p. 258.

Le mariage, selon moi, est l'école des grands producteurs contemporains.

3. Blanche Crackanthorpe, "A Last word on the Revolt," p. 428.

4. Ibid.

5. Francis Jammes, *Mémoires,* p. 159.

6. Frank Harris, "Lionel Johnson and Hubert Crackanthorpe," *Contemporary Portraits,* 2:184.

7. L. G. Pine, ed., *Genealogical and Heraldic History of the Peerage,* 101st ed. (London: Burke's Peerage, 1956), p. 1397.

The House of Macdonald derives in history from Somerled . . . provincial King of Argyll, who . . . left an eldest son and heir, Reginald . . . styled "King of the Isles."

8. *Dictionary of National Biography,* Supplement 2 (London: Smith, Elder, 1907), s.v. Grove, Sir William.

9. Francis Jammes, *Ma France poétique,* p. 63.

Ils avaient des iris et leur tabac anglais,
Leurs livres à côté, richement reliés,
Et qu'ils lisaient, une paupière mi-fermée
Lorsque les irritait la trop âcre fumée.
Leurs chambres, ils étaient de tout nouveaux époux,
Sentaient le maroquin, l'ambre et le caoutchouc.
Des cristaux au col d'or et des brosses d'ivoire,
Et des chiffres d'argent sur des écailles noires,
Etaient rangés avec soin méticuleux
Sur un meuble en bois blanc du logis peu coûteux.
Dans la grange, ils logeaient leurs deux juments tarbaises,
Nerveuses, mais sur qui leur grâce était à l'aise.

10. Edmond de Goncourt and Jules de Goncourt, *Journal des Goncourt,* 1:146.

Cette gaieté de surface venant d'un fond d'âme mélancolique.

11. Jammes, *Mémoires,* pp. 180–81.

J'ai parlé de cette sorte de guerrière qu'avait épousée mon ami Hubert Crackanthorpe. Dès les premiers jours de leur mariage, elle et lui vinrent s'installer aux environs d'Orthez dans une villa que j'avais louée pour eux. Nous voilà battant la campagne tous quatre, je dis tous quatre parce que Charles Lacoste était avec nous. On cueille des iris, on s'amuse d'une chèvre qui broutait comme de l'herbe le tabac de Virginie, on pique-nique et, naturellement, on prend le thé. Plutôt mourir que de n'avoir pas sous la main, à cinq heures où que l'on soit, sa bouilloire et sa lampe d'alcool! C'est ce dernier ustensile qui faillit causer un affreux malheur. Nous étions, Hubert et moi, à quelques cinquante mètres de sa femme, au bord du gave, quand nous la voyons se rouler à terre et l'entendons pousser des cris déchirants. Lacoste qui est avec elle a l'air de lui porter secours. Nous nous précipitons. L'esprit-de-vin a fait exploser la lampe que Madame Crackanthorpe était en train d'allumer et lui a brulé horriblement les yeux. On soulève les paupières et l'on ne distingue que deux ampoules sanguinolentes. . . . Durant les semaines qui suivaient cet accident si pénible nous nous rendions souvent chez nos amis, à neuf kilomètres d'Orthez. Lorsqu'il n'y eut plus de complications à redouter pour les yeux de la jeune femme, notre calme intimité reprit. Dans cet acide parfum de tabac blond et de cuir qu'exhale la vie anglaise, nous lisions les poètes: Shakespeare, Keats, La Fontaine, Mallarmé.

12. Robert Mallet, *Francis Jammes, une étude,* p. 27.

Et cependant, à quelle passion de non-conformisme répondaient les poèmes que, depuis trois ans, il écrivait en secret! Il lui fallait des approbations et des encouragements pour le décider à risquer le scandale, en risquant le succès. Ses anciens camarades de lycée, Charles Lacoste et Charles Veillet-Lavallée et surtout un jeune écrivain anglais en séjour à Orthez, Hubert Crackanthorpe, furent en 1893, les clairvoyants et persuasifs conseillers dont il avait besoin.

13. Robert Mallet, *Francis Jammes, sa vie, son oeuvre,* p. 60.

Crackanthorpe l'encouragea à persévérer dans le sens du non-conformisme.

14. Jammes, *Mémoires,* pp. 181–82.

Hubert Crackanthorpe voulut profiter du grand bruit que l'on menait autour de sa première oeuvre, *Wreckage,* pour me faire connaître. Il comprenait à merveille, et sans l'effort qu'il a fallu à certains Français déformés par des pions, les poèmes que déjà Lacoste et Clavand avaient lus, et que je lui avais confiés. Il marquait en mon avenir poétique une foi absolue. Il me pressa tellement qu'il triompha jusqu'à un certain point de ma résistance: je l'autorisai à faire un petit choix parmi mes vers et, non pas à les livrer à un éditeur, ce qu'il eut voulu, mais à en former une mince plaquette blanche, imprimée à Orthez . . . limitée à cinquante exemplaires, hors commerce.

15. Ibid.

Il exulta et fut charmant, et je le vois encore qui, pour fêter le petit livre, grimpait avec l'agilité d'un écureil dans les chênes sous lesquels nous allions dîner, pour y suspendre autant de flambeaux que je lui avais laissé publier de poèmes.

16. Francis Jammes, *Vers,* dedication.

A toi, Crackanthorpe, déjà célèbre en ton pays, et qui as senti passer en toi le souffle de l'amour et de la pitié humains.

17. Crackanthorpe to Image, April 21, 1893, in the author's possession.

18. Ibid., n.d.

19. Ibid., April 21, 1893.

20. Ibid.

21. Ibid.

22. Grant Richards, *Memories of a Misspent Youth*, p. 152.

23. Goncourt and Goncourt, *Journal*, 2:223.

Tout le laid de la vie.

24. Henry James, "Hubert Crackanthorpe," p. xx.

25. Arthur Symons, *Studies in Prose and Verse*, p. 65

26. Walter Pater, *Marius the Epicurean*, 2:19.

27. Edmond de Goncourt and Jules de Goncourt, *Germinie Lacerteux*, pp. viii, 5.

Que le roman ait cette religion que le siècle passé appelait de ce large et vaste nom: "Humanité"; il lui suffit de cette conscience, son droit est là.

28. Ibid., p. 5.

29. Hubert Crackanthorpe, *Wreckage*, pp. 1–2.

30. Ibid., p. 44.

31. Ibid., p. 53.

32. Goncourt and Goncourt, *Journal*, 2:6.

Le grand caractère de la fille tombée à la prostitution: c'est l'impersonalité. Elle n'est plus une personne, plus quelqu'un. . . . La conscience et la propriété du moi s'efface chez elle.

33. Crackanthorpe, *Wreckage*, p. 7.

34. Ibid., p. 18.

35. Ibid., p. 22.

36. Ibid., pp. 24–25.

37. Pater, *Marius*, 2:203.

38. Crackanthorpe, *Wreckage*, p. 24.

39. Ibid., p. 42.

40. Emile Zola, *La Curée*, p. 160.

Tout ce que la brutalité du désir et le contentement immédiat de l'instinct jettent à la rue, après l'avoir brisé et souillé.

41. Emile Zola, *Nana*, p. 236.

Corrompant et désorganisant Paris entre ses cuisses de neige.

42. Crackanthorpe, *Wreckage*, p. 43.

43. Zola, *Romanciers naturalistes*, p. 244.

C'est une lente dégradation morale qui la jette à la débauche des barrières, quand son amant la quitte. Elle a besoin de l'amour, comme on a besoin du pain qu'on mange.

44. Gustave Flaubert, *Lettres de Gustave Flaubert à George Sand*, p. 59.

Je ne veux avoir ni amour, ni haine, ni pitié, ni colère. Quant à de la sympathie, c'est différent: jamais on n'en a assez.

45. Gustave Flaubert, *Madame Bovary*, p. 361.

46. Crackanthorpe, *Wreckage,* p. 143.

47. J. M. Kennedy, *English Literature, 1880–1905,* p. 1; W. G. Blaikie Murdoch, *The Renaissance of the Nineties,* p. 49.

48. Crackanthorpe, *Wreckage,* p. 58.

49. Emile Zola, *L'Oeuvre,* p. 416.

Oui, oui, il travaille. Il veut tout finir avant de se remettre à la femme.

50. Crackanthorpe, *Wreckage,* p. 58.

51. Ibid., pp. 96–97, 99.

52. Ibid., p. 104.

53. Zola, *L'Oeuvre,* p. 464.

Claude, écoute-moi. . . . Reviens, oh! reviens, si tu ne veux pas que j'en meure, . . . d'avoir si froid et de t'attendre.

54. Pater, *Marius,* 2:231.

55. Emile Zola, *Le Roman expérimental,* p. 4.

56. Henry James, "Hubert Crackanthorpe," p. xviii.

57. "Our Literary Table," *Athenaeum* no. 3418, p. 535.

58. "A Decadent Proseman."

59. Crackanthorpe, *Wreckage,* p. 107.

60. Ibid., pp. 110–11.

61. Ibid., p. 112.

62. Ibid., p. 111.

63. Ibid., p. 110.

64. "New Novels," p. 384.

65. James, "Hubert Crackanthorpe," p. xix.

66. Flaubert, *Madame Bovary,* p. 385.

Je ne vous en veux pas. . . . Non, je ne vous en veux plus.

67. Emile Zola, *L'Assommoir,* p. 293.

Les hommes sont des hommes, n'est-ce pas? On est fait pour se comprendre.

68. Crackanthorpe, *Wreckage,* pp. 127–29.

69. Ibid., p. 136.

70. Ibid., pp. 137–38.

71. Ibid., p. 154.

72. Ibid., pp. 160–62.

73. William Archer, "Wreckage."

74. "A Decadant Proseman."

75. H. D. Traill, "Literature."

76. L. F. A., "The Book and its Story."

77. "New Books and Reprints."

78. Guy de Maupassant, "Gustave Flaubert," in *Lettres à George Sand* by Flaubert, p. lxxvi.

Il emplit le lecteur intelligent d'une mélancolie désolée devant la vie.

79. In the author's possession.

80. James, "Hubert Crackanthorpe," p. xv.

81. Dayrell Crackanthorpe to Leila Macdonald, November 25, 1896, a copy handwritten and signed by Dayrell and initialled by Montague Crackanthorpe, in the author's possession.

82. Dayrell Crackanthorpe to Ida Crackanthorpe, August 20, 1911.

83. Richard Le Gallienne, "Hubert Crackanthorpe: In Memoriam."

84. William Rothenstein, *Men and Memories,* 1:208.

85. Leila Crackanthorpe, draft will, December 16, 1893, in the author's possession.

86. W. C. Frierson, *The English Novel in Transition, 1885–1940,* p. 53.

87. Maurice Barrès, *Un Homme libre,* p. 272.

Sans argent, plus d'*Homme libre.*

88. Goncourt and Goncourt, *Journal,* 1:187.

Il faut à des hommes comme nous, une femme peu élevée, peu éduquée, qui ne soit que gaieté et esprit naturel, parce que celle-là nous réjouira et nous charmera ainsi qu'un agréable animal auquel nous pourrons nous attacher. Mais que si la maîtresse a été frottée d'un peu de monde, d'un peu d'art, d'un peu de littérature, et qu'elle veuille s'entretenir de plain-pied avec notre pensée et notre conscience du beau, et qu'elle ait l'ambition de se faire la compagne du livre en gestation ou de nos goûts; elle devient pour nous insupportable comme un piano faux—et bien vite un objet d'antipathie.

89. In the author's possession.

90. Frierson, *English Novel in Transition,* p. 52.

91. James, "Hubert Crackanthorpe," p. xviii.

92. Crackanthorpe to Gosse, January 23, 1894, Gosse papers, Brotherton Library, University of Leeds.

93. Sir Edmund Gosse, *Questions at Issue* (London: Heinemann, 1893), pp. 152–53.

94. Arthur Waugh, "Living Critics. 9—Mr. Edmund Gosse," *Bookman* (London), September 1896, p. 165.

95. Conal O'Riordan, "Foreword," p. 12.

96. W. C. Frierson, *L'Influence du naturalisme français sur les romanciers anglais de 1885 à 1900,* p. 132.

Les phases de l'oeuvre de Crackanthorpe . . . démontrent avec quel sérieux il s'est adonné à l'étude de l'humanité et avec quel compatissant compréhension il en a écrit.

97. Hubert Crackanthorpe, "Reticence in Literature," *Yellow Book* 2:262, 268.

98. Ibid., p. 269.

99. Zola, *Roman expérimental,* p. 111.

Il est certain qu'une oeuvre ne sera jamais qu'un coin de la nature vu à travers un tempérament.

100. Ibid., p. 94.

Il y a un abîme entre l'écrivain naturaliste qui va du connu à l'inconnu, et l'écrivain idéaliste qui a la prétention d'aller de l'inconnu au connu. . . . nous vous donnerons au moins la nature vrai, vue à travers notre humanité.

101. Crackanthorpe, "Reticence in Literature," p. 261.

102. Flaubert, *Lettres à George Sand,* p. 286.

Je ne puis pas avoir un autre tempérament que le mien, ni une autre esthétique que celle qui en est la conséquence.

103. Pater, *Appreciations,* p. 10.

104. Crackanthorpe, "Reticence in Literature," p. 264.

105. Ibid., p. 261. Paul Bourget's version is in *Essais de psychologie contemporaine,* 1:115.

Chacun de nous aperçoit non pas l'univers, mais *son* univers; non pas la réalité nue, mais, de cette réalité, ce que son tempérament lui permet de s'approprier. Nous ne racontons que notre songe de la vie humaine, et, en un certain sens, tout ouvrage d'imagination est une autobiographie, sinon strictement matérielle, du moins intimement exacte et profondément significative des arrière-fonds de notre nature.

106. Walter Pater, *Studies in the History of the Renaissance,* p. 209.

107. Crackanthorpe, "Reticence in Literature," p. 269.

108. Pater, *Marius,* 1:154.

109. Zola, *Romanciers naturalistes,* p. 123.

Stendhal n'a pris que la tête de l'homme, pour y faire des expériences de psychologue.

110. Paul Bourget, *Le Disciple,* p. 328.

Par quelles paroles empêcher que ce cerveau de vingt-deux ans fût ravagé d'orgueil et de sensualité, de curiosités malsaines et de dépravants paradoxes? Démontrerait-on à une vipère, si elle comprenait un raisonnement, qu'elle ne doit pas sécréter son venin? "Pourquoi suis-je une vipère?" répondrait-elle. . . . Changer quoi que ce fût dans une âme, ce serait arrêter la vie.

111. Georges Pellissier, *Le Mouvement littéraire au XIXe siècle,* p. 378.

Tel, parmi nos jeunes romanciers, ne voit dans la nature humaine que des instincts et des impulsions aveugles; ses récits francs, sobres, d'une touche vive et forte, d'une langue simple, robuste, crue, peignent avec un relief puissant des personnages dont l'activité est tout physique. . . . Tel porte au contraire dans la psychologie cette curiosité qui caractérise notre génération; disciple de Stendhal, comme l'autre de Flaubert et de Zola, il ne s'intéresse qu'à des "états d'âme," à des "cas de conscience," il fait des "planches d'anatomie morale."

112. Symons, *Studies in Prose and Verse,* p. 66.

113. Hubert Crackanthorpe, *Sentimental Studies,* p. 70.

114. Ibid., pp. 5–6.

115. Emile Zola, *Une Page d'amour,* pp. 63–65.

Les deux fenêtres de la chambre étaient grandes ouvertes, et Paris, dans l'abîme qui se creusait au pied de la maison . . . déroulait sa plaine immense. . . . Hélène depuis huit jours, avait cette distraction du grand Paris . . . devant elle. . . . Le livre glissa de ses mains. Elle rêvait, les yeux perdus.

116. Bourget, *Essais de psychologie,* 1:148.

La disproportion qui les fait souffrir provient, toujours et partout, de ce qu'ils se sont façonné une idée par avance sur les sentiments qu'ils éprouveront. . . . C'est donc la Pensée . . . qui condamne l'homme à un malheur assuré.

117. Crackanthorpe, *Sentimental Studies,* p. 91.

118. Zola, *Une Page d'amour,* p. 65.

Comme ces romans mentaient! . . . Et elle restait séduite pourtant. . . . Aimer, aimer! et ce mot qu'elle ne prononçait pas, . . . de lui-même vibrait en elle.

119. Crackanthorpe, *Sentimental Studies,* p. 91.

120. Edmond de Goncourt and Jules de Goncourt, *Charles Demailly,* p. 203.

L'homme de lettres . . . s'analyse quand il aime, et, quand il souffre, il s'analyse encore. . . . Savez-vous comment un homme de lettres s'attache à une femme? Comme Vernet au mât du vaisseau . . . pour étudier le tempête. . . . Nous ne vivons que nos livres . . . d'autres disent: "Voilà une femme!" Nous disons: "Voilà un roman!"

121. Crackanthorpe, *Sentimental Studies,* pp. 10–12.

122. Goncourt and Goncourt, *Demailly,* p. 208.

Plus encore en auteur qu'en amoureux.

123. Crackanthorpe, *Sentimental Studies,* p. 15.

124. Ibid., p. 18.

125. Ibid., p. 28.

126. Ibid., pp. 24–25.

127. Ibid., pp. 59–60.

128. Paul Bourget, *Un Crime d'amour,* p. 98.

Hélène ne se doutait pas que, même à cette minute, cet homme venait de trouver dans cette absolue soumission à ses désirs qui avait tant coûté à la pauvre femme, de quoi ne pas croire en elle.

129. Crackanthorpe, *Sentimental Studies,* p. 65.

130. Ibid., p. 85.

131. Ibid., pp. 100–101.

132. Ibid., pp. 102–3.

133. Ibid., p. 11.

134. Bourget, *Crime d'amour,* p. 273.

Il se rendait compte que le collège avait sali trop tôt son imagination.

135. Crackanthorpe, *Sentimental Studies,* p. 9.

136. Ibid., p. 37.

137. Ibid., p. 83.

138. Ibid., p. 93.

139. Richard Le Gallienne, *The Romantic '90s,* pp. 102–3.

Chapter 4

1. Evelyn Sharp, "A Group of the Nineties."

2. Holbrook Jackson, *The Eighteen Nineties,* p. 54.

3. *Times* (London), April 20, 1894, p. 3.

4. Henry James, *The Letters of Henry James,* ed., P. Lubbock (London: Macmillan, 1920), 1:222.

5. "A Yellow Impertinence."

6. *Oxford Magazine,* May 17, 1894, p. 2.

7. Edmond de Goncourt and Jules de Goncourt, *Journal des Goncourt,* 2:37–38.

Le docteur Simon va me dire, tout à l'heure, si notre vieille Rose vivra ou mourra. J'attends son coup de sonnette, qui est pour moi celui d'un jury des assises rentrant en séance . . . "C'est fini, plus d'espoir, une question de temps. . . ." Et il faut revenir à la malade, lui verser de la sérénité avec notre sourire.

8. Hubert Crackanthorpe, *Sentimental Studies,* p. 225.

9. Katherine Lyon Mix, *Study in Yellow,* p. 183.

10. Crackanthorpe to Image, April 21, 1894, in the author's possession.

11. Hubert Crackanthorpe, "Reticence in Literature," p. 266.

12. Crackanthorpe to Image, 1894, in the author's possession.

13. Hubert Crackanthorpe, *Vignettes,* pp. 29–30.

14. "La mort de M. Hubert Crackanthorpe."

15. Crackanthorpe, "Reticence in Literature," p. 267.

16. Crackanthorpe, *Sentimental Studies,* pp. 203–4.

17. Paul Bourget, *Mensonges,* p. 213.

C'est là un phénomène de mirage sentimental assez fréquent chez les hommes chastes, et qui les livre comme une proie sans défense aux plus grossières duperies. Cette incapacité de juger leurs propres sensations les rend plus incapables encore de juger les manoeuvres des femmes qui remuent en eux tous les trésors accumulés de la vie.

18. Crackanthorpe, *Sentimental Studies,* p. 197.

19. Henry Harland, "Books: A Letter to the Editor, from 'The Yellow Dwarf,' " p. 141.

20. Selwyn Image, *Selwyn Image Letters,* p. 87.

21. Richard Whittington-Egan and Geoffrey Smerdon, *The Quest of the Golden Boy,* p. 276.

22. Osbert Burdett, *The Beardsley Period,* p. 231.

23. Goncourt and Goncourt, *Journal,* 1:185.

Les émotions sont contraires à la gestation des livres. Ceux qui imaginent ne doivent pas vivre. Il faut des jours réguliers, calmes, apaisés . . . pour mettre au grand jour, du tourmenté, du dramatique.

24. Walter Pater, *Marius the Epicurean,* 2:208–9.

25. Victor Plarr, *Ernest Dowson, 1888–97,* p. 105.

26. J. Lewis May, *John Lane and the Nineties,* pp. 82–83.

27. Hubert Crackanthorpe, "Bread and the Circus," pp. 236, 246–47.

28. Crackanthorpe to Image, 1895, in the author's possession.

29. Crackanthorpe, *Sentimental Studies,* p. 227.

30. Ibid., pp. 228–29.
31. Jackson, *Eighteen Nineties,* p. 168.
32. Crackanthorpe, *Sentimental Studies,* pp. 235–36.
33. Pater, *Miscellaneous Studies* (London: Macmillan, 1895), p. 174.
34. Henry James, "Hubert Crackanthorpe," p. xxi.
35. Bourget, *Mensonges,* p. 232.

Elle y sentait un désir de sa personne, aussi passionné que craintif
et respectueux. Et que celà lui plaisait d'être désirée, avec cette
pudeur! Elle mesurait mieux l'abîme qui séparait son petit René
. . . des hardis et redoutables viveurs qui composaient son milieu
habituel.

36. Crackanthorpe, *Sentimental Studies,* pp. 130–31.
37. Ibid., p. 137.
38. Ibid., p. 136.
39. Ibid., p. 137.
40. Ibid., pp. 133–34.
41. Ibid., p. 156.
42. Ibid., pp. 160–61.
43. Ibid., pp. 163–64.
44. Ibid., p. 169.
45. William C. Frierson, *L'Influence du naturalisme français sur les romanciers anglais de 1885 à 1900,* p. 122.

Le mépris, l'émotion, l'ironie qui miroitent dans ses pages . . .
sont . . . la contexture même de ses récits, . . . les émanations de
sa logique mentalité.

46. Crackanthorpe, *Vignettes,* pp. 58–59.
47. James, "Hubert Crackanthorpe," p. xxi.
48. Richard Le Gallienne, *The Romantic '90s,* p. 179.
49. Wendell Harris, "Hubert Crackanthorpe as Realist," p. 80.
50. Frierson, *L'Influence du naturalisme français,* pp. 133–34.

C'est Flaubert qui lui a inspiré l'idéal de devenir le maître styliste
qu'il se montre dans "Lisa-la-folle".

51. Harris, "Hubert Crackanthorpe as Realist," p. 84.
52. Hubert Crackanthorpe, *A Set of Village Tales,* pp. 239–40.
53. Ibid.
54. Ibid., p. 241.
55. Ibid., p. 242.
56. Ibid.
57. Ibid., p. 244.
58. Ibid.
59. Emile Zola, *La Terre,* p. 109.

On ne distinguait, sur le sol, que la couche épaisse des grêlons, une
nappe blanchissante.

60. Crackanthorpe, *Set of Village Tales,* pp. 244–46.
61. Ibid., p. 247.
62. Ibid., pp. 247–48.
63. William Peden, "Introduction," p. xvii.
64. Crackanthorpe, *Village Tales,* pp. 250–51.

65. Ibid., pp. 266–67.

66. Ibid., p. 269.

67. Ibid., p. 252.

68. Ibid., pp. 254–57.

69. Ibid., p. 258.

70. Ibid.

71. Ibid., p. 259.

72. Ibid., p. 261.

73. Ibid., p. 263.

74. Ibid., p. 272.

75. Ibid., p. 273.

76. Ibid., p. 274.

77. Ibid.

78. Ibid., p. 273.

79. Ibid., p. 274.

80. Ibid., p. 277.

81. Ibid., pp. 277–78.

82. William Peden, "Introduction," p. xvii.

83. Crackanthorpe, *Vignettes,* pp. 59, 61.

84. Pierre Loti, *Aziyadé,* p. 177.
Si malheureux que vous soyez, faites en sorte d'avoir toujours un petit coin de vous-même que vous ne laissiez pas envahir par le mal et qui puisse raisonner sur le mal: ce petit coin sera votre boîte à médicaments.—*Amen.*

85. Harland, "The Yellow Dwarf," p. 141.

86. "Mr. Crackanthorpe's New Volume."

87. Lionel Johnson, "Sentimental Studies and A Set of Village Tales," p. 218.

88. Lionel Johnson, "Hubert Crackanthorpe," p. 428.

89. Bourget, *Mensonges,* p. 110.
Cette irritabilité qui est le signe le plus indiscutable d'un déclin d'amour.

90. Crackanthorpe, *Vignettes,* pp. 33–34.

91. Ibid., p. 38.

92. Jackson, *Eighteen Nineties,* pp. 170–72.

93. Dayrell to Blanche Crackanthorpe, December 3, 1895, in the author's possession.

94. Crackanthorpe, *Vignettes,* p. 47.

95. Ibid., p. 48.

96. Pater, *Marius,* 1:150.

97. Peter Kroyer, *The Story of Lindsey House, Chelsea,* pp. 72–79, 112–13.

98. Roger Fry, *The Letters of Roger Fry,* p. 165.

99. Dayrell Crackanthorpe to Leila Macdonald, November 25, 1896, in the author's possession. Some pages of Dayrell's letter exist in draft as well as in the final version: the reference to the miscarriage occurs only in the draft.

100. Ernest Dowson, *The Letters of Ernest Dowson,* p. 357.

101. Arthur Symons, "Hubert Crackanthorpe," *Saturday Review* 85:52.

102. Hubert Crackanthorpe to Ethel Clifford, May 5, 1896, in the possession of Mrs. Timothy Dilke (Ethel Clifford married, in 1905, Sir Fisher Wentworth Dilke Bt.).

103. Whittington-Egan and Smerdon, *Quest of the Golden Boy,* p. 306.

104. Ibid., p. 302.

Chapter 5

1. Grant Richards, *Memories of a Misspent Youth,* p. 236.

2. Richard Whittington-Egan and Geoffrey Smerdon, *The Quest of the Golden Boy,* p. 198.

3. Richard Le Gallienne, *The Romantic '90s,* p. 106.

4. Richards, *Memories of a Misspent Youth,* p. 236.

5. W. C. Frierson, "Realism in the Eighteen-Nineties and the Maupassant School in England," p. 38.

6. Whittington-Egan and Smerdon, *Quest of the Golden Boy,* p. 306.

7. Ibid., p. 425.

8. Ibid., p. 427.

9. Paul Bourget, *Un Crime d'amour,* p. 65.

10. "Mr. Crackanthorpe's Fate," December 14, 1896.

11. Ibid., December 15, 1896.

12. "Hubert Crackanthorpe," December 25, 1896.

13. Ibid., December 26, 1896.

14. "M. H. Crackanthorpe," *Le Petit Parisien.*

15. Richards, *Memories of a Misspent Youth,* p. 343.

16. Ibid., p. 344.

17. Grant Richards, *Author Hunting,* p. 18.

18. Holbrook Jackson, *The Eighteen-Nineties,* p. 53.

19. "Vignettes."

20. Hubert Crackanthorpe, *Vignettes,* pp. 16–18.

21. "Floods in France," *Times* (London), November 2, 1896, p. 5.

22. "Hubert Crackanthorpe," *Le Matin.*

23. Whittington-Egan and Smerdon, *Quest of the Golden Boy,* p. 306.

24. Aubrey Beardsley, *The Letters of Aubrey Beardsley,* p. 223.

25. Crackanthorpe, *Vignettes,* p. 61.

26. Paul Bourget, *Un Coeur de femme,* p. 313.
Elle a pour principe non plus la vision impure des caresses, mais la certitude que nous ne suffisons pas au bonheur de ce que nous aimons.

27. George Meredith, "Modern Love XL," in *Poems,* Memorial Edition (London: Constable, 1910), 1:220.

28. "La Mort de M. Hubert Crackanthorpe."

29. Vincent Starrett, *Buried Caesars: Essays in Literary Appreciation,* p. 136.

30. William Rothenstein, *Men and Memories,* 1:208.

31. "Hubert Crackanthorpe," *Le Journal,* December 26, 1896. Peut-être a-t-il été précipité dans la Seine à la suite d'une rixe.

32. "Mr. Crackanthorpe's Death."

33. Ethel Clifford, January 1, 1897, in the possession of Mrs. Timothy Dilke.

34. Walter Pater, *Marius the Epicurean,* 1:22.

35. Blanche Crackanthorpe to Ethel Clifford, January 30, 1897, in the possession of Mrs. Timothy Dilke.

36. Francis Jammes, *Mémoires,* p. 159. Son identité fut établie par une pierre bizarre qu'il portait au doigt, et qu'il m'avait montrée. Ses armes y étaient gravées. Il la disait unique au monde. Et lui aussi était unique, et je le regrette profondément! Ses cendres ont été déposées dans la crypte funéraire de son château familiale, crypte que je lui avais dépeinte pour l'avoir vue en songe deux ans avant sa mort.

37. Richard Le Gallienne, "Hubert Crackanthorpe: In Memoriam."

38. Jeannette Gilder, "The Lounger."

39. Lionel Johnson, "In Memory of Hubert Crackanthorpe," *The Complete Poems of Lionel Johnson,* p. 252.

40. Le Gallienne, *Romantic '90s,* pp. 121–22, 140, 179.

41. Holbrook Jackson, "Hubert Crackanthorpe," p. 10.

42. Starrett, *Buried Caesars,* p. 136.

43. Henri-Frédéric Amiel, *Fragments d'un journal intime,* 2:48. L'âpre sensation de l'inanité de la vie et de la fuite des choses.

44. Henry James, "Hubert Crackanthorpe," p. xxiii.

45. Amiel, *Journal intime,* 1:155. Dégoût et lassitude de la vie, tristesse mortelle.

46. Ibid., 2:279. La libellule n'en est pas encore un symbole assez frêle; c'est la bulle de savon qui traduit le mieux . . . cette apparence fugitive du petit moi qui est nous.

47. Edmond de Goncourt and Jules de Goncourt, *Journal des Goncourt,* 2:188. Nous sommes comme des gens, qui n'ont entre eux et le suicide, que la trêve de quelques oeuvres à faire.

48. Amiel, *Journal imtime,* 1:142. J'entre doucement dans le cercueil, de mon vivant. J'éprouve comme la paix indéfinissable de l'anéantissement et la quiétude . . . de Nirvana; je sens devant moi et en moi passer le fleuve rapide du temps.

49. Ernest Dowson, *The Letters of Ernest Dowson,* eds. D. Flower and H. Maas, p. 384.

50. Lawrence P. Jacks, *The Life and Letters of Stopford Brooke,* 2:528.

51. James, "Hubert Crackanthorpe," pp. xviii, xxii.

52. Hubert Crackanthorpe, *Sentimental Studies,* p. 7.

53. Hubert Crackanthorpe, *Last Studies*, p. 1.

54. Bernard Muddiman, *The Men of the Nineties*, p. 76.

55. Pater, *Marius*, 1:5, 8.

56. James, "Hubert Crackanthorpe," p. xxi.

57. Crackanthorpe, *Last Studies*, p. 52.

58. Ibid., p. 36.

59. Ibid., p. 29.

60. Ibid., p. 53.

61. Ibid., p. 39.

62. Ibid., p. 67.

63. Lionel Johnson, "Hubert Crackanthorpe," p. 428.

64. Crackanthorpe, *Last Studies*, pp. 73–75.

65. Ibid., p. 72.

66. Ibid., p. 75.

67. Maurice Barrès, *Sous l'oeil des barbares*, p. 25.
Le culte du Moi. . . . il nous faut le défendre chaque jour et chaque jour le créer.

68. Crackanthorpe, *Last Studies*, p. 81.

69. Pater, *Studies in the History of the Renaissance*, p. 211.

70. Crackanthorpe, *Last Studies*, pp. 80–81.

71. Ibid., pp. 83–84.

72. Ibid., p. 92.

73. Ibid., p. 89.

74. Ibid., p. 94.

75. Ibid., p. 96.

76. William Peden, "Introduction," p. xxi.

77. J. H. Rosny, *L'Imperieuse Bonté*, p. 256.
Une âme n'est indépendante que dans de très grosses réalités fixées par les siècles.

78. Crackanthorpe, *Last Studies*, p. 107.

79. Ibid., p. 137.

80. Ibid., pp. 155–56.

81. Ibid., pp. 203–4.

82. Ibid., p. 223.

83. Ibid., p. 96.

84. Jackson, "Hubert Crackanthorpe," p. 8.

85. Johnson, "Hubert Crackanthorpe," p. 424.

86. "Fiction," December 24, 1897.

87. Arthur Symons, "Hubert Crackanthorpe," *Saturday Review* 85 (1898): 52–53.

88. James, "Hubert Crackanthorpe," p. xv.

89. W. C. Frierson, *L'Influence du naturalisme français sur les romanciers anglais de 1885 à 1900*, p. 120.

90. "Short Stories," *Athenaeum*, no. 3657:746.

91. Johnson, "Hubert Crackanthorpe," p. 428.

92. Amiel, *Journal intime*, 2:210–11.
Extrêmement subjectif par le sentiment et objectif par la pensée. . . . tu mourras sans avoir vraiment deballé.

Bibliography

Works by Hubert Crackanthorpe
(in order of publication)

"Mr. Henry James as a Playwright." *Albemarle,* January 1892, pp. 34–35.

"Realism in France and England: An Interview with M. Emile Zola." *Albemarle,* February 1892, pp. 39–43.

"He Wins Who Loses." *Albemarle,* March 1892, pp. 104–11.

"After the Play: A Conversation." *Albemarle,* June 1892, pp. 216–18.

Wreckage. London: Heinemann, 1893.

"Reticence in Literature." *Yellow Book* 2 (1894): 259–69.

Sentimental Studies & A Set of Village Tales. London: Heinemann, 1895.

"Bread and the Circus." *Yellow Book* 7 (1895): 253–57.

Vignettes. London: Lane, The Bodley Head, 1896.

"Notes for a Paper on Barrès and Bourget." *To-Morrow* 3 (1897): 83–92.

Last Studies. London: Heinemann, 1897.

The Light Sovereign: A Farcical Comedy in Three Acts. (With Henry Harland). London: Lady Henry Harland, 1917.

Collected Stories (1893–1897) of Hubert Crackanthorpe. Edited and with an Introduction by William Peden. Gainesville, Fla.: Scholar's Facsimiles and Reprints, 1969.

Principal Works Cited: Books

(Editions of nineteenth-century works in French are those in Hubert Crackanthorpe's library).

Amiel, Henri-Frédéric. *Fragments d'un journal intime.* 2 vols. Geneva: Georg, 1887.

Barrès, Maurice. *Un Homme libre.* Paris: Perrin, 1889.

———. *Sous l'oeil des barbares.* Paris: Perrin, 1892.

Beardsley, Aubrey. *The Letters of Aubrey Beardsley.* Edited by Henry Maas, J. L. Duncan, and W. G. Good. London: Cassell, 1970.

Belloc Lowndes, Marie. *The Merry Wives of Westminster.* London: Macmillan, 1946.

Bourget, Paul. *Un Coeur de femme*. Paris: Lemerre, 1890.

———. *Un Crime d'amour*. Paris: Lemerre, 1886.

———. *Le Disciple*. Paris: Lemerre, 1889.

———. *Essais de psychologie contemporaine*. 2 vols. Paris: Lemerre, 1886–1889.

———. *Mensonges*. Paris: Lemerre, 1889.

Brooke, Stopford A. "Poem." In *Last Studies,* by Hubert Crackanthorpe. London: Heinemann, 1897.

Burdett, Osbert. *The Beardsley Period*. London: Lane, 1925.

Burke, Sir Bernard. *Burke's Genealogical and Heraldic History of the Landed Gentry of Great Britain*. 11th ed. London: Harrison, 1906.

Crackanthorpe, Blanche Alethea. *The Letters of Diana, Lady Chesterfield, to her Daughter and Sister*. London: Heinemann, 1909.

Crackanthorpe, Montague H. *Population and Progress*. London: Chapman and Hall, 1907.

Curwen, John F. *Castles and Towers of Cumberland and Westmorland*. Kendal, Eng.: Titus Wilson, 1913.

Dowson, Ernest. *The Letters of Ernest Dowson*. Edited by D. Flower and H. Maas. London: Cassell, 1967.

Flaubert, Gustave. *Lettres de Gustave Flaubert à George Sand*. Paris: Charpentier, 1889.

———. *Madame Bovary*. Paris: Charpentier, 1887.

Frierson, William C. *The English Novel in Transition, 1885–1940*. Norman, Okla.: University of Oklahoma, 1942.

———. *L'Influence du naturalisme français sur les romanciers anglais de 1885 à 1900*. Paris: Giard, 1925.

Fry, Roger. *The Letters of Roger Fry*. Edited by D. Sutton. London: Chatto and Windus, 1972.

Gissing, Algernon, and Gissing, Ellen. *Letters of George Gissing to Members of his Family*. London: Constable, 1927.

Goncourt, Edmond de, and Goncourt, Jules de. *Charles Demailly*. Paris: Charpentier, 1877.

———. *Germine Lacerteux*. Paris: Charpentier, 1889.

———. *Journal des Goncourt,* vols. 1–3. Paris: Charpentier, 1887–1888.

Goncourt, Edmond de. *Journal des Goncourt,* vol. 5. Paris: Charpentier, 1891.

Hardy, Florence E. *The Later Years of Thomas Hardy, 1892–1928*. London: Macmillan, 1930.

Harris, Frank. *Contemporary Portraits,* 2d. series. New York: Frank Harris, 1919.

Image, Selwyn. *Selwyn Image Letters*. Edited by A. H. Mackmurdo. London: Grant Richards, 1932.

Jacks, Lawrence P. *The Life and Letters of Stopford Brooke*. 2 vols. London: John Murray, 1917.

Jackson, Holbrook. *The Eighteen Nineties*. London: Grant Richards, 1913.

James, Henry. "Hubert Crackanthorpe." In *Last Studies,* by Hubert Crackanthorpe. London: Heinemann, 1897.

Jammes, Francis. *Ma France poétique*. Paris: Mercure de France, 1926.
———. *Mémoires*. Paris: Mercure de France, 1971.
———. *Vers*. Privately printed, 1893.
Jepson, Edgar. *Memories of a Victorian*. London: Gollancz, 1933.
Johnson, Lionel. *The Complete Poems of Lionel Johnson*. Edited by Iain Fletcher. London: Unicorn, 1953.
Kennedy, J. M. *English Literature, 1880–1905*. London: Swift, 1912.
Kroyer, Peter. *The Story of Lindsey House Chelsea*. London: Country Life, 1956.
Le Gallienne, Eva. *At 33*. New York: Longman, 1934.
Le Gallienne, Richard. *The Lonely Dancer and Other Poems*. London: Lane, 1914.
———. *Retrospective Reviews: A Literary Log*. London: Lane, 1896.
———. *The Romantic '90s*. London: Putnam, 1926.
Longaker, Mark. *Ernest Dowson*. Philadelphia: University of Pennsylvania, 1944.
Loti, Pierre. *Aziyadé*. Paris: Calmann Levy, 1881.
Lyttelton, Hon. Edward. "Old Public School Who's Who." In *Eton School List Comprising the Years between 1853 and 1892,* by H. E. C. Stapylton. Eton: School Press, 1900.
Macdonald, Leila. *A Wanderer, and Other Poems*. London: Fisher Unwin, 1904.
Mallet, Robert. *Francis Jammes, une étude*. Paris: Seghers, 1950.
———. *Francis Jammes, sa vie, son oeuvre*. Paris: Mercure de France, 1961.
Maupassant, Guy de. "Gustave Flaubert." In *Lettres de Gustave Flaubert à George Sand*. Paris: Charpentier, 1889.
———. "Imprudence." In *Monsieur Parent*. Paris: Ollendorff, 1891.
May, J. Lewis. *John Lane and the Nineties*. London: Lane, 1936.
Mix, Katherine L. *A Study in Yellow*. London: Constable, 1960.
Montgomery-Massingberd, Hugh, ed. *Burke's Genealogical and Heraldic History of the Landed Gentry*. 18th ed. vol. 3. London: Burke's Peerage, 1972.
Moore, George. *Confessions of a Young Man*. London: Heinemann, 1928.
Moorman, Mary. *William Wordsworth, The Early Years: 1770–1803*. Oxford: Clarendon, 1957.
Muddiman, Bernard. *The Men of the Nineties*. London: Danielson, 1920.
Murdoch, W. G. Blaikie. *The Renaissance of the Nineties*. London: Moring, De La More Press, 1911.
O'Riordan, Conal. Foreword to *J. T. Grein, the Story of a Pioneer,* by Michael Orme. London: Murray, 1936.
Orme, Michael [Mrs. J. T. Grein]. *J. T. Grein, the Story of a Pioneer 1862–1935*. London: Murray, 1936.
Parker, Eric. *Eton in the Eighties*. London: Smith, Elder, 1914.
Pater, Walter H. *Appreciations*. London: Macmillan, 1904.
———. *Marius the Epicurean. 2 Vols*. London: Macmillan, 1885.

—————. *Studies in the History of the Renaissance.* London: Macmillan, 1873.

Peden, William. Introduction to *Collected Stories of Hubert Crackanthorpe.* Gainsville, Fla.: Scholars' Facsimiles and Reprints, 1969.

Pellissier, Georges. *Le Mouvement littéraire au XIXe siècle.* Paris: Hachette, 1889.

Plarr, Victor G. *Ernest Dowson, 1888–97.* London: Elkin Mathews, 1941.

Richards, Grant. *Author Hunting.* New York: Coward-McCann, 1934.

—————. *Memories of a Misspent Youth.* London: Heinemann, 1932.

Robins, Elizabeth. *Theatre and Friendship: Some Henry James Letters with a Commentary.* London: Cape, 1932.

Rosny, J. H. *L'Impérieuse Bonté.* Paris: Plon, 1894.

Rothenstein, William. *Men and Memories.* 2 vols. London: Faber, 1931.

Schneider, Ben Ross. *Wordsworth's Cambridge Education.* Cambridge: Cambridge University Press, 1957.

Starrett, Vincent. *Buried Caesars: Essays in Literary Appreciation.* Chicago: Covici-McGee, 1923.

Symons, Arthur. *Studies in Prose and Verse.* London: Dent, 1904.

Taylor, Michael W. *Manorial Halls in Westmorland.* Kendal, Eng.: Cumberland and Westmorland Antiquarian and Archaeological Society, 1892.

Vadier, Berthe. *Henri-Frédéric Amiel étude biographique.* Paris: Fischbacher, 1886.

Whittington-Egan, Richard, and Smerdon, Geoffrey. *The Quest of the Golden Boy.* London: Unicorn Press, 1960.

Wordsworth, William, and Wordsworth, Dorothy. *The Early Letters of William and Dorothy Wordsworth.* Edited by Ernest de Selincourt. Oxford: Clarendon, 1935.

—————. *The Letters of William and Dorothy Wordsworth: The Middle Years,* 3 vols. Edited by Ernest de Selincourt. Oxford: Clarendon, 1937.

Zola, Emile. *L'Assommoir.* Paris: Charpentier, 1888.

—————. *La Curée.* Paris: Charpentier, 1886.

—————. *Mes haines.* Paris: Charpentier, 1880.

—————. *Nana.* Paris: Charpentier, 1885.

—————. *L'Oeuvre.* Paris: Charpentier, 1886.

—————. *Une Page d'amour.* Paris: Charpentier, 1878.

—————. *Les Romanciers naturalistes.* Paris: Charpentier, 1890.

—————. *Le Roman expérimental.* Paris: Charpentier, 1890.

—————. *La Terre.* Paris: Charpentier, 1889.

Essays, Articles, Reviews

Archer, William. "Wreckage." *Westminster Gazette,* March 25, 1893, p. 3.

"Books of the Week." *Times* (London), November 6, 1896, p. 10; November 13, 1897, p. 10.

Crackanthorpe, Blanche Alethea. "A Last Word on the Revolt." *Nineteenth Century* 35 (1894):424–29.

———. "The Revolt of the Daughters." *Nineteenth Century* 35 (1894):23–31.

———. "Sex in Modern Literature." *Nineteenth Century* 37 (1895):607–16.

"A Decadent Proseman." *Daily Chronicle,* March 23, 1893.

Decker, Clarence R. "Zola's Literary Reputation in England." *PMLA* 49 (1934):1149.

"Fiction." *Speaker,* May 27, 1893, p. 609; December 24, 1897, pp. 723–24.

Frierson, William C. "Realism in the Eighteen-Nineties and the Maupassant School in England." *French Quarterly* 10, no. 1 (1928), pp. 31–43.

Furse, Charles W. "Modern French Art and its Critics." *Albermarle,* August 1892, pp. 47–48.

Gilder, Jeannette. "The Lounger." *Critic* 27 (1897):9.

Harland, Henry. "Books: A Letter to the Editor from 'The Yellow Dwarf.' " *Yellow Book* 7 (1895):125–43.

Harris, Wendell. "Hubert Crackanthorpe as Realist." *English Literature in Transition* 6 (1963):76–91.

Harrison, Austin. "George Gissing." *Nineteenth Century and After* 60 (1906):456.

Jackson, Holbrook. "Hubert Crackanthorpe." *Windmill* 1, no. 4 (1946), pp. 8–16.

Johnson, Lionel. "Hubert Crackanthorpe." *Academy* 52 (1897):428–29.

———. "Sentimental Studies and A Set of Village Tales." *Academy* 45 (1895):218–19.

Le Gallienne, Richard. "Hubert Crackanthorpe: In Memoriam." *Star,* January 2, 1897.

L. F. A. "The Book and its Story." *Sketch* 3, no. 37 (1893), p. 553.

MacColl, D. S. "The Logic of Painting." *Albemarle,* September 1892, pp. 87–88.

"Mr. Crackanthorpe's New Volume." *Saturday Review* 80 (1895):117–18.

"New Books and Reprints." *Saturday Review* 75 (1893):361.

"New Novels." *Black and White* 5 (1893).

"Our Literary Table." *Athenaeum,* no. 3418 (1893), p. 535; no. 3604 (1896), pp. 714–15.

"Pages in Waiting." *World,* May 31, 1893, p. 29.

Saintsbury, George. "New Novels." *Academy,* 43 (1893):414.

Sharp, Evelyn. "A Group of the Nineties." *Manchester Guardian,* January 19, 1924.

Shaw, George Bernard. "Shaming the Devil about Shelley." *Albemarle,* September 1892, p. 98.

"Short Stories." *Athenaeum,* no. 3543 (1895), p. 383; no. 3657 (1897), p. 746.

Traill, H. D. "Literature." *New Review* 8 (1893):607–8.

"Vignettes." *Saturday Review* 82 (1896):678.

"A Yellow Impertinence." *Critic* 21 (1894):360.

Newspaper Items

"Court Circular." *Times* (London), January 2, 1897, p. 6.

"Crackanthorpe Mystery." *Daily Mail,* December 18, 1896.

"Death of Mr. Crackanthorpe: Mysterious Contradictions." *Daily Graphic,* December 26, 1896.

"Death of Mr. H. Crackanthorpe," *Times* (London), December 25, 1896, p. 3.

"Floods in France." *Times* (London), November 1, 2, 1896, p. 1.

"Hubert Crackanthorpe." *Le Journal* (Paris), December 25, 26, 1896.

"Hubert Crackanthorpe." *Le Matin* (Paris), November 2, 1896.

"The Late Mr. Hubert Crackanthorpe." *Daily Graphic,* December 28, 1896.

"The Late Mr. Hubert Crackanthorpe." *Daily News,* December 28, 1896.

"The Lost Author." *Daily Mail,* December 25, 1896.

"Lost in Paris." *Daily News,* December 15, 1896.

"M. H. Crackanthorpe." *Le Figaro* (Paris), December 26, 1896.

"M. H. Crackanthorpe." *Le Petit Parisien,* December 25, 1896.

"La Mort de M. Hubert Crackanthorpe." *Le Matin* (Paris), December 26, 1896.

"Mr. Crackanthorpe." *Daily Mail,* December 15, 28, 1896.

"Mr. Crackanthorpe's Death." *Daily News,* December 26, 1896.

"Mr. Crackanthorpe's Disappearance." *Daily Graphic,* December 14, 1896.

"Mr. Crackanthorpe's Fate." *Daily Mail,* December 14, 15, 1896.

"Mr. Hubert Crackanthorpe." *Kendal Mercury and Times,* December 25, 1896.

"Obituary: Mr. Crackanthorpe, K. C." *Times* (London), November 17, 1913, p. 11.

"Obituary: Mr. Montague Crackanthorpe K. C." *Eugenics Review* 5 (April 1913–January 1914):352–53.

"Obituary: Mrs. Crackanthorpe." *Times* (London), June 6, 1928, p. 22.

Index